Praise for
What Lawyers Do

"I'm in awe of the myriad of paths the Class of 1958 has taken. Some are lawyer's lawyers. Some are lawyers writ large. But all are deeply engaged with the world and the problems of their time. These stories confirm the extraordinary effect that Yale Law School has had on a generation and the extraordinary leadership roles our graduates serve."

HEATHER GERKEN
Dean of the Yale Law School

"*What Lawyers Do* is a fascinating look into incredible careers of some impressive members of the generation of lawyers who practiced at a time of explosive growth in the profession. Many of the stories were familiar newspaper headlines in their day, allowing the reader now to gain a new perspective on the event. Each chapter is written in the author's unique style, showing that talent as a writer is often a trait of an excellent lawyer."

LINDA KLEIN
President
American Bar Association, 2016-17

"*What Lawyers Do* seems like the title for a civics lesson. But it's much more than that. The Yale Law School class of 1958 was a fascinating mix of people who produced an equally fascinating mix of achievements in law, public affairs, academia, and many other fields (so much so that I once toyed with writing a feature article about the class). Their narratives of the ups and downs of their lives and work is great reading."

STEVEN BRILL
founder of The American Lawyer & Court TV
and author of *Tailspin: The People and Forces Behind
America's Fifty Year Fall—and Those Fighting to Reverse It*

"Through stories of the past, this book highlights the many possibilities that exist for a lawyer's future. Law students, especially—and not just those at Yale—should take a moment and read *What Lawyers Do* to better understand the incredible future that can be theirs."

ROBERT E. HIRSHON
President
American Bar Association, 2001-02

What Lawyers Do

Classmate Peter Fleming arguing to the jury in the Mitchell-Vesco case, 1971

What Lawyers Do

NARRATIVES FROM THE
YALE LAW SCHOOL
CLASS OF 1958

EDITED BY BILL FELSTINER

EL BOSQUE
EDITIONS
2018

ISBN 978-1-5323-7088-5

First Edition
Printed in the United States

BOOK DESIGN BY JOHN BALKWILL
LUMINO PRESS / SANTA BARBARA

Typeset in Monotype Baskerville

This book is dedicated
to all one hundred fifty-five
graduating members of our class
and to the faculty of the
Yale Law School
from 1955–58
who shared our
intellectual and emotional journey

and to

Bill, the Brittany spaniel,
who waited patiently for Walter
every day in the front hall
for all three years

CONTENTS

What Lawyers Do

Prologue

BILL FELSTINER

WHAT DO LAWYERS DO? Lawyers do lots of things, but mostly they practice law. Early on they develop a specialty and ride it right into the sunset. Our classmate Milton DeVane and I went to the same firm in 1958. I left in 1965: he was still there in 2008 when the firm split into pieces after 161 years, practicing wills and estates from first to last. Another classmate, Pat Flaherty, began a litigation practice in 1959 and is still at it as I write. But some lawyers do other things.

Our classmate Dick Ravitch was counsel to a congressional committee, ran a construction company, ran the New York City transportation system, ran New York State's urban development program, was head of major league baseball's player relations committee and became New York's lieutenant governor. He is probably doing something else right now. Carla Hills was secretary of HUD in the Ford administration and US Trade Representative in Reagan's as well as being a partner in several mega law firms. Guido Calabresi virtually invented the field of law and economics, managed fifteen years as dean of the Yale Law School and became a federal judge. Cliff Alexander was secretary of the army. Steve Shulman was general counsel to the air force before he was thirty. I was a trial lawyer for seven years, an aid administrator, a law school administrator, a law teacher, a professor of sociology, ran two research institutions and a Red Cross shelter, and founded a nonprofit working in central Africa.

The readers of this book will catch more than a glimpse of this incredible variety of professional practice. They will meet a judge deciding cases, a young tax lawyer developing a new form of business enterprise (sports agencies), lawyers working in the Peace Corps and the army, lawyers working on the federation of African states and in Ford's cabinet. They will read about lawyers in copyright cases, speech cases, land use cases, responding to Hurricane Katrina and teaching constitutional law.

As the class of 1958's corresponding secretary, I am more aware than most of what our classmates are up to. In the fall of 2016 I asked them each whether they wanted to share some of their professional experience with a general audience. Here were the instructions:

> Perhaps it would help if I more explicitly described what I see as the objective/purpose/goal of the volume. We shared an educational experience. Although our previous lives and general inclinations may have differed some, we had the same teachers, took the same courses, and did so at the same historical time. We each began professional life with at least three incredible advantages—a Yale Law School degree, a Yale Law School education, and graduating into a hot job market. How did we capitalize on those advantages?
>
> One way to capture that notion would be to present career time lines or histories. First I did that, then I did this, that led to this other thing which enabled me to do that other one, etc. Such recitals would be accurate in a way, but rather tedious. I don't think they would appeal to anyone, may be even not to our children (if we have children).
>
> On the other hand, I am convinced that we all have had exciting, interesting, challenging episodes in our professional lives. No one episode or series of episodes will describe or reflect an entire individual

career. But my expectation is that twenty-five of them could give the wider public an idea of how varied and useful the life of a competent lawyer can be, has been, in the American social milieu in which we lived. And because these episodes are interesting, challenging, even important, they would be worth reading.

This book then took shape. I've done some editing, but authors had the final say on their contributions. As you read these chapters it would be worthwhile recalling that they were all written by people in their eighties, sixty-three years after we started law school together. Remarkable folk.

Introduction

LAURA KALMAN

SEPTEMBER 15, 1955, 9:10 A.M. Imagine 169 students about to begin their first term of law school. While they hailed from about three-quarters of the country's states, over half of them claimed New York or Connecticut as their permanent residence. So, too, though they represented seventy-six colleges and universities, 44 percent were Ivy League graduates. Yale College contributed a whopping thirty-six members of the first-year class. Harvard gave eleven; and the other Ivies together donated an additional twenty-eight. Another seven were Amherst grads. The remainder came in smaller numbers or solo from institutions ranging not quite from A–Z, but A–Y: Allegheny to Yeshiva. Fourteen, 8 percent, of the first-years were women.

Some of the fledgling law students possessed unusual backgrounds. After repeated arrests and jailings, Pat Eames organized a garment plant in South Carolina. Bud Klauser had worked for the CIA. The Naval Reserve had denied a commission to Eugene Landy, who had graduated second in his US Merchant Marine Academy class, because his mother was a former communist. Ed Woodsum had played football for the Chicago Cardinals.

The class went to work at a building that occupied a block of prime Yale real estate across from Sterling Memorial Library and the Hall of Graduate Studies. Designed by James Gamble Rogers, Sterling Law Building was an imposing stone quadrangle in Collegiate Gothic modeled after the Inns of Court. But the somberness of the place was relieved by its playful gargoyles and stone figures that depicted, among other things, the lawyer as fox, the judge as owl, the client as goat, the professor lecturing to the sleeping class, and the lawyer arguing before the dozing judge. Carved over one entrance was the announcement, "Law Is a Living Growth, Not a Changeless Code."

Yale was hardly the first to spread that message. Fifty years before the Sterling Law Building opened in 1931, Oliver Wendell Holmes Jr. had said that judges made law in accordance with contemporary social, political, and economic needs, and the sentiment was not unique then, either. But it was the embrace of a living law that breathed new life into Yale, where professors had begun talking up jurisprudence, public law, and interdisciplinarity during the 1870s, and that created the modern law school, beginning in the late 1920s. Taking the helm at the age of twenty-seven in 1927 and building on the earlier twentieth-century labors of Arthur Corbin, Wesley N. Hohfeld, and Dean Thomas Swan, Dean Robert Maynard Hutchins launched Yale's venture into legal realism. He hired three members without law degrees—a psychologist, a political scientist, and an economist—and announced that professors and the small student body that would differentiate Yale from Columbia and Harvard would engage in interdisciplinary scholarship. Stuck in the backwater of New Haven between two great law schools in two great cities, Hutchins had to do something drastic to win a place for his struggling institution with its weak student body!

When Hutchins became president of the University of Chicago two years later, his successor, Charles Clark, who steered the Law School through the 1930s while drafting the Federal Rules of Civil Procedure, inherited and added to a marquee of figures who made the school ground zero for legal realism and liberalism. Call the roll of those professors frequently ranked among the realists during the 1920s and 1930s, and you will find many teaching at Yale and/or extolling its attempted modernization of legal education and its challenge to Harvard doctrinalists—in addition to Clark and Hutchins, Thurman Arnold, Walter Wheeler Cook, William O. Douglas, Abe Fortas, Jerome Frank, Leon Green, Walton Hamilton, Karl Llewellyn, Underhill Moore, Wesley Sturges, and Leon Tulin. When judicial decisionmakers and those who studied them reached out to the social sciences; realized that the fact-patterns involved in a case, as well as legal doctrine, affected its resolution; and recognized the role of human idiosyncrasy, along with precedent, in accounting for outcomes, legal realists told their students, law would be understood as indeterminate and therefore malleable.

And lawyers would become policymakers and social reformers. Yale became the place where intellectuals went to study law's relationship to society and where liberals went to learn statecraft from professors like Arnold, Douglas, Fortas, and Hamilton who were commuting to Washington to shape the New Deal. While law professors from other institutions also enlisted in Roosevelt's crusade, of course, Clark differed from most of their deans by glorying in it. He understood that FDR provided his faculty with much of its élan. Unlike most deans, he supported Roosevelt's Court Packing Plan, just one of many acts that earned his school a reputation for "radicalism." In 1939, the notoriously conservative *Chicago Tribune* featured a cartoon of a Yale law professor hoisting the hammer and sickle of the Soviet Union up the school's flagpole. The faculty defined itself by its progressive politics, legal thought, and approach to legal education. Yale found its contemporary niche as the boutique school for legal intellectuals and policy wonks and as the anti-Harvard.

As the members of the class of 1958 began thinking about law school during the 1940s and 1950s, Yale's professors continued laboring in the vineyard that had earlier taken root. They tried, often more successfully than their 1930s predecessors, to fulfill the realist program for education by writing casebooks (or "cases and materials" books) that incorporated the social sciences and treated law as policy. They championed civil rights and civil liberties. They worked with the NAACP to litigate *Brown v. Board of Education*. They brought cases claiming a right to birth control. They defended communists and government employees accused of disloyalty during the heyday of the Second Red Scare, and they urged abolition of the House Committee on Un-American Activities. Their work was controversial and took guts, just as it had during the 1930s.

Yale law professors' approaches to legal education and politics tested the university's presidents at the same time that they gave the school its offbeat reputation. Indeed during the late 1940s, it underwent an investigation sparked by the accusation that Yale was not really a law school, but "a school of government, economics, philosophy, and law in which the emphasis is not placed upon the law," and one where courses about the development of river valley regions; law, science, and policy; the world community and the law; and law and the arts abounded. Yale administrators must have breathed a sigh of relief that William F. Buckley Jr. attacked Yale College for its liberalism in his 1951 bestseller, *God and Man, at Yale*, for, as Buckley sardonically—and accurately—observed, "some of the graduate departments, the Yale Law School in particular, would provide far more flamboyant copy." Buckley would later claim that a wealthy conservative alumnus tried to talk him out of publishing the book by reassuring him that Yale University President A. Whitney Griswold would "clean up" Yale by firing law professor Thomas "Tommy the Commie" Emerson and by "shutting up" law professor Eugene Victor Debs Rostow, who had boldly condemned the Supreme Court's behavior in the Japanese-American internment cases and urged the reorganization of the American oil industry. Fortunately, Griswold, though skeptical of some faculty members, lacked such intentions.

By the time those in the class of '58 applied to Yale in 1954, then, it had acquired its mystique as "the only law school that wasn't like a law school," as Robert Stevens, an author in this volume, observed. Yale occupied a special place in the hierarchy. Harvard Law still reigned preeminent, and Yale played Avis to Harvard's Hertz. Still, Eugene Rostow reasonably claimed that by now, Yale was "universally accepted as one of the two best law schools in the country, and by many is regarded as the best law school." Victor Navasky (YLS '59) summed up the clichés about the two schools for the *New York Times Magazine*: "Yale trains judges, Harvard trains lawyers; Yale doesn't teach you any law, Harvard teaches you nothing but; Yale turns out socially conscious policymakers, Harvard turns out narrow legal technicians; Yale thinks that judges invent the law, Harvard thinks that judges discover the law; Yale is preoccupied with social values, Harvard is preoccupied with abstract concepts; Yale is interested in personalities, Harvard is interested in cases; Yale thinks most legal doctrine is ritual mumbo-jumbo, Harvard thinks it comprises a self-contained logical system; Yale cares about results, Harvard cares about precedents; Yale thinks the law is what the judge had for breakfast, Harvard thinks it is a brooding omnipresence in the sky." The *Yale Daily News* might grumble about "the Law School parlor pinks, misty-eyed liberals, and left-wing political seers," but because of its reputation, Yale snatched some of the best and brightest law students away from Harvard.

Yet as the members of the class of 1958 received their offers of admission and weighed their options in the spring of 1955, the Law School was operating with smoke and mirrors. Less than a year after becoming dean, Harry Shulman died of cancer in March 1955. The school lost a third of its faculty over a fifteen-month period because of deaths, retirements, and separations. Professors' 1954 reversal of their 1953 decision to tenure Vern Countryman—taken, some suspected, because of Countryman's work defending victims of McCarthyism—had made the *New York Times* and split the faculty into two separate camps. The Law School possessed a sturdy cadre of professors in 1955—Boris Bittker, Ralph Brown, Eli Clark, Richard Donnelly, Thomas Emerson, Grant Gilmore, Ashbel Gulliver, Fowler Harper, Fleming James Jr., Nicholas Katzenbach, Friedrich Kessler, Harold Lasswell, Addison Mueller, Louis Pollak, Myres McDougal, James William Moore, F. S. C. Northrop, Fred Rodell, Wesley Sturges, Jack Tate, Samuel Thorne, and John Thompson. But Katzenbach, Mueller, Thorne, and Thompson would soon leave. Professors' numbers were diminished, and morale was low.

As it turned out, although members of the class of 1958 opted for Yale Law School at a perilous moment in its history, they made a great choice. At Shulman's death in 1955, the faculty chose Rostow, "a shovel-carrying legal realist," as its dean. The polished, deliberately jocular Rostow, a great friend of Griswold's, proved the only Yale Law School dean to get along with the central university administration since Hutchins. Rostow was an inspired fund-raiser and leader. He introduced the tradition of one seminar-style course and "small group" experience for each first-termer. Rostow also ushered in the divisional program that required each student to choose a specialty for serious scholarship. These changes only took effect for 1956 entrants. But those who started Yale in 1955 nevertheless reaped their benefits because the dean used the new requirements to justify doubling the size of his faculty, which enabled him to boast of the school's 17:1 student-faculty ratio. A considerable portion of the new professors had arrived by the time the class of '58 approached graduation. In addition to two members of the class, Guido Calabresi and Robert Stevens, Rostow's recruits included other quirky, intellectually restless, and interdisciplinary scholars who left a lasting impact on the school: Alexander Bickel, Charles Black, Robert Bork, Ronald Dworkin, Abraham Goldstein, Joseph Goldstein, Leon Lipson, Ellen Peters, Charles Reich, Clyde Summers, and Harry Wellington.

What was life at Yale like for the members of the class of '58? By contemporary standards, tuition was a bargain, just $750 per year (about the equivalent of $6,800 today). It was hard to flunk out of the Law School, but not impossible. While most of those who entered in 1955 ultimately graduated, not all did so with their class. Some left for a year or two to serve in the military or do something else. Some dropped out for longer. One first-year law student in 1955 received his law degree in 1979.

There was a lively social scene. Four members of the class of '58 married classmates. Many of them ate at Corbey Court and at Mory's on special occasions. The anecdotal evidence suggests that most studied and partied hard.

We know our students faced cold calls the first term in Contracts I (from Nicholas Katzenbach, Friedrich Kessler, or Addison Mueller); Introduction to Public Law (Thomas Emerson, Louis Pollak, or Eugene Rostow), Legal Research (Katzenbach), Procedure I (Fleming James or Quentin Johnstone), and Torts I (Fowler

Harper or Fleming James). Beyond that, and the required Moot Court, Property, and Criminal Law in the second term, stretched a wide array of electives whose titles paid obeisance to the enduring influence of the "Yale approach"—Dynamics of Human Behavior; Law and Public Opinion; Law, Science & Policy: Jurisprudence for a Free Society; Regional Planning and Natural Resource Development; Scientific and Philosophical Foundations of Legal Institutions, etc.

Given the individualistic nature of legal instruction at Yale, it's difficult to generalize about what those in the class of '58 learned there. Without a doubt, though, they came to understand that lawyers and law could solve, as well as create, problems. Mark Tushnet (YLS '70) jokes about "the 'lawyer as astrophysicist' assumption: We are people who have a generalized intelligence and can absorb and utilize the products of any other discipline in which we happen to become interested." That means they can "read a physics book over the weekend and send a rocket to the moon on Monday." Who but Yale law graduates would possess such refreshing chutzpah?

But chutzpah can empower. To single out some in the class of '58 for what they did after graduation risks omitting others but provides a sense of the members' versatility. There were careers in government. For example, Clifford Alexander and Stephen Shulman each chaired the Equal Employment Opportunity Commission. Grace Berg Schaible became Alaska's first woman attorney general; Robert Del Tufo, attorney general of New Jersey; Carla Anderson Hills, secretary of Housing and Urban Development, then US trade representative; Milton Gwirtzman, a public policy consultant and confidant to three Kennedys; Richard Ravitch, lieutenant governor of New York. There were many storied careers in private practice. Among them, Tom Barr transformed big-case litigation; criminal defense lawyer Peter Fleming won an acquittal for former Attorney General John Mitchell (who was subsequently reindicted and eventually served time); Max Truitt became a founding partner of Wilmer, Cutler & Pickering; Robert Weinberg, founding partner of Williams & Connolly. There were careers in public interest law. Leonard Weinglass represented (in)famous radicals, including the Chicago Seven and Kathy Boudin; Larry Levine was a founding partner of the public interest law firm that successfully represented Hurricane Carter and four of the Central Park Five; and Jack Golodner became a founder and president of the Department for Professional Employees, AFL-CIO. There were judges—Circuit Court of Appeals Judges Guido Calabresi and John Farrell, District Judge Edward Cahn, Administrative Law Judge Jesse Etelson, Connecticut Superior Court Judge William Burke Lewis, and Florida Appellate Judge Daniel Pearson. There were careers in the legal academy. Jerome Barron became professor at George Washington; Guido Calabresi, professor at and dean of Yale Law School; Bill Felstiner, director of both the American Bar Foundation and the International Institute for the Sociology of Law; Howard Fink, professor at Ohio State; Thomas Headrick, professor of law, dean of the Law School, and provost at SUNY Buffalo; Henry Monaghan, professor at Columbia; Jerome Reichman, professor at Duke; Robert Stevens, professor of law at Yale, president of Haverford, chancellor of UC Santa Cruz, and master of Pembroke College, Oxford.

Alumni ventured into less traditional realms too. There were careers in business. At McDonalds, Paul Duncan brought Big Macs to Beijing and Moscow. Jay Lafave became a founder of International Management Group; Eugene Landy, a pioneer of the Real Estate Investment Trusts industry; Richard Maidman, a Manhattan real-estate tycoon; Stan Ebner, an aerospace executive. There were scholarly careers outside the legal academy for computer scientist Eugene Lawler, philosopher Louis Hammer, biblicist Walter Lamp, poet and translator Burton Raffel, education professor David Schimmel, and political scientist Theodore Vestal. There were two second careers as prep school teachers for Charles Bates and James Boorsch. There were two publishers who were also novelists, one of whom also became a screenwriter, playwright, producer, director, and prodigious litigator: Laura Chapman Hruska and Alan Hruska. There were two medical doctors: cardiovascular surgeon Irwin Boruchow and transfusion medicine specialist Thomas Zuck. Ed Woodsum became Yale's athletic director for six years (during which time he also served as president of the National Audubon Society). There was even a colorful journalist. "Rumpled and Runyonesque, a habitué of Gallagher's, Elaine's, Sardi's, and other celebrity watering holes, Mr. [Sidney] Zion was a loud, cigar-smoking, storytelling, die-hard New York Giants fan who railed against what he called fitness fascists, passionately defended Israel, and counted horse-players, mobsters, actors, and politicians among his friends," the *New York Times* obituary noted of its onetime reporter.

A complete list of achievements of the class of '58 would fill this volume. But you get the idea. Its members were a remarkable bunch. Enjoy their stories of what these lawyers have done.

I

CASES AND CONTROVERSIES

GUIDO CALABRESI

A Failure, Redeemed In Part

MY CAREER HAS BEEN A LUCKY ONE. BUT rather than write about incidents that I am proud of, I'd rather describe a failure to do the right thing, and how this failure came, in a sense, to be redeemed.

I was a relatively young (in years of sitting but not in age) judge, when I was on a panel reviewing a habeas petition brought by a young man who had been convicted in a state court of murdering his parents when he was barely eighteen. Generally, in habeas cases one can see possible errors—often serious ones—made at trial, but one has little doubt as to the guilt of the petitioner. This case, however, was different. Though the petitioner had confessed, after grueling and highly misleading questioning, he had immediately renounced his confession. More important there were a thousand and one things—behavior on the part of the investigators, tactics by the prosecutor at trial, and unexplained failures to look into the likely guilt of potential murderers who were unrelated to the petitioner—that made the case smell. I read the record, again and again, and came away convinced that there was a significant likelihood that the youngster was innocent. Moreover, it seemed clear to me that if he were given another trial, with a decent lawyer, he might very well be acquitted. But finding reversible error cognizable on habeas was anything but easy. The "wrong" things that had been done were, each, only at the edge of what a federal court can find to be so wrong as to require a state retrial. Nonetheless, I was ready to grant habeas, because the case just did not feel right.

The federal district judge, a good one, had denied habeas. And my fellow appellate panelists agreed with him that habeas should not be granted. These were two highly experienced former federal district judges. Both had been appointed to the Second Circuit when I was, but slightly after me. One, the more senior of the two, was (and is) very tough in criminal cases. He rarely finds error and tends, often with good reason, to be sympathetic to the police. The other, a slow, thoughtful, and very wise judge, almost always got it right. Over the years he became the judge who most often caused me—as quick as he was careful—to rethink my initial instincts for the better. They both said that, given the law as it was, granting habeas was clearly wrong. I struggled but could not sway them.

What then was I to do? If I disagreed with them, the youngster would stay in jail nonetheless. I could, sounding very good, write a forceful dissent, emphasizing my doubts as to his guilt, and underscoring the possible errors that had been made. But if I did so, the majority opinion, denying habeas, would be written by the conservative panel member. He would write a precedential opinion in which the possible errors were totally discounted, thereby making habeas in future and probably worse cases of prosecutorial misbehavior less likely. Indeed, my dissent, pointing out what had been done wrong, would, by the very fact that it had been rejected by the majority, serve only to protect such police behavior from future reversals.

I decided to go along and to write the opinion denying habeas. I was able to get the panel to agree to require a Batson reexamination based on the possible exclusion of some jurors on racial grounds. This, if the reexamination confirmed racial exclusions, could lead to a retrial—as I earnestly hoped. But, such reexaminations rarely succeed, and so my "going along" would likely mean, and did in fact result, in a unanimous court rejecting the youngster's pleas.

When it was over, I felt pretty good about it. After all, whether I had gone along or not, the kid would stay in jail. A decent, future harm reducing, opinion got written by me. And I had avoided the temptation to grandstand, to write for history, to no purpose except to look good. What was there to be troubled by? Over the years, I learned! As time passed the youngster, from an awful jail, tried again and again to demonstrate his innocence. He was able to accumulate more and more evidence to that effect. And yet it was never enough. The state courts which, after his failed habeas, were as a practical matter his only recourse, kept repeating the need for finality in such matters. They emphasized how many opportunities he had had to prove his innocence. They noted that neither other state courts nor the federal ones had been convinced. And they reiterated the law that at such a stage it was his burden to demonstrate innocence beyond peradventure. This was not something that from his cell he could possibly do.

I kept following the case and became more and more agitated. What, I thought, would have happened had I dissented and had stated my belief that the kid might well be innocent? Would the state courts, reading of my doubts and seeing the powerful listing of misbehaviors in the investigation and trial, be more receptive to his pleas and to the increasing evidence of innocence now? They would certainly have viewed his additional requests more sympathetically, I thought. And so I agonized.

I even asked the chief judge of our circuit if I could write the state courts and tell them of my original doubts and my reasons for them. He told me that I could not write, but that the panel I had chaired could do so, if they shared my worries. This, however, was not possible. The conservative judge was not inclined that way. And the third judge, who might well have joined me, had died. So there was nothing I could do.

The case became a kind of object lesson for me and for my law clerks. When the question of whether one should dissent or go along and insist on a narrower opinion would come up—as it does every year—I would make all the, often valid, arguments for going along. But I would then mention this case and express my anguish, while explaining that there are situations in which "useless" dissents are anything but useless. This case had taught me a lesson and I was passing the lesson on to the clerks.

As it happened at least one of my clerks heard the lesson and my deep unhappiness with the consequences. When his clerkship had ended, he had gone to work in a major New York law firm. And lo and behold the sometime youngster, still in jail (he was sentenced to life in prison), had written to the firm begging them to take his case on, pro bono, now after many years. He listed his evidence of innocence. But more in point my clerk recognized his name. The former clerk talked the firm into taking the case, and that changed everything.

With the means and skill of top New York lawyers on the case, it was not long before so much evidence of the convicted murderer's guiltlessness was put together, that even the state courts had to take notice. Additional evidence pointing to a potential guilty party—the dead father's business partner, who had long since left the jurisdiction under doubtful conditions—was gathered. And the suspicious reasons why, originally, this possibly guilty party had never been adequately investigated were underscored.

It became all too clear. There could be no doubt. And so, after seventeen years in jail, the man, now some thirty-five years old, whose habeas I had denied was released. He had been a young high school kid when he was jailed. He had lost his youth and years of vitality in prison but now he was free!

My former clerk, who had been significantly responsible for his freedom, then had the gall to ask him if he wanted to meet the judge whose opinion had denied him habeas. Did he want to get to know the person who had failed to act on his behalf, and so, possibly, had been responsible for his extended prison time? Amazingly, he said yes!

We met, and I liked him. And he was extraordinarily generous to me. We talked about what he had lost and whether it could be made up, at least in part. He determined to make it up. In due course he went to college and graduated well. He then went on to a local law school, where I had the pleasure of being a judge in the moot court program, which he helped run. He also invited me to his graduation.

The state, incidentally, now recognizing the many wrong things that had adhered to his initial conviction, as well as the awful years he had spent in jail, settled a significant number of millions of dollars on him. Financially independent, he currently dedicates his life to working on "innocence projects" and to lecturing to schools and bar groups on the flaws in our criminal process. In time, he married, and, neither he nor his wife being that young, has recently joyously adopted a child.

A happy ending you might say. But what can make up for seventeen years in jail? One's youth, with all that entails in pleasures, sexuality, and, yes, uncertainties, lost behind bars. And what does it say about our criminal system, about judging and about judgments? There are no easy answers to these questions. My fellow panelists might well suggest that, had this youngster been freed way back then, that same decision would have led to the release of some clearly guilty defendants in other cases. And, should judges like me be allowed to trust their instincts rather than the law in cases like this one? I trust my instincts, but all in all I trust the law—flawed as it is—more than I trust the instincts of my fellow judges.

I still think I was wrong not to dissent long, long ago in this case. And that is why I write this piece rather than describing cases where I am confident that I did the right thing, even when doing that took considerable courage. Having said that, I thank God for the youngster's release and return to a reasonable life ... despite and yet, in a peculiar sense, because of me. And most of all, I am grateful that, rather than making me feel the pain that my weakness helped to cause him, the youngster has let me be part of his, and hence of my, redemption.

ALVIN DEUTSCH

How a Lost Copyright Led Nixon to China

IN THE LATE 1960s EDGAR SNOW WAS REFERRED TO me by one of his friends in book publishing. Snow's best-selling *Red Star Over China* was first published in the United States by Random House in 1938, following its original publication in the United Kingdom. The book was the culmination of Snow's many trips to China as a reporter in the 1930s during which he lived in Shanghai. In 1936 his articles dealing with the rise of communist-controlled areas of China were the only reliable reports from the scene of the Long March. During a four-month period in mid-1936 he interviewed Mao and became the first American to interview the nascent leaders of what became the Communist Republic of China (CRC) following the fall of the National Government of Chiang Kai-shek.

At our meeting, Snow complained that writers in Chinese studies were rapaciously citing what had become his classic work without attribution of authorship. He assured me that he was not looking for compensation; just proper recognition.

When dealing with a question of unauthorized citation, I pointed out as usual that the US copyright law allowed people to cite from copyrighted works under the doctrine of "fair use"—a concept I explained to Snow. He nonetheless felt that many citations transcended that "doctrine" to "unfair use."

My second inquiry dealing with a work published in 1938 was to enquire whether the US copyright had been duly renewed in

1965, the twenty-eighth year following publication. Snow's blank look led me to ask whether his publisher or literary agent had renewed the copyright in his name. He responded that *Red Star* was first published in England in 1937 (whose Copyright Act vested protection on publication for a then duration of 50 years following the author's death: no concept of "renewal" existed in the UK). But the original US edition was out of print, all rights had reverted to him, and he had long ago discharged his agent. Hence, no one with proper knowledge had been in place to renew the copyright, it had not been renewed and thus it entered the public domain in the US.

What to do? I suggested that he revise the book and include a new introduction.

It turned out to be a propitious time to produce a revised version. President Nixon early in his first term sought to achieve a working relationship with the CRC. He had his national security adviser, Henry Kissinger, commence sub-silento overtures in that direction. The original edition of *Red Star* was out of print and the revised version published by Grove Press in 1968 with a new introduction filled a yawning gap in the available commentary on the CRC.

By the late 1960s and early 1970s there were indications that China and the US were "considering" rapprochement. Following publication of the revised edition, Snow visited China where Chairman Mao advised him that he would be pleased to meet with Nixon. Snow carried that message to the White House. The Nixon-Mao meeting occurred in 1972 and the two countries set out on the path that led to formal US recognition of the People's Republic of China in 1979.

In all humility I suggest that my discovery of the unrenewed copyright which triggered the publication of the revised edition of *Red Star*, which brought renewed public attention to Snow's unique position vis-à-vis the Chinese leadership, followed by Snow's visit to Mao which triggered the Nixon visit, might not have occurred but for the incident of the unrenewed copyright. Who is to say?

Snow did not live to see the story unravel. During the McCarthy era he was hounded because of his relationship with the Chinese Communist Party and could no longer make a living as a correspondent in the US. He moved with his wife, the actress Lois Wheeler, to Switzerland. On hearing that Snow was suffering from pancreatic cancer, Zhou Enlai sent a team of physicians to aid in his treatment. Snow died on February 15, 1972, the very week Nixon was en route to China.

Stanley Ebner

The Commanding General Wants to See You

"THE COMMANDING GENERAL WANTS TO SEE YOU ... now." I was awakened from a mild reverie by the sharp-edged tone of our office administrator's words, which were completely unambiguous. The head of our office, the staff judge advocate of our command, was on travel. As his deputy I was left in charge—and charge I did, right over to the headquarters building. It turned out that the subject was a court-martial, on which I had signed off earlier that day. The case was a pretty straightforward matter of Absence Without Leave (AWOL), but I could see that the sentence troubled the general. The court had sentenced the accused to a bad conduct discharge plus a year's confinement. When I reviewed the record it was clear that the prisoner should never have been in the army to begin with, and that the form of discharge was appropriate. But the year in jail seemed excessive. I could not see that the cost of confinement would yield any tangible benefits to the government. And the prisoner, given the realities of life in prison, was unlikely to emerge from jail a man changed for the better—at least for military service, that was.

The general, who was quite bright, wanted to discuss the case at some length—and so we did. Now, a discussion between a major and a major general is something akin to oral argument at the Supreme Court between a seasoned associate justice and a junior law partner with limited appellate experience. Finally, and not surprisingly, he overruled my recommendation and decided to restore the court's original sentence.

He handed me the case file and said he'd be sure to sign it promptly once I changed it to align my recommendation with his decision. When I tried to explain that the staff judge advocate's recommendation was part of the official trial record and could not be changed after the fact, he wouldn't hear of it. "How would it look for a commanding general to be overruling his own attorney?" he asked. My attempt to reassure him that it does happen did not help. "If I go along with you the senior Pentagon brass will think I'm getting soft by letting this guy off without any jail time," he muttered. I got the distinct feeling, as the discussion ranged back and forth, that he actually appreciated the chance to argue with someone who wasn't totally intimidated by his position and aggressive manner. Nevertheless, I tried not to show my extreme relief as he pulled the file to him, gave one last grunt, and signed it "as is." My relief was compounded the very next day when I learned that a prisoner had escaped from our stockade, and that our general had relieved the provost marshal of his duties on the spot with the words "No one escapes from my jail."

When the lieutenant colonel who normally served as the staff judge advocate and my boss returned from his trip he learned of my interface with the general, which disturbed him more than I felt it should have. He vacillated over any follow-up that might be required. I insisted that if there was, then I should be present. He wasn't overly keen on that prospect either. Actually the lieutenant colonel vacillated over almost everything, having been passed over several times for full colonel and knowing this assignment was his last chance. His relationship with the commanding general was okay, but hadn't been tested. He knew that I'd defend my position strongly, and wasn't sure where he should come out in front of the CG. So he did nothing, which in this case was right for him. In actuality, he retired from that job as a lieutenant colonel. Ultimately the subject died of its own weight and, as busy people tend to do, we moved on. But this episode has a post script. During the traditional farewell party the office gave for me, who should show up but the commanding general. Not only did he offer up some very kind comments, but he also pinned the Army Commendation Medal on my lapel. Totally unexpected, this said more about him than me. Rounding things out, I later learned that he had earned a promotion to lieutenant general and retired with three stars. I can still recall his comment to me at my farewell that lawyers played a key role in the life of our democracy because "they are the generalists of our society." Indeed. But I had been learning that, and much more, earlier in my limited army career. Such as in a case somewhat the obverse of the one above, where I actually had the full support of the leadership at a different earlier post. I was a staffer in a larger judge advocate office led by a well-regarded full colonel who, although not exactly burning with ambition, did have a sentencing legacy of sorts he wanted to try and leave behind. It involved an AWOL case also but, unlike the later case I described above, the court had sentenced the accused to one-year confinement but with no discharge. Evidently someone on the panel had persuaded the others that a year in jail would improve the prisoner's outlook and make him a viable soldier. I'm sure, but couldn't prove, that an element of punishment crept into the deliberations of a somewhat jaded court whose docket included at least one too many AWOL cases. My boss wanted my opinion as to whether this case might be a suitable vehicle for commutation, something he'd wanted to try for a time. He picked me I suppose because we got along, because he liked my work, and because he hoped (but never said) that my Yale law degree might produce a useful element of originality. He was right on that score, as I didn't know the first thing about it. There wasn't much to know, actually, given the lack of a successful commutation case in military law. So the brief I wrote had few footnotes but lots of imagination. The staff judge advocate liked it, especially because he believed that commuting this prisoner's sentence from confinement to a bad-conduct discharge would be doing him and the army each a service. And so, consistent with our policy and especially sensible in this case, I had the accused and his counsel in my office to explain the procedures we would follow in moving the case forward. It took very little time before it became obvious that we had lost our prisoner (figuratively) whose eyes had begun to glass over before I had gotten very far. With the end in sight, however, I pressed on, until I got to the phrase "Now when they execute the sentence ...." The prisoner turned pale, his eyes got big as saucers, and he sat bolt upright in his chair. In a quavering voice he asked "execute?" It took a bit of time to calm him down and explain what we meant, but we needn't have bothered. The government appealed, the case was reversed, and I pressed on with my education as a lawyer and person. Quite a journey. Not through yet.

ALAN HRUSKA

The Clifford Irving Fandango

IN OUR DAY (INVIDIOUS PHRASE), ATTENDANCE AT class was left entirely to our discretion. So I exercised mine most often against. I regret that, since the professors of "our day" were great showmen in addition to being great scholars. But I did set a record that will not likely be broken: teaching more classes than I attended.

Despite the tolerance of the attendance policy, I was, of course, repeatedly punished for cutting class—e.g., when I complained to Dean Sturges that the exam paper to which he'd given a D deserved an A grade, he blithely replied, "I wouldn't know. I never read it." And I was certainly not rewarded for my teaching. Boris Bittker, when working on my *Yale Law Journal* comment regarding corporate reorganizations—a subject of which I retain absolutely nothing—conceived the dubious idea of having me join him in the teaching of Tax III. Soon thereafter, he departed for more pressing work, infrequently to return, leaving me to finish most of the term. I still apologize to the members of that class—in my imagination, if not in person.

I went to Cravath to be a tax lawyer. That decision did not survive the day. I received my first tax assignments, proceeded directly to the tax library, stared at the binders for maybe an hour, and experienced—I'd say, apocalyptically—a revelation: I did not want to do this for the rest of my life. By the end of the day I was in litigation, supposedly "helping out" for a month. The case to which I was assigned, the tetracycline price-fixing litigation, was then railroaded to trial by Senator Estes Kefauver, as part of his strategy to capture the Democratic nomination for President. Looking back, it's not hard to appreciate why that "month" as a litigator lasted forty-four years.

By the end of that "month," the partner who rescued me from Tax was himself rerouted into another emergency, abandoning E. R. Squibb & Sons to my questionable care in the biggest antitrust suit of the late '50s. Remarkably, Squibb's general counsel agreed to this—a decision that would be unthinkable in today's world. So there I was, weeks out of law school, trying a case I could read about daily in the *New York Times*. I did so for the better part of two years, well protected by the likes of Walter Mansfield, Gary Gesell, and other great trial lawyers of the period, who were representing other defendants. But the first time I rose to speak, I was nervous enough to knock the water pitcher off the table. The guy who caught it was a young Covington associate, Bill Baxter, who, many years later, played a somewhat more significant role— bailing me and hundreds of others out of a thirteen-year judicial travesty known as *US v. IBM*. The day Baxter was appointed head of the antitrust division, I called Nick Katzenbach, then general counsel of IBM, and said, "The case is over. Bill Baxter will throw out this case." And he did.

After tetracycline, which we won following a two-year trial (great story, which I've no space to tell here), I tried fourteen other cases as an associate, including the American Express salad oil case in Supreme, New York County, and the jury trial involving the National Sugar plant closings. As a partner, I did, for various long stretches of time, all the litigation for CBS and Time Inc., and very large cases for IBM, Westinghouse, Warner-Lambert, Studebaker, Price Waterhouse, most of the financial industry, half the steel industry, much of the magazine publishing industry, and many other companies, institutions, and individuals. During the latter part of this career, Nick Katzenbach strolled into my office and said, "You're now my patent lawyer." I said, "I was a liberal arts major." He said, "That's why you're now my patent lawyer." He then presented me as such to his prior patent firm sitting en banc for the occasion. Lovely moment: Daniel enjoyed warmer welcomes from the lions. But many patent cases for IBM and others followed (including one for Trimble Navigation, which required me to understand GPS well enough to explain it to a reasonably intelligent ten-year old, which is the level one should aim for in a patent case). The individuals I represented in a variety of cases and matters included Henry Kissinger, Bill Paley, Frank Stanton, Tom Watson, Dick Watson, Kay Graham, Sam Walton, and Bill Simon. All in all, I won a bit more than 250 cases, and settled an equal number.

I did lose one. When ASCAP and BMI tried to triple their rates, Bill Paley asked me to get them out of the business of licensing music to TV networks. I told him the case would go to the US Supreme Court, where it would become another *Toolson v. New York Yankees*—which, of course, is what happened. After a lengthy trial, the district court dismissed the complaint; the Second Circuit reversed, ruling for CBS on per se grounds; the Supreme Court reversed but remanded for a reappraisal under the rule of reason; Murray Gurfein wrote a Second Circuit opinion in CBS's favor, but died, leaving it unsigned on his dining room table; another panel reached the opposite conclusion, without doing the appraisal for which the Supreme Court had asked and somehow managing nowhere to address CBS's principal argument; but the high court declined another certiorari review (Thurgood said, years later, "What the hell did you expect," to which I responded, "Nothing"). Bill Paley, however, felt more content with the result than I. During the ten years of that litigation, ASCAP and BMI refrained from seeking any hike in the rates.

But I digress. The assignment is to write about one "episode" that was "interesting [to 'the general public'], challenging, [and] even important." ASCAP would not qualify on most of those grounds, except for someone fascinated by the realities of the judicial system. Other episodes would take too long to tell, are too confidential to relate in detail, or both—e.g., the second round of the turbine generator price-fixing litigation in which Westinghouse (my client) made go away a multibillion dollar, potentially business-crippling exposure by talking 500 public utility lawyers and executives out of a suit in a speech at the Sheraton Hotel and procuring a consent decree from the antitrust division that cost Westinghouse nothing and significantly improved its competitive position against GE; the first "insider trading" case (for Merrill Lynch); the trade secrets case, *IBM v. Cogar*, tried in Arthur Liman's conference room, with Artie sitting in judgment on his own client and ultimately agreeing to a decree allowing Arthur D. Little to police, and Williard Wirtz to act as master, to ensure no further use of IBM's secrets; the circuit court initiative to wrest *US v. IBM* from David Edelstein's grasp by having me persuade my client, IBM (quite willing), and the Department of Justice (ultimately unpersuadable) to arbitrate the issues before a judge of the court of appeals; the many cases brought for Republic, Inland, Jones & Loughlin, and National Steel in the International Trade Commission and the Court of International Trade in an attempt to save the American steel industry; the prosecution of the newsman's privilege in the Supreme Court and throughout the states; the nationwide program to convert *Sullivan v. NY Times* and *Hill v. Time Inc.* into engines for the summary disposal of libel and privacy actions; and the work done, never to be revealed (including here), in connection with the Pentagon Papers litigation.

So I chose an episode, highly public and brief, which I think of as the "Clifford Irving Fandango." Frankly, I doubt its importance to anyone but the participants, but it did seem at the time to interest most everyone in the world. I remember one woman, Nina van Pallandt, who made herself an international celebrity overnight, and launched a movie career, simply by claiming to have slept with the con man, Irving. And Irving himself was later flatteringly portrayed by Richard Gere in a film, based on Irving's own book, which left out (understandably) most everything that was interesting legally.

It began for me in December 1971 with a call from Time Inc.'s editorial counsel, Jack Dowd. He told me there was this guy, Clifford Irving, who claimed to be representing the autobiography of

Howard Hughes—a manuscript Irving purportedly helped write. McGraw-Hill had bought the book rights for $750,000 (about $4.5 million in today's money) and wanted *Life* to serialize the edition. To publicize the deal, McGraw was holding a press conference that afternoon, and Dowd asked me to meet him at the event.

Irving put on quite a show. There is something about a man asserting an utterly preposterous story with self-deprecating humor and awkward sincerity, while managing to look everyone straight in the eye. Irving himself brought up the book he wrote about his Ibiza neighbor, Elmyr de Hory, the notorious art forger. That book, prophetically entitled *Fake*, should have served—one would have thought—as a stunningly obvious tip-off that Irving was simply one-upping his neighbor. But as Irving spun it that day, it was the skillful writing of *Fake* that led Hughes to seek Irving's assistance.

As we walked back to Jack Dowd's office, he asked, "Have you ever seen anything like that?" I told him I had. Several times, actually. People doing things so outrageous, with such implausible explanations, that they had to know they'd be caught—and so acted precisely because they wanted to be punished. (Later, another such matter I dealt with involved a Yale Law School grad who stole Roswell Gilpatric's private correspondence with Jackie Kennedy, claiming the letters had been abandoned in a wastepaper basket.)

"In any event," Dowd said, "*Life* will buy a ticket to the show. It's a small down payment, nothing more to be paid, and that refundable, if the manuscript is proven to be fraudulent—proof we've already launched a team from *Time* to gather. Shouldn't take long."

Hughes, of course, sued (though his alter ego, Rosemont) to enjoin the McGraw-Hill book and the prospective *Life* series. What he asked for was no less than a prior restraint on freedom of the press, which no civilized court in the nation would grant. In New York, however, he drew the Honorable Gerald P. Culkin, whom *New York* magazine dubbed the worst judge in the state. Culkin's assignment to the case might have been the result of a lucky spin of the wheel at Supreme Court, New York County. But the attorney Hughes retained, Dave Shivitz, was the go-to man for Tammany Hall.

McGraw-Hill retained the famous handwriting experts, the Osborn brothers, who opined that the handwriting in the manuscript and the endorsement on the McGraw-Hill check matched Hughes's signature on his application for a Nevada gambling license. And a Time Inc. reporter, Frank McCulloch, who knew Hughes well, initially formed the belief that the manuscript was genuine. At the hearing on Hughes's motion for a preliminary injunction, I called the court's attention to those facts, but emphasized that it was the rule against prior restraints that defeated the motion, whether the manuscript was genuine or a hoax.

The day after that hearing, the first bit of real evidence emerged: the McGraw-Hill check written (at Irving's request) to H. R. Hughes had been endorsed and deposited in a Swiss bank, not by Howard, but by a woman calling herself Helga R. Hughes, who turned out to be none other than Irving's wife, Edith. I told the court that Hughes's pending motion was moot, at least against my client, since *Life* no longer had any interest in serializing this manuscript.

By the end of the week, the *Time* team, led by Frank McCulloch, had tracked down the full story. I informed the court and opposing counsel; a hearing was scheduled; and strange bedfellows came together: Howard Hughes, McGraw-Hill, and Clifford Irving all aligned to stop *Time* magazine's proposed printing of any part of the manuscript, even (or in Irving's case, especially) for the purpose of exposing it as a fraud. Again, I got a call from Jack Dowd. Jim Shepley, president of the company, wanted to talk.

Shepley's office was an eight-window corner expanse surrounded by a honeycomb of rooms for dining and caucusing, and an outer chamber for his secretaries and staff. The man himself was a feisty bantam, all energy and smarts. "As you know," Shepley said, "we now have our hands on what apparently inspired this hoax—a bio of Hughes written by a reporter named James Phelan who collaborated with Noah Dietrich. It was Dietrich who helped build Hughes's empire—and then the two had a spat. Apparently, the Phelan-Dietrich manuscript was offered to a batch of publishers and movie producers, which is probably how Irving got it—it's how we did—but no one would bite. Scared off by Hughes, no doubt, who is known to sue anyone who publishes anything about him he doesn't like. Irving added a lot to his piece—publically known stuff—but the Dietrich material is what gives it enough appearance of authenticity to let Irving palm it off as Hughes's own work. We're doing a side-by-side. Printing passages of the Phelan-Dietrich manuscript alongside Irving's plagiarized work. That should be the end of Mr. Irving."

"Great story," I said.

"We like it," said Shepley. "And, for you, piece of cake, right? Getting their motion denied?"

"Wouldn't say that, no."

Shepley put on a show of surprise. "Irving's a swindler. We're printing a news story. First Amendment. Case closed. What'd I miss?"

"You can write what you want about Irving," I said, "but if you prove it with a side-by-side, there's a competing policy: copyright."

"On a fraudulent manuscript? You can't be serious!"

"The problem is timing," I said. "The court hearing is scheduled for an emergency session tomorrow morning, Saturday. You go to press tomorrow night. The trial judge will rule against us. We need time to take an emergency appeal on a Saturday afternoon. Which cuts out the time for an evidentiary hearing—even assuming, contrary to fact, that the trial judge would allow one. So we have to win immediately in the appellate division on the papers. And all we have is our paper allegation that the manuscript is a hoax. Without live witnesses—and without the time for these judges actually to read both manuscripts side by side—this is not a slam dunk."

"How much of the thing do they have to read, for chrissakes? Look at four or five passages, and you know that Irving is a plagiarist."

"He'll probably claim Phelan plagiarized from him."

"That's absolute nonsense!"

"No doubt. But you can't cross-examine an affidavit. And if there's no evidentiary hearing, Irving's sworn statement, for the time being, will be taken as true."

"But you will win the case," Shepley said.

"I'll win what I think you need."

"Meaning?"

"How much of the Irving manuscript were you planning to print?"

Shepley looked down the table. Andrew Heiskell, the Time Inc. chairman, had just joined the meeting. Heiskell was a natural leader who also looked the part: a tall, tanned, handsome man with a courtly manner and a warm smile. "About a thousand words should do it," he said.

"Okay," I said. "A thousand words. You got it."

"What about the copyright problem?" Shepley asked.

"Just went away. With the doctrine of fair use. Assuming we can find some appellate judge who understands it."

"Why are you so sure we're losers in the lower court?"

"The judge," I said. "Some are fairly predictable. He's a sure thing."

"You know," Heiskell said, "when this case started, I asked your senior partner, Bruce Bromley, to handle it."

"He turn you down?"

"He said I was better off with you, and he'd carry your bags. That true?"

"The bags part, probably."

As I got back to our office downtown, it was Bromley himself who pulled me into his suite. In his habitual dark raiment—suit, vest, tie—he looked like a preoccupied pallbearer. "While you were palavering with the client," he said, "Hughes's papers came in from Dave Shivitz's office."

"So what is he arguing?"

"Libel," Bromley said. "And exclusive right to his own bio."

"Pretty baseless."

"Not at the trial-court level."

"No, they could argue anything there."

"So, whatta you need?" Bromley asked, sitting back in his desk chair, running fingers through his wisps of gray hair. "In an appellate judge?"

"We get to pick our own judge?" I said.

"This is the appellate division. Still in the Dark Ages. No

emergency judge is designated. You got an emergency? Go find a judge yourself. On a Saturday."

"A single judge can stay an injunction," I said, thinking aloud. "Not reverse it, but stay it until the full court can review weeks later. Right?"

"Right."

"And a stay on a Saturday afternoon is all we need to go to press Saturday night."

"Now you're getting on top of the problem. So what kind of judge do you need?"

"First of all, he can't be a Democrat. Dave Shivitz is totally plugged into Tammany Hall. Secondly, we need a smart judge. We've got the better case. Be nice if we had a judge who understood it."

"You also want someone who knows something about copyrights."

"Yeah, great," I said. "In state court? A smart Republican scholar of a federal doctrine?"

"There actually is such a person," Bromley said. "Teddy Kupferman. Big copyright expert before going on the bench. Won a huge case in that field. Landmark decision."

"Sounds ideal."

"Yes, he is," Bromley said, getting up, going to the window.

"There's a problem. I can see it in that look you're giving me."

Bromley gazed out on the late afternoon view, the sun dying in the gristle of his complexion.

"Yeah, there's a problem. Case he won was against your client, Time Inc. And he won it by defeating the very doctrine you'll be relying on—the fair-use exception to a copyright."

"The Zapruder film case," I said. "The JFK assassination. *Life* wanted to publish two or three frames of the film, arguing it would be a fair use. The Supreme Court ruled otherwise."

"You remember the facts, but not the lawyers."

I said carefully, "You were on the other side?"

"Whatta you think?" Bromley said with a smile. "You win every case?"

"Our facts are a lot better than those in Zapruder."

"A bit. So are you going to call Mr. Justice Kupferman, or am I going to have to do that for you, too?" The trick about not being nervous, I thought, as I dialed Justice Kupferman's chambers, was not to think about all the things that should be making you nervous. It also helps if the thing you're calling about is the front page story of every newspaper on the planet.

I told the judge's secretary why I was calling, and the Honorable Theodore Kupferman immediately took the call. Ingesting a complicated situation netted out tersely caused the jurist briefly to pause.

"I'll be at home tomorrow afternoon," Kupferman said. "If your papers are in order—which includes proof of appropriate notice to your opponents—I'll hear your application for a stay. In my living room. I'll put my secretary back on to give you the telephone number and address."

While I waited, I mused over an interesting fact. Not even Kupferman had any doubt but that Gerald Culkin would issue an injunction.

I had little sleep that night, though Bromley and others had worked on the papers so I could get some. And it was a cold February morning when I stepped into a cab. Stoically, I rode it downtown, spied the commotion going on in front of the courthouse, and got out on the west end of Foley Square.

Crossing a small park of tall, spindly trees, I watched the press mob swarming over the courthouse steps, vans in front, camera equipment being assembled. I stopped for a moment, took a deep breath, and looked up. Black limbs patterned a pewter sky, like an abstract canvas. The sun was up there somewhere between the branches, behind the cloud covering. The crowd was there because of Howard Hughes, but in a couple of hours, they'll be swarming the lawyers. I made for the courthouse. The reporters let me pass with only mild curiosity. No one had any idea who I was, and I looked straight ahead. Wind swirled in the square like wet paint.

*　*　*

Lawyers were haranguing a bleary-eyed judge. He wanted no reporters to witness this, so the argument was in chambers. He looked put upon and confused: a round man in a bulging vest, slouched in his chair and peering at you like a hound dog. For all the comprehension Justice Culkin displayed, the attorneys before him might have been speaking in tongues.

Clifford Irving had somehow conned Maurice Nessen into representing him. Maury was a sleek little man who had won more cases than anyone in the room. And, predictably, he argued for the injunction on the ground that the planned *Time* exposé of the Irving manuscript would infringe his client's copyright on that work. The publishing company lawyer, Haliburton Fales, wagged his impressive jaw in harmony with Nessen's point, adding that, without an evidentiary hearing, the court could not accept as true Time Inc.'s allegation that the manuscript was fraudulent, undeserving of copyright protection.

Culkin turned to Dave Shivitz, whose client, Hughes, owned no copyright on Irving's manuscript, which Hughes had himself denounced, or on the work Irving plagiarized, which Hughes claimed was defamatory and an invasion of privacy. So, apart from complaining about the sufficiency of notice, Shivitz argued that the prospective *Time* article—though he'd never seen it— must also be libelous and an invasion of privacy, and therefore restrained until the court had an opportunity to study it. Culkin glanced at me, as if he agreed.

"Can't do it, Your Honor."

"Oh, really!" said the judge, stirring himself into an upright position. "Why is that, Mr. Hruska?"

"The doctrine prohibiting prior restraint. One of the oldest First Amendment principles—and the most clearly established."

"I want to stop this article, counsel—I just issue the order."

"Which, Your Honor—and I say this with all due respect to the court—would be overturned by the appellate division in approximately twenty minutes, the time of a cab ride uptown."

"You planning to take such a cab ride, Mr. Hruska?"

"At one o'clock, Your Honor."

Culkin looked at me cagily. "I may not rule by one o'clock."

"Then that's appealable."

"My not ruling?"

"Of course," I said. "The magazine's printing deadline is to-night. Which means everything has to be submitted this afternoon. Everyone knows that, especially the hundred or so press people waiting outside. Holding a prospective injunction over our heads all afternoon would itself impose a chilling effect. And when a trial court deliberately delays an injunction until the last minute before the enjoined act can be taken—the delay done to prevent an appeal—that itself is an appealable event. At least by mandamus. Basic rules of appellate procedure."

"It would be just a temporary restraint."

"Makes no difference, Your Honor. No prior restraint means no prior restraint without a clear and present danger to the nation. Even the threat and delay of such an order is appealable, as I just said."

Culkin said warily to Shivitz, "You know about such a rule?"

Shivitz, shaking his head, looked uncertain.

"Would Your Honor like authority on the point?" I said. "I take it that the appealability of a deliberate attempt by a trial judge to avoid an appeal is of interest to Your Honor."

"No, it isn't!" Culkin snapped. "Why should it be? I'll have my decision out well before one o'clock!"

Back in the office, waiting for Culkin's decision, Bruce Bromley said to me, "You actually have cases on the appealability of trial judges delaying rulings to avoid appeals?"

I shrugged. "No. Looked last night. Couldn't find any."

Bromley, smiling, said, "More balls than brains."

"I dunno. If I couldn't find any, Culkin's not likely to."

"Which means, for this bluff to work, he's got to believe you're smarter than he is—and not bluffing."

"Right."

Bromley's secretary walked in, white-faced and excited. "Call from the courthouse! The judge has issued an injunction!"

Bromley glanced at his watch and laughed. "You step in shit, kiddo."

I left to call Shivitz, and got him on the first ring. "You heard, Dave?"

"Yeah, have. Sorry, Alan, but we both know it's only the first round."

"What I was thinking."

"So," said Shivitz smoothly, "looking ahead, knowing one of us would want to appeal, I've lined up an emergency judge in the appellate division. To hear us this afternoon. He's available in his apartment at two thirty."

"Who'd you get, Dave?"

He named his man. I said, "Wasn't he the former Tammany leader in the Bronx?"

"Hmm," said Shivitz. "I think he might have been."

"Thing is, I'm going to be moving before Teddy Kupferman at one thirty. You can join me in his apartment if you like— this call is notice."

"Kupferman? He's a Republican!"

"Only nominally."

"I've already lined up the other guy," Shivitz said—I thought, unnecessarily loudly.

"I'm the appellant, Dave. It's my appeal. All I need is any judge of the appellate court to stay the decision below. So you go to the other guy's apartment, if you prefer. But if Kupferman issues the stay, doesn't matter what happens elsewhere, until the full court can be assembled."

*   *   *

I stepped out of the Checker cab, leaving Bruce Bromley to deal with the driver. It was the protocol of the firm: "first chair" never pays. And Bromley, former court of appeals judge and greatest trial lawyer of the century, observed the rule to the letter. I, waiting, peered up at the white brick high-rise. "Whatta you doing?" said Bromley. "Thinking about the ways you can fuck up this case?" He was right. That's what I was doing.

Riding up in the elevator, Bromley sniffed. "You think too much."

"No doubt," I said.

No trouble finding the apartment; reporters spilled out of it into the hall. The Honorable Theodore Kupferman, enthroned on the wing chair within the bay window of his living room, gazed out on the more than a dozen lawyers occupying his sofas and floor. Kupferman was a professorial sort of man with thinning hair, a high-domed forehead, and a trim-waisted medium frame. His khakis and pink open-collared button-down shirt distinguished him from the lawyers in suits. He had the demeanor of a host who wanted to move on with the party so he could clear all these people out of his home.

Maury Nessen argued the copyright point. I countered with the obvious proposition that copyrights are given only to original works, not to plagiarized manuscripts.

"And how," Kupferman asked, "within the approximately one hour you've given me to rule, am I to determine that this six-hundred-page manuscript submitted by Clifford Irving is nothing more—or little more—than an act of plagiarism?"

"You obviously can't," I said, "but I have here two things that will allow Your Honor to rule in a lot less time than an hour. The first is a four-hundred-page manuscript by a man named Phelan, who collaborated on the work with Hughes's closest associate, Noah Dietrich. Their agent sent a copy to several publishers and movie producers. Almost certainly, Irving got a copy from somebody in one of those offices."

"So both books—about a thousand pages, you say—" The judge held up the manuscripts and gave me a look that said, You surely don't expect me to read these.

"I show Your Honor the Phelan manuscript," I said, "only to verify the second item—which is a side-by-side layout of about twenty excerpts from the Irving manuscript and the Phelan passages that Irving stole from. As Your Honor will quickly see, they're virtually identical. Same anecdotes. Almost the same words."

On the judge's coffee-table sat an ashtray milled with a replica of the scales of justice. Maury Nessen lifted it above his head.

"Yes, Maury?" said Kupferman.

"There are a lot of people in Your Honor's living room at the moment, but none of them, so far as I know, is named Phelan." Nessen carefully returned the ashtray to the table. "So right now, we have only Mr. Hruska's statement that such a person exists, much less that he wrote this manuscript. In other words, Mr. Hruska offers us classic hearsay. And the vice of hearsay is that the actual witness, whom we're being asked to believe—Mr. Phelan—is not here to be cross-examined. And if he were—assuming he exists, and assuming this were an evidentiary hearing—he might well tell us, under vigorous cross, that it was he who copied his manuscript from the manuscript written by Mr. Irving—not vice-versa."

"Mr. Hruska?" the judge said. "Would you like Mr. Nessen to pass you the scales of justice?"

"Don't need them, Your Honor. I have the doctrine of fair use."

"I thought we'd be getting to that."

"It's the way the copyright laws reconcile the conflict between the act's restraint on the publication of copies and the First Amendment's prohibition of restraint on publication. So even if Your Honor were to assume that the Irving manuscript were genuine, we'd still be entitled to publish our opinion to the contrary and support it with excerpts from both manuscripts. As a fair use."

"I happen to know something about this doctrine."

"I know you do, Your Honor."

"I suspected you might. And there are limits to what constitutes fair use. Very important limits."

"And we're well within them. In the Zapruder film case, for example, *Life* published without license the entirety of the film that gave it any value—the several frames showing the assassination. Here, we're publishing a few excerpts from a six-hundred-page book."

Justice Kupferman looked me in the eye. "How many words?"

I didn't hesitate. "Twelve hundred, Your Honor."

"I'll give you a thousand."

I opened my mouth to protest, but the judge came down hard. "Don't push it, counsel!"

"Right," I said.

"All right, everybody," the judge said. "You heard it. I'm staying the order of injunction below. *Time* magazine can publish 1,000 words from the Irving manuscript. You'll have my opinion on Monday."

The lawyers were silent, but shouting reporters thronged the hallway, and several tried to interview Judge Bromley and me on the elevator going down. On the pavement outside, Bromley pushed me into the TV cameras.

Out rattled out the first question: "You won a great victory for the First Amendment! How does that feel?"

"These are pretty standard doctrines," I said. "Prior restraint. Fair use. Most people are aware of them."

"Apparently not Judge Culkin."

"Oh, I think he was aware of them," I said. "Just had a problem applying them to our case."

* * *

Quick epilogue. About a week after the *Time* issue in question was published, Dave Shivitz called and said, "Ain't over yet, Alan. Kupferman's ruling didn't dispose of the case. You'll lose because you breached your promise to Culkin that you'd give fair notice if your client decided to publish."

With unprintable expletives, I said, "I gave notice; it was fair in the circumstances; and the damn case is moot, Dave! Get over it!"

He didn't. He insisted on prosecuting the appeal and got the appellate division to agree with him, although there was utterly no consequence to the ruling.

In the lobby after the argument, he said, "This time I picked the judges."

I said, and I meant it, "I've no doubt that's true."

Marvin L. Karp

Tumult in "Browns Town"

How Art Modell abused his position as majority owner
of the Cleveland Browns, the highly publicized litigation that ensued,
and some of its indirect consequences.

IN 1961, ART MODELL, A THIRTY-FIVE-YEAR-OLD New Yorker who had been working in television advertising, put together a group that purchased the Cleveland Browns football team for $4 million. Modell's personal investment was only $250,000; nevertheless, he became, in the eyes of the general public, "the owner" of the Browns. Modell immediately moved to Cleveland, where he reveled in his newfound prominence and being depicted in the press as the full-time, "hands-on owner" of Ohio's most celebrated sports team.

However, Modell's concept of his position soon brought him into conflict with Paul Brown, the Browns' very famous coach. Since the formation of the team in 1945, each successive group of owners had given Brown a free hand in running the organization, and Brown personally came to be its embodiment. The Browns had, in fact, been named after him. It therefore didn't take long for Modell's visualization of his authority as "owner" to clash with Brown's understanding of their respective roles: in January 1963, Modell fired Paul Brown as coach and general manager of the Cleveland Browns.

At that point, Modell became the "public face" of the Browns.

He was regularly quoted in the newspapers and on television with respect to team matters, was noted for his "one-liners," and was constantly approached by autograph seekers wherever he went. Modell further promoted his image by taking an active role in various civic activities, including becoming treasurer of the Ohio Republican Party. In 1969, he married Patricia Breslin, a television actress, and adopted her two sons.

Contrary, however, to the impression he conveyed to the general public, Modell was not the sole owner of the Cleveland Browns. In fact, he owned only 52.5 percent of the company's outstanding stock, whereas roughly 45 percent was owned by members of the Gries family, an old-line Cleveland family whose roots in the community went back many years. The family's involvement with Cleveland professional football had begun in 1936 when Robert Hays Gries (then an executive with the May Department Stores Company) became a shareholder in the newly formed Cleveland Rams, which shares he held for several years. In 1945, after the Rams moved to Los Angeles, a group of Clevelanders (led by Arthur "Mickey" McBride, the owner of several local taxicab companies) organized the Cleveland Browns to play in the new All-America Football Conference. Robert Hays Gries was a shareholder in that group. In the years that followed he joined succeeding ownership groups, including the one that was put together by Modell in 1961. Robert Hays Gries died in 1966, but by that time his eldest son, Robert D. ("Bob") Gries, had become the de facto head of the Gries family. A graduate of Yale College, Bob had worked for roughly a dozen years at the May Company, like his father before him. He then formed Gries Investment Company, a venture capital enterprise that became his main business activity. Bob was also heavily involved in civic and philanthropic activities, serving diligently on the boards of a number of hospitals, foundations, charities, and social agencies.

By 1965, Gries Sports Enterprises Inc.—a family holding company originally established by Robert Hays Gries, but of which Bob was now president—owned 38.5 percent of the stock of the Browns. Bob himself owned an additional 4.5 percent in his own name, as did his then brother-in-law, Richard ("Dick") Cole. In December of that year, Gries Sports Enterprises, Bob Gries, Robert Hays Gries, and Cole entered into a shareholders voting agreement with Modell. That agreement provided that, so long as Modell and the Gries family owned, in the aggregate, at least 50 percent of the common stock of the Browns, Modell would vote his shares so as to elect, as directors of the Cleveland Browns Football Company, two persons designated by the Gries family. From 1966 through 1981, the two individuals named by the family were Bob Gries and Dick Cole. Modell selected all of the other Browns directors, usually five or six in number.

People outside of the Browns organization knew none of these ownership details. Indeed, whenever Bob Gries happened to travel on the team plane to or from out-of-town football games (which he did from time to time), members of the team thought that he was simply a good friend of Modell's.

The public image of Art Modell as the "sole owner" of the Cleveland Browns, however, was shattered on March 18, 1982, when the front page of the *Cleveland Plain Dealer* (Ohio's largest newspaper) was emblazoned with a startling headline:

"SUIT ACCUSES MODELL OF MISUSING FUNDS"

The story that followed reported that "Robert D. Gries, who had kept a low profile as a major stockholder of the Cleveland Browns," was the owner of 43 percent of the team; that Modell owned 53 percent; and that the lawsuit filed by Gries was asking the Common Pleas Court to rescind a business deal, approved by the directors of the Browns, because it would waste assets of the Browns "while conferring a personal benefit upon" Modell.

I was the lawyer who prepared and filed that lawsuit. The "Gries-Modell litigation" (as it came to be known) then remained front-page news in Cleveland and Akron for the next four-and-a-half years. And, as that initial article briefly explained, it arose out of Modell's efforts to cause the Cleveland Browns Football Company to purchase, over the vigorous objections of Bob Gries, the stock of a company known as Cleveland Stadium Corporation, 80 percent of which was owned by Modell.

THE SAGA OF
CLEVELAND STADIUM CORPORATION

During the 1950s and 1960s, both the Cleveland Browns and the Cleveland Indians played all of their home games in Cleveland Municipal Stadium. That 82,000-seat facility, located on the shore of Lake Erie, was owned by the City of Cleveland. By 1973, however, the stadium had become much too expensive for the city to operate and maintain. The mayor and other city officials therefore approached Modell for help. Modell agreed to form a new company—Cleveland Stadium Corporation (CSC)—that would lease the stadium from the city for a period of twenty-five years (at a rental of one dollar a year), assume all operating and maintenance costs, expend several million dollars on physical improvements, and enter into subleases with both the Browns and the Indians.

Eventually, Modell sold a 10 percent interest in CSC to Bob Gries, Dick Cole, and Gries Sports Enterprises and another 10 percent to three of Modell's colleagues: Jim Bailey (vice president and general counsel of the Browns), Nate Wallach (a long-time Browns employee), and Jim Berick (outside counsel for the Browns). Modell retained the remaining 80 percent.

By the year 1981, CSC owned two other assets in addition to its lease of Municipal Stadium. The first was a two-hundred-acre parcel of vacant land in Strongsville, Ohio, a suburb of Cleveland. Back around 1973, Modell had purchased that land in his own name for $800,000, with the thought of possibly using it as the site for a new football stadium. In 1975, Modell sold the Strongsville land to CSC for $4 million. CSC borrowed $3 million of that total from Central National Bank, which was immediately turned over to Modell along with a promissory note for the remaining $1 million. By the summer of 1981, CSC still owed $2.65 million on that loan.

CSC's other asset was a 2/7 interest in a long-term promissory note ("the hotel note") received from the purchasers of a downtown Cleveland hotel. CSC had previously owned a fractional interest in that hotel, and, as of 1981, still owed $1.5 million to a Cleveland bank because of that abortive investment.

Modell's Attempts to Solve His Personal Financial Problems

This was an era when interest rates being charged by banks were in the neighborhood of 20 percent, an astronomical level by today's standards. Modell was seriously impacted by that situation. In 1981, his personal bank indebtedness exceeded $8 million, and the interest payments he had to make thereon were now in excess of $1.15 million a year. In addition, CSC—which, it will be recalled, was 80 percent owned by Modell—had to make annual interest payments in a similar amount because of the $8 million that CSC had borrowed from local banks in order to (a) cover the costs of maintaining and refurbishing the Cleveland Municipal Stadium and (b) deliver to Model $3 million in cash for the Strongsville land. Accordingly, in the spring of 1981 Modell and his chief aide, Jim Bailey—who was vice president and general counsel of both the Browns and CSC—met with officers of Central National Bank and Union Commerce Bank to discuss ways in which Modell might reduce his bank loans.

What Modell and Bailey proposed was as follows: First, Modell would sell most of his principal "outside investments" (consisting almost entirely of oil and gas drilling ventures), the sale of which would, hopefully, generate enough funds to extinguish a $3.5 million loan that Modell had with Central National Bank. Second—and this was the most critical element of the proposal—Modell would cause the Cleveland Browns Football Company to purchase all of the stock of CSC for somewhere between $5 million and $7 million. Modell would then use his 80 percent share of the proceeds to pay off the $4 million bank loan that he had outstanding with Union Commerce Bank. Recognizing that the principal minority shareholders of the Browns (namely, the Gries family) might resist such a transaction, Modell asked a local brokerage and investment banking firm, McDonald & Company, to prepare a written "valuation" of CSC that would justify the price.

Accordingly, on August 12, 1981, McDonald & Company submitted to Modell, as president of CSC, a "valuation report" that opined that the net value of CSC—whose assets, it will be recalled, consisted of the Strongsville land, the lease of Cleveland Municipal Stadium and the 2/7 interest in the hotel note—was between $5.2 million and $5.9 million, after deducting CSC's outstanding debts of $8 million. Critical to that report was the $3.8 million valuation that McDonald & Company placed on the Strongsville land, even though the report stated that McDonald & Company had "no demonstrated expertise at valuing real estate."

After reviewing the report, Modell and Bailey asked McDonald & Company to send Modell a supplemental letter setting forth the increased value that CSC might have to the Browns, as distinguished from the value that it might have to a third-party purchaser. On October 8, 1981, McDonald & Company sent such a letter, stating that CSC would be worth an additional $1 million over the valuation stated in the August 12 report if the Browns were the purchaser.

MODELL'S DISCLOSURE TO GRIES OF HIS PLAN, AND THE ENSUING PREPARATIONS FOR A SHOWDOWN

Six weeks later, on November 24, 1981, Modell and Bailey, along with Browns outside counsel (and board member), Jim Berick, met with Bob Gries and Dick Cole at the Browns' office. Modell stated that he and Bailey had "decided that the Browns would be a logical buyer for the Stadium Corporation" and that the price would be $6 million, which would be borrowed by the Browns from Central National Bank. Modell then gave Gries copies of McDonald & Company's August 12, 1981, report and October 8, 1981, letter.

Gries responded that he would "get back" to Modell after he had had an opportunity to evaluate the proposed transaction.

Modell and Bailey, however, did not wait before proceeding with their preparations. They immediately instructed Berick to have lawyers in his office start drafting all of the legal documents that would be necessary to finalize the acquisition. They also asked McDonald & Company to issue a revised report, this one to be addressed to Modell as president of the Browns, rather than as president of CSC. That revised report, dated January 12, 1982, valued CSC at $7.1 million to $8 million.

In addition, on January 13, 1982—and without yet having heard back from Gries—Modell retained a very large (and nationally prominent) Cleveland-based law firm to defend against any litigation that the Gries family might institute. On that same date, Modell entered into a written agreement with Dick Cole that converted Cole into a Modell ally insofar as the proposed acquisition was concerned.

This latter development came about because, a couple of months earlier, in November 1981, Cole had separated from his wife (Bob Gries's sister, Ellen), and their separation agreement stipulated that Cole would "forthwith" resign from all entities controlled by, or involving the affairs of, the Gries family. Nevertheless, Cole's personal relationship with Gries was still amicable on November 24, when the two of them had met with Modell, Bailey, and Berick about Modell's plan to have the Browns acquire CSC. By early January, 1982, however, Cole's divorce from Ellen had become final and Cole found himself confronted with serious financial problems of his own. Modell learned of these changes in Cole's circumstances and quickly moved to take advantage of them. Thus, on January 13, 1982, Modell entered into a written agreement with Cole wherein Modell agreed to (a) cause the Browns to redeem Cole's stock in the Browns (4.5 percent of the total) for $665,000; (b) personally purchase Cole's shares of Cleveland Stadium Corporation (CSC) for $192,000 if such shares were not redeemed by CSC on or before March 1, 1982; (c) support Cole's "reelection as a director [of the Browns] so long as we mutually agree that it is in our joint best interests and in the best interest of all the shareholders" of the Browns; and (d) continue Cole's salary as a vice president of the Browns ($5,000 per year), and Cole's participation in the Browns' Blue Cross medical insurance program, for a period of five years. In addition, Modell arranged for a travel agency that was 50 percent owned by the Browns to provide Cole with a job.

As a consequence of this agreement, Modell could now count on Cole's vote whenever the CSC acquisition came before the Browns' board of directors for approval.

Gries was also busy after November 24, 1981. He consulted a number of experts with respect to the valuations placed by McDonald & Company on the three assets of Cleveland Stadium Corporation. Then, in early December, he met with his principal attorney, Jordan Band. Jordan—one of my law partners at Ulmer, Berne, Laronge, Glickman & Curtis—was an extremely able business lawyer who since 1973 had been representing Bob and several of the Gries family businesses, including Gries Investment Company and Gries Sports Enterprises. Jordan immediately recognized that the proposed acquisition might well result in litigation. He therefore brought me into the meeting (I was then chair of our firm's litigation department) so that I could begin to prepare for such an eventuality. That was the first time I ever met Bob Gries.

On January 19, 1982, Gries had his promised follow-up meeting with Modell and Bailey—this time, however, without the presence of Cole. Gries informed Modell and Bailey that, as a result of his personal analysis of the August 12, 1981, McDonald & Company report and his having met with several knowledgeable individuals (including two experienced Cleveland realtors), he had concluded that the Browns should not acquire CSC for $6 million, a price which Gries deemed highly excessive. He especially objected to the inclusion of the Strongsville land and the hotel note in the proposed purchase. On the other hand, he stated that he would not object to the Browns acquiring CSC's lease of Cleveland Municipal Stadium if a fair price for that lease were arrived at through arm's-length negotiation. Modell, however, rejected that proposed compromise, insisting that the acquisition had to include all of the assets and liabilities of CSC and that the purchase price had to be at least $6 million.

At that juncture, Modell left for a six-week vacation in California. Gries and Band then had several follow-up meetings with Bailey and other officers of the Browns, but no progress was made. A special meeting of the Browns Board of Directors, to consider and vote on the proposed acquisition, was therefore scheduled for March 16, 1982.

Two weeks before that date—and in accordance with a procedure that had been previously worked out by Berick's law firm and Bailey—CSC redeemed, for $120 a share, all of the CSC stock that was owned by persons and entities other than Modell. The sole reason for this redemption was to enable the minority shareholders to obtain capital gains tax treatment on the moneys that they received for their shares. According to the tax lawyers, this was a tax benefit those shareholders would not be able to realize if they sold their shares to the Browns. As a result of that March 2 redemption, Cole received $192,000, Berick $6,000, Wallach $48,000, and Bailey $24,000. (The CSC shares owned by Bob Gries and Gries Sports Enterprises were also redeemed.) The $1.2 million that CSC needed in order to fund the redemption was borrowed by CSC from Central National Bank, with the plan being that CSC would repay that loan after the Browns purchased CSC.

On March 12, 1982, just four days before the scheduled board meeting, Bailey sent each of the directors a letter stating that "matters pertaining to the proposed acquisition of Cleveland Stadium Corporation" would be on the agenda and enclosing, as "basic background information," copies of the January 12, 1982, McDonald & Company report (the one that was addressed to Modell as president of the Browns) and the October 8, 1981, McDonald & Company letter. By the morning of March 16, 1982, all of the documents needed to carry out the acquisition (including, in particular, the documents authorizing the borrowing of $6 million from Central National Bank to pay for it) had been prepared by Berick's law firm and signed by appropriate Browns officers. The only thing now needed was a vote by a majority of the directors approving the transaction.

THE BOARD MEETING

On March 16, 1982, the Browns' board of directors was comprised of six individuals: Art Modell; his wife, Patricia Modell; Nate Wallach, a long-time employee of the Browns; Jim Berick, the Browns' outside legal counsel; Dick Cole; and Bob Gries. When the board formally convened that afternoon, Modell asked that Browns Vice President Jim Bailey be elected as a new director, which was immediately done. At that point Gries stated that, since Dick Cole was no longer a member of the Gries family, Modell should cause Jordan Band (who had accompanied Gries to the meeting) to be elected to the board so that the Gries family could continue to have two directors of their choosing, as provided in the 1965 shareholders agreement. Modell, however, declared that Gries's request was "out of order."

When the meeting turned to the proposed purchase of CSC, Gries explained, at some length, his objections to the acquisition and described several of the reports that he had obtained from outside experts. He stated that those experts had concluded that two of CSC's three assets—namely, the Strongsville land and the hotel note—had an aggregate value that was actually $4 million less than the valuations set forth in the McDonald & Company report. Although several of the other directors immediately challenged Gries's comments, none of them asked any questions of Modell, who had argued strongly in favor of the acquisition. Nor did any of the directors ask whether the Browns could acquire CSC for less than $6 million or whether the Browns might simply purchase just the stadium lease, as Gries had suggested. Nor did any of them express any concern over the fact that one result of the proposed acquisition would be to increase the Browns' total corporate indebtedness from its current level of $2 million all the way up to $16 million, since the transaction would not only require the Browns to borrow $6 million from Central National Bank, but would also necessitate assumption by the Browns of the existing $8 million bank debt owed by CSC. Instead, by a vote of four to one (with Bailey, Berick, Cole, and Wallach all voting "yes," Gries voting "no," and Modell and his wife abstaining), the board proceeded to approve the acquisition.

As soon as the meeting ended, I received a telephone call from Jordan Band, authorizing me to proceed with the filing of the derivative shareholders lawsuit that I had already prepared. This I did, at 8:30 a.m. the following morning.

THE FIRST LAWSUIT

The complaint that I filed in the Common Pleas Court for Cuyahoga County on March 17, 1982, alleged that Modell, along with the four directors who had voted in favor of the acquisition, had breached the fiduciary duties that they owed to the Cleveland Browns Football Company and to the corporation's minority shareholders—in particular, plaintiffs Gries Sports Enterprises and Robert D. Gries. The complaint therefore asked the court to enjoin the proposed purchase.

The case was immediately assigned to Judge John Angelotta, an avid baseball fan who enjoyed socializing with local sports personalities such as Gabe Paul, president of the Cleveland Indians, and George Steinbrenner. Although he had been on the Common Pleas bench for a number of years, Judge Angelotta was not viewed by Cleveland trial lawyers as being particularly scholarly. Nevertheless, as another Common Pleas judge (and a fellow Yale Law School alum) said to me during this period: "You know, Marv, Angelotta really wants to be a good judge." And events so proved in the months (and years) that followed.

Before heading up to Judge Angelotta's chambers, on the morning of March 17, to ask the judge to issue a temporary restraining order, I telephoned the lead trial lawyer of the large firm that had been retained by Modell, informing him of the filing of the lawsuit and that I was on my way to see the judge. When that lawyer (accompanied by three of his partners) arrived at the courthouse, he informed Judge Angelotta that the Browns had already completed the mechanics of the acquisition: Central National Bank had transferred $4.8 million (80 percent) into Modell's personal bank account the previous evening, and the $1.2 million loan that CSC had obtained two weeks earlier in order to redeem the stock of CSC's minority shareholders had been paid off.

I therefore went back to my office and prepared an amended complaint that asked the court for an order rescinding the acquisition rather than for an injunction.

THE SECOND LAWSUIT

On June 11, 1982, I filed a second lawsuit against Modell, based on his March 16 refusal to honor Bob Gries's request that Jordan Band be elected as the Gries family's second Browns director. Specifically, the complaint asked the Common Pleas Court to specifically enforce the 1965 shareholders' agreement. This new case was assigned to Judge Richard McMonagle, a highly respected trial judge.

The defense asserted by Modell's attorneys was that, since the Cleveland Browns Football Company was a Delaware corporation, Delaware law governed the shareholders' agreement. In 1967, Delaware had enacted a statute that limited the duration of a shareholders voting agreement to ten years. Therefore, the agreement entered into by Modell with members of the Gries family in 1965 was no longer valid.

The history of this second lawsuit—which moved very quickly through the Ohio courts—foreshadowed what subsequently transpired in our lawsuit to rescind the CSC acquisition. First, we prevailed in the Common Pleas Court, with Judge McMonagle granting (on March 15, 1983) a summary judgment in our favor. (The judge held that the validity of the shareholders voting agreement was governed by Ohio law, not by the statutes of Delaware, inasmuch as the 1965 agreement had been negotiated and signed in Ohio by Ohio residents and was intended to be performed in Ohio.) Modell's attorneys immediately appealed that ruling to the court of appeals for Cuyahoga County, and, on December 1, 1983, a three-judge panel reversed Judge McMonagle. We (i.e., plaintiffs Bob Gries and Gries Sports Enterprises) then filed a notice of appeal to the Supreme Court of Ohio, together with a motion asking that court to accept jurisdiction (on the ground that the case was of "great public interest"). A few months later, the Supreme Court granted our motion. Subsequently, one of the seven elected Supreme Court judges, Justice Ralph Locher, recused himself, apparently for reasons stemming from his acquaintanceship with Modell (Locher had been mayor of the City of Cleveland from 1962 to 1967 and, before that, law director for many years). Chief Justice Frank Celebrezze thereupon appointed Judge Earle Wise of the Fifth District Court of Appeals to sit for Justice Locher when this case was heard. Ultimately, on December 31, 1984, the Supreme Court, by a vote of five to two, reversed the court of appeals and reinstated Judge McMonagle's summary judgment order. Judge Wise wrote the majority opinion, the thrust of which was that Ohio had a more significant relationship to the Gries-Modell shareholders agreement than did Delaware; therefore that agreement was governed by Ohio, not Delaware, law. (See *Gries Sports Enterprises Inc. v. Modell*, 15 Ohio St.3d 284, 473 NE 2d 807, 1984.)

The Third Lawsuit

On October 31, 1982, I filed, on behalf of Gries Sports Enterprises and Bob Gries, yet a third lawsuit against Modell. The complaint in that case accused Modell of having wrongfully abused his authority as president and majority shareholder of the Browns in various ways, and sought an accounting of all of the personal expenses for which he had been reimbursed by the Browns since 1975. That lawsuit, however, was essentially "put on hold" for the next four years while everyone concentrated on the CSC case.

The Prelude to the 1984 Trial

A large number of depositions were taken in connection with the CSC lawsuit, most of them by Modell's attorneys, who deposed virtually everyone with whom Bob Gries had consulted relative to CSC, whether before or after the March 1982 board meeting. Those attorneys also deposed several people who clearly knew nothing about the case and who, in my opinion, were interrogated primarily for the purpose of harassment. These latter deponents included one of Bob's sons (who lived in New York City), Bob's older sister Betty (who was an invalid and had been living in Los Angeles for almost thirty years), and his younger brother Tommy (who had been living in rural northern California during that same period of time). Betty was questioned about such things as the personal inscription that Paul Brown had inserted into the copy of his autobiography that he had given her, while Tommy's only recollection of the Cleveland Browns was that he and his brother Bob "used to go to games together, back in the late '40s or the early '50s, or something like that."

Moreover, totally unlike my past experience with other lawyers in that law firm during the preceding twenty years, those depositions were generally extremely hostile in tone and conducted in such a way as to make the experience as unpleasant as possible for the deponent. The manner in which those depositions were handled made a lasting impression on me and gave rise to some indirect consequences that I will discuss at the end of this chapter.

One further observation about events prior to the trial. After depositions began, I selected one of our firm's associates to assist me as "second chair." Whether, however, I chose unwisely or because I failed to provide proper guidance to the associate, I soon concluded that I was not receiving any significant help in terms of ideas, suggestions, etc. I therefore decided to handle the Gries-Modell cases "solo," with my only assistance coming from the client, Bob Gries, and his colleague at Gries Investment Company, Dick Brezic (who was both a CPA and a licensed attorney). Yet that assistance proved to be extraordinary. Bob and Dick (both of whom were exceedingly bright and knowledgeable) devoted enormous amounts of time to the litigation. Their work included analyzing the 80,000 documents that were produced during discovery, meeting with potential expert witnesses, helping map out deposition strategy, and providing reams of technical backup with respect to the complicated accounting and financial issues that were at the heart of the case, i.e., the value of Cleveland Stadium Corporation. Indeed, their contributions were so enormous that, at the end of the case, I included the value of their time in the plaintiffs' application for reimbursement of attorneys fees, as I will describe later.

The absence of an Ulmer Berne associate did, however, turn out to have an intangible benefit. Every day during the four-week trial that took place in the summer of 1984 I walked into Judge Angelotta's courtroom alone, toting two very large briefcases. I then sat at the plaintiffs' trial table alone, except for my client, Bob Gries. At the other trial table, on the other hand, there sat at least three lawyers from the large law firm representing Modell and directors Berick, Bailey, and Cole (Wallach had died before the trial), along with a fourth attorney (from yet another law firm) who had been hired to represent the Cleveland Browns Football Company, a nominal defendant in that derivative shareholders lawsuit. In addition, Modell's law firm had several paralegals regularly sprinting in and out of the courtroom. Judge Angelotta observed this imbalance of lawyers and clearly took note of it.

THE TRIAL: "YOU CAN PROVE ANYTHING YOU WANT WITH NUMBERS"

The trial of our lawsuit to rescind the CSC acquisition was scheduled to begin on June 18, 1984. This was a bit sooner than normal for a civil case in Judge Angelotta's room. The judge, however, had been continually beseeched by members of the press as to when "the Gries-Modell trial" was going to start. Also, Modell wanted the courtroom activity to be concluded before the start of Browns training camp in mid-July. However, a multiweek trial in early summer would seriously interfere with Judge Angelotta's long-standing devotion to summertime golf. The judge therefore asked all counsel if we would agree to starting court each day at 8:00 a.m. and then recessing by 1:00 p.m. And that is what happened. Court adjourned each day promptly at 1:00 p.m., at which point Gries, Brezic, and I would retreat to my office where we would spend the rest of the afternoon (and early evening) preparing for the next day. In the meantime, Judge Angelotta enjoyed his afternoon on the golf course.

On Sunday, June 17, both the *Cleveland Plain Dealer* and the *Akron Beacon Journal* ran, on their front pages, lengthy articles with respect to the trial that was scheduled to begin the following day. On Monday morning, Judge Angelotta's courtroom was filled with reporters and other observers. In the jury box sat cameramen from all of the local television stations. However, after opening statements and the testimony of Modell—whom I had called on cross-examination, as our first witness—the television people realized that this trial was going to be relatively dry, with most of the testimony being focused on the financial intricacies of Cleveland Stadium Corporation and the amount of revenue that that company might be able to generate from its operation of the stadium. Hence, after three days the television cameras disappeared from the courtroom, returning only for the final arguments of counsel on July 16, although the *Plain Dealer* (and the *Akron Beacon Journal*) ran daily articles on what was transpiring.

The central legal issue undergirding the trial was whether the decision made by the Browns' directors on March 16, 1982—that the Browns should purchase CSC for $6 million—was protected by the Delaware business judgment rule. That rule precludes courts from interfering with, or second-guessing, decisions made by corporate directors and was therefore the principal defense asserted by Modell and his codefendants counsel against the claims of breach of fiduciary duty. Our position as plaintiffs, however, was that the four directors who voted in favor of the acquisition—Bailey, Berick, Cole, and Wallach—could not rely on the business judgment rule as a defense because (a) those defendants were not "disinterested" with respect to the CSC acquisition (since each of them had received a personal financial benefit from the redemption of their own CSC stock); (b) they were not "independent" (since each of them was beholden to, or "dominated by," a controlling person, i.e., Modell); and (c) they had not fulfilled their duty to inform themselves of all material information reasonably available to them relative to the proposed transaction. Under Delaware law, a director may not rely on the business judgment rule if any one of those three preconditions has not been met. Instead, in such a situation the burden shifts to the interested-dominated-uninformed director to prove that the transaction was "intrinsically fair" to the corporation and to the minority shareholders. If the director fails to meet that burden, the court must conclude that the director has breached his fiduciary duty.

The evidence as to the defendant directors being interested, dominated, etc., at the time of their vote on the CSC acquisition did not take long to present. Hence, most of the evidence during the four-week trial related to the value of the Strongsville land, the value of the hotel note and, especially, the value of CSC's lease of Cleveland Municipal Stadium 2, all of which evidence went to the issue of whether the acquisition was "intrinsically fair" to the Browns. The evidence regarding the value of the stadium lease came from several purported experts and was particularly complex and contentious, reflecting, in part, the difficulty of valuing the operations of a sports stadium. Yet—at least from Judge Angelotta's viewpoint—most of that testimony was a waste of time, since the judge already held strongly negative views with respect to the nonreliability (and hence the nonutility) of expert testimony in general. The judge's skepticism was then bolstered by a statement made by the defendants' final expert witness, Glenn Desmond. For when asked by one of the defendants' attorneys how he had correlated the three different "indications of value" of the stadium lease that he had considered in reaching his expert conclusions,

Desmond responded:

"Well, taking the various value indications that we have discussed here and pulling away from the numbers, you can prove anything you want with numbers. That's easy."

That answer evoked an immediate reaction from Judge Angelotta.

BY THE COURT:

Q: I am interested in that statement: "You can prove anything with numbers. That is easy."
A: [by Mr. Desmond]: You are right, Your Honor.
Q: And I have got numbers here. In two-and-a-half weeks I have got numbers that range from a minus $69,000 to a plus $12.4 million. If you can prove anything with numbers, I suppose maybe I should disregard the numbers, and then what should I make the decision on, Mr. Desmond?
A: I think that you have to use the numbers.
Q: But just explain that to me. This isn't my business.
A: Okay, Your Honor. I will try my best.
Q: And I purposely ask you at this point, prior to [counsel for the defendants] and Mr. Karp speaking with you again, because I do have that range of things. It is a problem ... you seemed to agree that you can prove anything with arithmetic. And I admit that by changing the rate a little bit, changing the multiplier, using a different formula, you can do all kinds of things to give you a number. Ultimately the appraiser, if he is doing his job, has to be intuitive about value. Where is that value?

Moreover, it had been manifest from early in the trial that Modell's promotion of the Browns' acquisition of CSC was not motivated by any belief that it would confer a particular benefit on the Browns corporation. Rather, Modell's sole objective in pushing the transaction was so that he himself could obtain at least $4 million with which to pay off his personal bank loans. And the only way that he could realize that amount of money would be to include all of CSC's assets in the acquisition. Thus, when asked under cross-examination whether the Browns could have simply acquired from CSC the stadium lease alone, i.e., without the Strongsville land and the hotel note, Modell testified as follows:

Q: [by Mr. Karp]: Now, mechanically, it was possible to do this, is that right?

A: [by Mr. Modell]: Oh, I guess you can spin off assets, and mechanically—

Q: However, you refused to separate the land and the hotel notes out of the acquisition?

A: I considered the transaction one complete and I might add—

Q: Please answer my question.

A: I answered it.

Q: You refused to separate them out?

A: I did not want to separate it out. It was one package.

Q: And you therefore, as 80 percent owner of Cleveland Stadium Corporation, insisted that the Browns had to take the whole package for $6 million?

A: That was going to be my recommendation to the board.

Q: You took the position, I gather, to Mr. Gries, that Cleveland Stadium Corporation had to be sold intact?

A: That was my position and recommendation to the board.

To the same effect was the testimony of director Jim Berick, whose own law firm had been given the assignment of preparing, prior to the March 1982 board meeting, all of the necessary legal documents. Berick testified that he was "enthusiastic about the acquisition" from the moment he first learned of it in November 1981, even though he admitted that he never "looked . . . at the individual asset valuations" by McDonald & Company. And why not? Because he "didn't think it was necessary to the value the trees. I was valuing the forest."

The actual value of the Strongsville land, however, was very significant to Judge Angelotta, who believed himself to be knowledgeable with respect to Cleveland real estate. Accordingly, as the trial progressed the judge became increasingly disdainful of the $3.8 million value that McDonald & Company had placed on the Strongsville land in its 1981–1982 reports. That disdain deepened even further when the defendants failed to call anyone from McDonald & Company to testify, but relied, instead, on a local real estate appraiser who placed the value of that land at only $1.1 million.

JUDGE ANGELOTTA'S DECISION: "IN THIS CASE I PLACE NO VALUE ON THE TESTIMONY OF EXPERTS."

The banner, six-column headline that appeared at the top of page one of the August 3, 1984, issue of the *Cleveland Plain Dealer*, read:

"COURT UPSETS BROWNS-STADIUM CORP. DEAL"

The article that followed described Judge Angelotta's decision, set forth in a four-page letter that he had delivered to counsel, copies of which the judge had released to members of the press. That letter, dated August 2, 1984, stated that the judge was "grant[ing] rescission" and that

Proposed Findings of Fact and Conclusions of Law are to be submitted [by counsel] on or before August 16, 1984. The court will make Findings of Fact and Conclusions of Law, filing them simultaneously on August 30, 1984, with an entry of judgment.

There then followed a brief description of the March 16, 1982, board meeting and of the information that had been sent to the directors by Bailey on March 12, namely, the January 12, 1982, McDonald & Company "Valuation of Cleveland Stadium Corporation." Judge Angelotta went on to state that if he himself had been a member of the board, he "would have voted nay" on the proposed acquisition because, "to be profitable to the Browns," the CSC transaction had to be worth in excess of $14 million (i.e., the total of the amount that the Browns would be borrowing in order to pay for the acquisition and the amount of CSC debt that the Browns would be assuming). Moreover, McDonald & Company had "proved that they had no expertise at valuing real estate," and Judge Angelotta had concluded from the evidence presented at trial that, "at most, the land was worth $750,000." Hence, a "knowledgeable buyer under no restraint and without compulsion to act would not consummate the transaction."

Judge Angelotta then explained why he was rejecting most of the expert testimony that he had heard during the trial relating to the value of the stadium lease:

> I am told that Oscar Wilde once described a cynic as a person "who knows the cost of everything and the value of nothing." Mr. Wilde describes an expert. If I had any reservation about the value of the experts, that is, any good reservation, it was totally destroyed by Mr. Desmond when he stated, "you can prove anything you want with numbers, that's easy." Now, really, when a judge listens to testimony from experts who testify that CSC has a value ranging from negative $69,000 to plus $12.4 million, the whole subject becomes somewhat ludicrous. No responsible person could make an intelligent judgment from such testimony. I charge myself with the applicable law to weigh expert testimony, to apply the usual rules for testing credibility, and to determine the weight to be given to the testimony of experts. In this case I place no value on the testimony of experts.

The judge also rejected the "business judgment rule" defense relied upon by the defendants, because he had concluded that Modell "dominated" the board of directors. Therefore, under Delaware law, the defendants had the "burden of proof of establishing that the transaction was intrinsically fair to the minority shareholders." In the judge's view, the defendants had not sustained that burden.

Nevertheless, Judge Angelotta stated that he would not enter an order of rescission if, "within thirty days hereafter, the Browns convey the land and [hotel note] back to Modell." He therefore ended his letter with a plea to the parties that they now resolve the case through negotiation:

> Coach Sam Rutigliano expressed the belief that these lawsuits were detrimental to Cleveland Browns football. To this observation, I agreed with the coach in open court.
>
> The parties should effect a settlement of all pending cases. Two intelligent men of means, committed to God and family, men who have demonstrated civic awareness and accomplishment, ought certainly be able to amicably resolve these matters without further recourse to legal proceedings.
>
> Gentlemen, the people of this community want the Cleveland Browns to get on with the business of bringing a national football league championship to the City of Cleveland.

Needless to say, the judge's plea was ignored by Modell.

I, of course, was very pleased with Judge Angelotta's request, in the opening paragraph of his letter, that counsel submit to him, within two weeks, Proposed Findings of Fact and Conclusions of Law. I knew that that would give me the opportunity to put before the judge, for his eventual adoption, carefully crafted findings that would provide a solid evidentiary basis for the legal conclusions that followed. Those conclusions, in turn, would establish our legal right to a rescission of the CSC transaction, and, since those conclusions would be grounded on specific factual findings made by the trial judge, they would be very difficult for any reviewing court to overturn.

Thus, the Proposed Findings of Fact that I drafted (and submitted to the court on August 16) established that directors Bailey, Berick, Cole, and Wallach were interested, dominated, and uninformed, which findings would negate the defendants' reliance on the business judgment rule. They included the following:

23. As of March 16, 1982, directors Berick, Bailey, and Wallach were dependent upon Arthur J. Modell, in that the continuation of their employment (as outside counsel in the case of Mr. Berick, and as full-time employees of the Browns in the case of Mr. Bailey and Mr. Wallach) was entirely dependent upon their retaining the goodwill of Mr. Modell, who, as chief executive officer of the Browns, had the power to discharge them. Director Cole, the former brother-in-law of plaintiff Robert D. Gries, was similarly beholden to defendant Modell, for on January 13, 1982, Modell and Cole had entered into a written agreement wherein Modell agreed: (a) To cause the Browns to buy Cole's stock in the Browns for $665,000; (b) to personally purchase Cole's shares in CSC for $192,000, if such shares were not redeemed by CSC, at that price, by March 1, 1982; (c) to support Cole's "reelection as a director so long as we mutually agree that it is in our joint best interests and in the best interest of all the shareholders of CBFC."; (d) to continue Cole's salary and Blue Cross coverage as a vice president of the Browns for a period of five years. In addition, prior to the March 16, 1982, board meeting, director Cole had obtained employment with a travel agency, 50 percent of which was owned by the Browns. The board of directors of the Browns was therefore dominated by Arthur J. Modell.

*   *   *

32. The decision to acquire the Strongsville land and the hotel notes, when such assets were so heavily burdened with debt in excess of $4 million, cannot be attributed to any responsible business purpose.

33. Rather than serving the best interests of the Browns and all of the Browns' stockholders, the effect of this transaction was to benefit the majority shareholder of the Browns (who thereby reduced his ownership interest in the assets and liabili-

ties of CSC from 80 percent to 53 percent) at the expense of the principal minority shareholders (who, as a consequence, saw their interest in such assets and liabilities increase from 7 percent to 43 percent).

34. Defendants have failed to prove that the acquisition of CSC was intrinsically fair to the Browns and to its minority shareholders.

35. Defendants have failed to prove that $6 million was a fair price for the Browns to pay for CSC. The directors who voted in favor of the transaction did not exercise due care to inform themselves of all material and relevant information pertaining to the proposed transaction. The four directors who voted in favor of the transaction abused their discretion.

These Proposed Findings were then followed by twelve Proposed Conclusions of Law, of which the following were the most significant:

6. . . . The manner in which the subject transaction was initiated, structured, negotiated, and disclosed to plaintiffs . . . did not satisfy any reasonable concept of fair dealing.

7. Defendants failed to sustain their burden of proving that the transaction was intrinsically fair to the corporation and to the minority shareholders.

8. Even if the intrinsic fairness test were not applicable here, directors Cole, Bailey and Berick still could not claim the protection of the "business judgment" rule, since that rule does not apply to actions taken by directors with respect to a transaction which confers personal financial benefits upon the directors. (See *Gottlieb v. Hayden Chemical Corp.*, 90 A.2d 660, 1952.) Directors Cole, Bailey, and Berick all derived personal financial benefits from the subject transaction. Accordingly, a majority consisting of disinterested directors did not approve the transaction. (See *Aronagon v. Lewis*, 473 A.2d 805, 812; Del., 1984.)

Much to my surprise (and, indeed, delight), the law firm representing Modell, et al., did not file any proposed findings and conclusions, although Judge Angelotta's August 2 letter had clearly invited them to do so. Instead, on August 27 those attorneys filed "Objections to Plaintiffs' Proposed Findings of Fact and Conclusions of Law." The central thrust of those objections was that, since "the court's letter of August 2 already contains its findings of fact and conclusions of law," the plaintiffs' Proposed Findings and Conclusions "must be rejected." Modell's attorneys further pointed out that, on August 2 and 3, Judge Angelotta had granted interviews to members of the press in which he had explained some of the reasoning behind his decision. They therefore argued that those statements to the press rendered any additional findings and conclusions superfluous.

Judge Angelotta, however, rejected defendants' objections, on August 30, three days after they were filed. On that same day, the judge signed and filed formal Findings of Fact and Conclusions of Law that tracked, almost word for word, the proposed findings and conclusions that I had submitted to him. The next day (August 31), the headline on the front page of the *Cleveland Plain Dealer* read:

"COURT ORDER BLISTERS MODELL"

MODELL'S APPEAL, AND SOME EXTRAORDINARY LEAKS

Modell's attorneys immediately filed a notice of appeal to the court of appeals for Cuyahoga County and asked that court to "expedite the appellate proceedings." That request was promptly granted, with the chief administrative judge issuing an order stating that "the case will be scheduled for oral arguments at the earliest feasible date." That date turned out to be December 12, 1984. On that day, the panel of judges allowed each side to argue for more than forty minutes, even though oral arguments in that court are normally limited to fifteen minutes.

While the case was in the court of appeals, something occurred that I never experienced, before or after, in all my years of practice: I received several anonymous phone calls from an apparent employee of the court. The first call (prior to oral argument) informed me that the composition of the three-judge panel that was going to hear the case had been changed and that one of the judges originally assigned to the panel had been replaced by the chief administrative judge himself. The second call came in early February 1985, two months after oral argument. This time I was told that the panel was going to reverse Judge Angelotta's decision and that "a lot of people" at the court of appeals were very upset about that. The anonymous court employee went on to say that Gries had "initially stood in a good position with the panel," but the chief administrative judge had persuaded one of the other judges to go the other way, even though that judge had previously "been sympathetic" to Gries. The employee further stated that it would be a while before a formal written opinion would be issued.

That occurred on April 25, 1985, with two of the judges holding that Judge Angelotta's order of rescission should be vacated and final judgment entered in favor of Modell and his fellow directors. That opinion, written by the chief administrative judge, avoided any discussion of whether the $6 million purchase price was fair to the Browns or to the minority shareholders. Instead, the two majority judges concluded that "regardless of the unfairness of the price or the manner in which the transaction was handled," the acquisition was "protected" from judicial scrutiny by reason of the business judgment rule. In those judges' view, that rule was controlling in this case because, notwithstanding Judge Angelotta's specific factual findings to the contrary, at least two of the four directors who voted in favor of the acquisition were "disinterested" and "independent" and had taken "adequate steps to inform themselves before voting." The majority opinion further concluded that none of those four directors received any "personal financial gain from the acquisition"—which would have rendered them "interested"—inasmuch as their individual shares in CSC had been redeemed back on March 2, 1982, two weeks before those directors voted to approve the transaction.

The third member of the court of appeals panel, Judge Leo Jackson, filed a strongly worded forty-six-page dissent in which he vigorously disputed the majority's rejection of Judge Angelotta's specific factual findings that had rendered the business judgment rule inapplicable. Judge Jackson pointed out that those factual findings were supported not only by "some competent, credible evidence" but by "substantial competent, credible evidence," and, hence, could not be disregarded by an appellate court. "Clearly," wrote Judge Jackson, "this evidence supports the conclusion that Directors Berick, Bailey, and Cole were interested, dominated and uninformed with respect to the acquisition of CSC." Substantial evidence also supported Judge Angelotta's further conclusion that "the acquisition of CSC was unfair to both the Cleveland Browns and its minority shareholders." Consequently, the appellate court should have affirmed that decision: "In my judgment, the trial court's conclusion is not only evidenced by the record, it is compelled by the record."

Judge Jackson took particular issue with the majority's conclusion that the directors who voted in favor of the acquisition had not received a personal financial benefit from the transaction. He pointed out that the March 2, 1982, stock redemption "was an integral part of the March 16, 1982 acquisition: there would not have been a redemption, but for the impending acquisition of CSC." Indeed, the only reason that the transaction took place in two steps—with CSC first redeeming the stock of all of the shareholders except Modell, and with the Browns then purchasing the stock owned by Modell—was to enable the minority shareholders to pay only capital gains tax on the moneys that they would be receiving. Judge Jackson further noted that director Berick had admitted under cross-examination that the "higher the price paid by the Browns for CSC's stock would mean the more money [he] would receive and the more money that Mr. Bailey and the other directors would receive for their CSC stock." It was therefore "inconceivable that the majority can conclude that the directors had no financial interest in the Browns acquisition of CSC."

ONCE AGAIN, THE SUPREME COURT: "OUR DECISION TODAY IS IN THE FINEST TRADITION OF JUDICIAL INSIGHT."

As we had done two years earlier—after a court of appeals panel had overturned Judge Richard McMonagle's enforcement of the 1965 shareholders voting agreement—we filed a notice of appeal to the Ohio Supreme Court, together with a motion asking that court to accept jurisdiction (a case of "great public interest," etc.). Once again the Supreme Court granted our motion. Once again Justice Locher recused himself. And, once again, Judge Wise of the Fifth District Court of Appeals was assigned to sit in his stead.

Oral argument in the Supreme Court took place on February 19, 1986. Six days later, on February 25, Jim Bailey sent a letter to Gries and Jordan Band—who, by then, was a director of the Browns, as a result of the Supreme Court's December 31, 1984 decision enforcing the 1965 shareholders voting agreement—informing them that the Browns intended to immediately "resell" all of the stock of Cleveland Stadium Corporation (now called "Clesta Inc.") to Lake Erie Radio Company, a company owned 50 percent by Modell and 50 percent by his good (and extremely wealthy) friend, Alfred Lerner, for $7 million. A special board meeting was scheduled for March 17 to vote on that proposed transaction. Bailey's letter caused us to file in the Supreme Court, on March 12, a motion asking that court to enjoin any sale of the stock of Clesta until after the pending appeal was adjudicated. Otherwise, there could be no rescission of the March 16, 1982, transaction, and the Browns could not be "made whole" should the Supreme Court reverse the court of appeals and reinstate Judge Angelotta's August 30, 1984, order. On the very next day (March 13, 1986), the Supreme Court granted our motion. We took that order as a favorable sign as to how the Supreme Court would ultimately rule on the merits of our appeal.

Six months later that anticipation became a reality. On August 21, 1986, the front page of the *Cleveland Plain Dealer* carried the following six-column headline:

"HIGH COURT BACKS GRIES OVER MODELL"

By a vote of four to three, the Supreme Court had upheld Judge Angelotta's decision that the Browns' purchase of CSC was unfair to the minority shareholders. The majority opinion, written once again by Judge Wise, concluded that there was competent and credible evidence in the trial record to support Judge Angelotta's findings that the defendant directors (a) were not "disinterested" (each of them having received a personal financial benefit from the sale/redemption of their CSC stock); (b) were not "independent" (to the contrary, they were dominated by Modell; Judge Wise, for example, quoted the statement in the court of appeals majority opinion that "as outside counsel for the Browns, it was Berick's job to do what Modell requested"); and (c) had not properly informed themselves of pertinent facts readily available to them. Hence, the four directors who had voted in favor of the acquisition could not invoke the protection of the business judgment rule. Instead, they had the burden of showing that the transaction was intrinsically fair to the minority shareholders, which burden they had failed to meet, as stated in Judge Angelotta's Finding of Fact No. 34 and Conclusion of Law No. 7.

Justice Clifford Brown of the Supreme Court filed a separate concurring opinion, which ended with the following statement:

> Our decision today, in holding that the business judgment rule
> does not protect the challenged CSC stock purchase by the
> Browns, and in requiring application of the intrinsic fairness
> test is in the finest tradition of judicial insight. It avoids mixing
> a conglomeration of corporate legal principles and concepts
> to reach an absurd and unjust result, thereby sidestepping the

preordained results desired by the critics of our majority decision (i.e., the three dissenting justices). (See *Gries Sports Enterprises, Inc. v. Cleveland Browns Football Co., Inc.*, 26 Ohio St.3d 15, 496 NE2d 959,1986.)

All three of the dissenting justices were Republicans. Their votes therefore came as no great surprise to me, given the fact that (as pointed out earlier) Modell had been the treasurer of the Ohio Republican Party for a number of years. Moreover, the separate dissents that those three judges wrote were quite bitter, replete with comments like "paragraph two of the syllabus of the majority opinion illustrates the [majority's] abject ignorance of corporate matters," and "certain members of the majority are fond of talking about preordained results. Now it is clear why they are able to speak with such authority on the subject."

Several weeks later an anonymous voicemail message was left on my telephone: "Congratulations on *Gries v. Modell*. This is sent by voice from the court of appeals."

THE APPLICATION FOR ATTORNEYS' FEES, AND THE STEPS TAKEN TO AVERT FUTURE LITIGATION

In the fall of 1986, the Cleveland Browns Football Company returned the stock of CSC to Modell, and Modell began making repayment to the Browns of $6 million, plus $1.4 million in interest. It then fell to Judge Angelotta to make one final ruling, namely, the awarding of attorneys' fees and expenses to the prevailing plaintiffs, which reimbursement had become the responsibility of the Browns under Ohio law pertaining to derivative shareholders actions. However, in the fee application that I filed with Judge Angelotta, I asked him to do something that was rather unusual: in addition to ordering the Browns to reimburse Robert Gries and Gries Sports Enterprises for the attorneys' fees and out-of-pocket expenses that those plaintiffs had paid to Ulmer, Berne, Laronge, Glickman & Curtis (as well as other out-of-pocket expenses such as the fees they had paid to experts and consultants), I asked him to order the Browns to reimburse Gries Investment Company for the many hours that Bob Gries and Dick Brezic had personally devoted to the CSC litigation. Specifically, I asked for $121,320 for Bob's time and $223,800 for Dick's. I described all the work that the two of them had done and how invaluable their efforts had been to our winning the case. Modell's attorneys, of course, strongly opposed the latter request, arguing that it was "unprecedented."

The oral hearing on our fee application took place on October 14, 1986, and lasted more than seven hours (i.e., until 9:00 p.m. that night). However, as it turned out, Judge Angelotta never had to issue any order with respect to that application.

The reason was that the October 14 hearing had triggered another round of newspaper articles, which were not very favorable to Modell's public image. A few days later, Modell's lead attorney called me to say that Modell had now "recognized that it is advisable to stop all this." Modell therefore agreed that the Browns would voluntarily pay a total of $900,000 to cover all of the fees and expenses we were seeking, including the amounts sought for Gries and Brezic's time, without the necessity of having Judge Angelotta issue any order to that effect. Modell's lead attorney further asked if we could now settle Gries's still-pending third lawsuit and, more fundamentally, establish some procedures that might obviate any future court actions between Gries and Modell. After some thought, I came up with a suggestion, to which Modell's attorney agreed. The result was a letter agreement that was signed by Gries and Modell in mid-December 1986.

That letter provided, first, that our third (and remaining) lawsuit would be dismissed with prejudice. Second, so long as Bob Gries or Gries Sports Enterprises owned any stock in the Cleveland Browns, Gries and Modell would, upon the written request of either, personally discuss any proposed transaction by the Browns that might arguably confer a financial benefit, or inflict a financial detriment, on Gries, Gries Sports Enterprises, or Modell that would be disproportionate to their respective shareholdings in the Browns. Should that discussion not resolve the issue, the parties would engage in mediation, and, if the mediation failed, arbitration. Modell and Gries would then advise the Browns Board of Directors of the result of the arbitration and "use their best efforts" to cause the board to act in accordance with that ruling. If, however, any director attempted to have the board take action contrary to what the arbitrators had decided, both Modell and Gries would immediately take steps to remove that director from the board.

OCTOBER, 1995: MODELL MOVES THE BROWNS TO BALTIMORE

The dispute-resolution procedures outlined in the December 1986 letter agreement were never triggered. Rather, that 1986 agreement ceased to exist at the end of October 1995, when the Browns redeemed all of the Gries family's stock in the Cleveland Browns Football Company. That redemption was precipitated by Modell's decision to move the football team to Baltimore. Modell had informed Gries of that decision at a special meeting of the Browns' board held on the afternoon of Friday, October 20. ("The team was losing money," it had a "huge debt," it would need $15 million of additional revenue each year, Baltimore was offering the Browns a $200 million stadium deal, which offer would expire at the end of the month, etc.) Immediately after the meeting Bob attempted to reach me, but I was out of town, as was Jordan Band (who, by then, had retired from the law firm). When I got back to Cleveland two nights later, I immediately went to Bob's home to discuss what was happening and what Bob's options might be, including Bob's potential financial exposure (to Modell and others) if he attempted to somehow block the move, which move would have definite financial advantages for the corporation. That weekend Bob arrived at several conclusions: In all probability he could not successfully block the move (not, at least, without potential financial consequences to himself); however, he and his family would not participate in any way whatever in what was about to occur. Therefore, all of the Gries family's stock had to be bought out in its entirety by the Browns (or by some third party) before the planned move was revealed to the public. Bob made his position in that regard absolutely clear to Modell and to Modell's close friend and ally, Al Lerner, who was now a director of the Browns. By Monday noon, a price for all of the Gries stock had been agreed upon, and by 10:00 p.m. Tuesday night (the 24th) all necessary documents to accomplish the redemption (payable by the Browns over a ten-year period) had been worked out and signed. A few days later Modell and Lerner flew, on Lerner's private plane, to Baltimore, where Modell announced the relocation of the team and signed various papers to that effect. Modell's stunning announcement made him an instant pariah in Cleveland, and he never again set foot in that city. And, with that, the tumult between Gries and Modell finally came to an end.

SOME PERSONAL CONSEQUENCES

As a result of the Gries-Modell litigation, the nature of my trial practice changed considerably. Prior to 1982 my work had concentrated primarily on the defense of fire insurance claims (usually predicated on allegations that the plaintiff insured had committed arson), the defense of legal malpractice claims, and the prosecution of large property damage subrogation claims grounded on negligence. The extensive (and long-running) publicity surrounding the Gries-Modell cases, however, resulted in an influx of new litigation matters arising out of business or corporate disputes, and cases of that nature became the principal focus of my practice, and remained so, until I retired at the end of 2014.

But the most unusual—and, in some ways, enduring—consequence of my four-and-a-half-year immersion in the Gries-Modell lawsuits was an indirect one. As mentioned earlier, I had been very much taken aback by the manner in which Modell's attorneys had conducted depositions in those cases, as well as by the hostility exhibited by some of those lawyers in our day-to-day dealings.

Prior to 1982 I (and most experienced Cleveland trial lawyers of my acquaintance) generally viewed depositions as being a valuable tool for eliciting information. Depositions, therefore, were usually handled in a relatively courteous manner, since such an approach had a tendency to relax deponents and cause them to be more voluble in their answers to questions. In the Gries-Modell litigation, however, I saw depositions being used to intimidate witnesses and being conducted in an atmosphere of, at times, outright nastiness. Even worse, I began to observe that other lawyers, in Cleveland and elsewhere, were beginning to employ a similar "hardball" approach to litigation. Deliberate rudeness became those lawyers' operating norm; requests for reasonable accommodations in scheduling were rejected out of hand or acceded to only grudgingly; opposing parties and witnesses were verbally abused; and ad hominem attacks were frequently made on the character, competence, and integrity of opposing counsel. In short, whether because there were now too many lawyers, too much economic pressure, too much competition, or too little understanding of the true meaning of our adversary system, a "Rambo" mentality had begun to infect many of our brethren. For such lawyers, litigation had become synonymous with all-out war, their principal objective being to win at any cost. And if, in the process, they could destroy the other side and humiliate the opposing lawyer, so much the better. Why? "Because," we were told, "this is what clients want, a lawyer who is mean and tough. So either you play hardball, or you won't be able to play at all."

Such an approach understandably evoked retaliation in the same mean spirit. As a consequence, there was a growing escalation in both the financial and emotional costs of litigation, not to mention the creation and hardening of animosities between opposing counsel that made an early, let alone amicable, resolution of the underlying dispute increasingly difficult.

I brooded over this burgeoning trend for some time. Then, fortuitously, I was given an opportunity to do something about it. In the summer of 1987, I became president-elect of the Cleveland Bar Association, and the association's then president, Liz Moody—also a Yale Law School alum, by the way—asked me to chair an ad hoc committee on professionalism. At roughly the same time, I was appointed chair of a special committee on professionalism established by the Council of the Tort and Insurance Practice Section (TIPS) of the American Bar Association, of which section, incidentally, I would become chair a few years later. Both the Cleveland Bar committee and the TIPS committee were comprised of a number of experienced trial lawyers, along with several distinguished judges. With my personal experience in the Gries-Modell cases still fresh in mind, I suggested to both committees that we develop what we ultimately called a "Lawyer's Creed of Professionalism." That creed would consist of a list of very specific "dos and don'ts" that could serve as a primer as to how a lawyer should conduct himself/herself in the lawyer's dealings with opposing counsel, with judges and, indeed, with the lawyer's own clients. The creed would, for example, stress the importance of courtesy and civility between lawyers; of cooperating in scheduling; of refraining from utilizing litigation to harass the opposing party; of not filing frivolous motions and pleadings; of stipulating to facts as to which there was no genuine dispute; and of recognizing that excessive zeal can be detrimental to the interests of one's clients and to the proper functioning of our system of justice. The creed would also point out that a lawyer has certain professional responsibilities that transcend the lawyer's duties to his or her clients. For while a lawyer must always be loyal and committed to the client's cause—and while it may be true, as someone once said, that the ideal client is rich, angry, and wrong—a lawyer also has an obligation to advise his/her client against pursuing a course of action that is of dubious merit or insisting on tactics that are intended to delay, harass, or drain the financial resources of the other side.

Because I was simultaneously chairing (and acting as scrivener for) both committees, they both ended up with the same work product, i.e., the text of the Lawyer's Creed of Professionalism. In the early summer of 1988, the board of trustees of the Cleveland Bar Association adopted that text. In addition, the board authorized the printing of 6,000 copies, on sixteen-by-twenty-inch heavy decorated paper, which copies were then mailed to all of the association's members and all of the judges (state and federal) in Cuyahoga County, Ohio. That mailing was accompanied by a letter from the president of the association (who, by then, was me), urging each recipient to hang the creed on his or her office wall, where it would be a constant reminder to the lawyer, as well as to the lawyer's clients, of the professionalism standards that the lawyer intended to abide by in his or her everyday practice. And a lot of lawyers and judges did just that. Indeed, it is still possible today to see copies of the creed in Cleveland law offices, as well as in the chambers of some of the local judges.

That same summer (1988), the council of the TIPS Section of the ABA submitted to the ABA House of Delegates a Report and Recommendation that urged the ABA to recommend to all state and local bar associations across the country that such associations do what the Cleveland Bar Association had done, namely, adopt a creed of professionalism and distribute printed copies to their members, to be hung on their office walls as a reminder.

The House of Delegates at the ABA annual meeting in Toronto approved that Report and Recommendation. The TIPS Section then proceeded to mail, to approximately 250 state and local bar associations, a letter describing the House of Delegates' recommendations and enclosing a copy of the TIPS/Cleveland Bar Lawyer's Creed of Professionalism as a model. Quite a number of bar associations took those recommendations to heart, adopting the Lawyer's Creed of Professionalism as their own and sending out printed copies to their members. In addition—thanks to a favorable article by David Margolick that appeared in The *New York Times* on August 5, 1988—the Cleveland Bar Association received requests for copies from quite a large number of judges and lawyers around the country. Subsequently, the TIPS/Cleveland Bar Association creed, along with similar creeds adopted by other bar associations, was specifically mentioned in the April 1991 Interim Report of the US Court of Appeals for the Seventh Circuit's Committee on Civility. (See 143

Federal Rules Decisions 371 at 422.)

My efforts to promote civility and professionalism didn't end there. In a series of successive leaderships positions that I held—including president of the Cleveland Bar Association, chair of the TIPS section of the ABA, president of the Federation of Defense and Corporate Counsel, chair of the ABA Standing Committee on Ethics and Professional Responsibility, and chair of the Ohio Supreme Court's Commission on Professionalism—I gave a number of speeches, and published several articles, on lawyer professionalism. Most of those speeches and articles tied back, in one way or another, to the Lawyers Creed.

In 2014—twenty-five years after the creed's initial promulgation—the Cleveland Metropolitan Bar Association (the association's current name) asked me to chair a task force that would review and update the 1988–89 creed. The new task force did exactly that. Once again, the bar association printed copies of the revised creed and asked the association's members and local judges to hang them on their office walls. In addition, the task force urged the Bar Association Board of Trustees to establish a Professionalism Conciliation Panel that local lawyers could contact for informal assistance if they were having problems due to nonprofessional behavior by other lawyers. Such a panel was duly established.

These, then, are some of the indirect consequences of the Gries-Modell lawsuits that wended their way through the Ohio courts more than thirty years ago. And that is why it might be said—with perhaps only a slight amount of hyperbole—that those lawsuits begat a legacy that, in some ways, endures to this day.

II

FIRMS, LAW, AND OTHERWISE

James T. Boorsch

How I Forgot Pearl Harbor

A FEW MONTHS AGO AMERICANS OF A CERTAIN age, those over 80, observed the seventy-fifth anniversary of Pearl Harbor. I was seven when we were attacked in what was then the worst day of our history. I still "Remember Pearl Harbor" as we were taught to do way back then.

I loved the late fall in Connecticut. That day I was out back of our house raking and burning the last of the fallen leaves from our many oak trees. This was in North Haven; my father was a professor in the French department at Yale, and my parents had built our house in a new development reachable by the Whitney Avenue bus. In midafternoon that day, both my mother and father came out to tell me that the regular Sunday afternoon radio broadcast of the New York Philharmonic had been interrupted with the news of a Japanese air attack on Pearl Harbor. They told me that Pearl Harbor was in Hawaii, and was the main base of our Pacific fleet. Apparently there was a lot of damage to the fleet, and great loss of life.

At that age, in third grade, I knew a little geography but nothing of the recent history of rising antagonism between the US and Japan. My parents and our teacher at Spring Glen public school talked about the treachery and villainy of the sudden brutal attack. We were encouraged to think of the "Japs" (or "Nips") as a backward, uncivilized, aggressive, even subhuman, race. The phrase "yellow peril" was revived from earlier days when it was applied to Chinese laborers. Cartoons showed the ordinary Japanese soldier as a short, wiry, bucktoothed, thick-glasses-wearing, sneaky, alien enemy. Their leaders, Emperor Hirohito and Prime Minister Tojo, were caricatured as totally evil devil antagonists. "Remember Pearl Harbor" was a slogan drilled into us to collect and focus all of the enmity and hatred we could muster, and to build patriotism and encourage enlistment. President Roosevelt's words about the date which would "live in infamy," December 7, 1941(he pronounced *forty* "fawty"), were shown over and over in the inevitable newsreels which preceded feature films.

There was a newsreel showing many of the thousands of "Japs" (actually a majority were American citizens) being shipped off to "internment" (never "concentration") camps, which Governor Warren and President Roosevelt considered a prudent step to prevent espionage or other forms of aiding the enemy. The movie audience applauded.

During the war years themselves, I began to read the newspapers, first the *New Haven Register*, which I delivered as a newsboy toward the end of the war, and then the *New York Times*. And our family listened to the radio every evening, though with more focus on the European theater, where my father's parents, my grandparents, were caught up in the Nazi occupation of France, and when letters arrived through the Red Cross months late.

For my part, I collected US Army toys, trucks, tanks, and soldiers. My main interest was a large wall map that my parents bought me with sets of paper flags of the warring nations, which I could pin into the map as faraway places changed hands. I had to push in the Rising Sun over Corregidor and Manila. I read of the brutal Bataan Death March. Later on, of course, I was able to put the '48 Stars and Stripes in Guadalcanal and Iwo Jima, as well as Omaha Beach and ultimately Paris. Finally came V-E Day, and after the A-bombs were dropped on Japan in August of 1945, V-J Day. I was only ten, but I still remember all of our neighbors pouring out of their houses to celebrate that warm August evening when President Truman assured us the war was over. We rejoiced, and the next day gas rationing and the thirty-five-mile-per-hour speed limit were lifted.

During the war, my father, a French citizen living abroad, was not called into military service by either Vichy France or the US. But I got some feeling for the agonies of the struggle against Japan when he was hired by Elmer Davis of the Office of War Information to translate some of John Hersey's books on specific battles. I remember Tarawa and Guadalcanal especially. My mother helped my father understand the American idiom, while he prepared texts for Francophone readers, in particular navy and army officers who were learning French in his immersion courses at Yale, prior to the North African and European invasions.

At both Exeter and Yale I took as many history courses as I could, and I learned a fair amount of Japan's history, at least from Commodore Perry onward. The Meiji Restoration and the rapid industrialization were impressive, as was the Japanese victory over Russia in their war. I don't remember learning much about the Japanese contribution to World War I, except that Japan was on the Allied side. Nor their occupation of Korea and the subsequent invasion of Manchuria that became the Japanese province of Manchukuo. The invasion of China, which included the Rape of Nanking, was not highlighted, nor was the growing dependence of Japan on oil imports from Indonesia and other Far East places. The lead-up to Pearl Harbor, including the American embargo and sanctions, at least helped me understand the Japanese motivation and reasoning for a military challenge to the US, but never justified it in my mind either legally or morally.

Now fast forward to the 1960s. I had not followed the MacArthur suzerainty (he governed like the old shoguns) in Japan, and depended on a series of letters from a former roommate who was stationed in Japan with the American occupation. (Curiously this roommate had acquired the nickname of "Jap" at Exeter, supposedly for "welshing" on agreements and playing nasty tricks on people. It was wholly undeserved). His letters gave me a feel for conditions there, at least from an American's point of view, which he described quite favorably. At Yale, I had made a Japanese friend (named Yamamoto, which is a common name; contrary to rumor, he was not related to the admiral who had led the Pearl Harbor attack). But other than these two sources I did not learn much or even try to follow what was happening in Japan.

After graduating from law school, I went to Wall Street with many classmates, to an old-line, white-shoe law firm. I was an associate in the litigation group, mostly working on antitrust cases. One day in the summer of 1966 the chief executive of a corporate client's Hong Kong office jumped to his death from a high floor in his office building. Almost immediately, problems with his clients were uncovered. He had not observed the US margin rules. When the market sagged, his customers could not meet margin calls, and he saw his firm was foundering, so he ended his own life rather than face the shame and the investigations that would ensue.

Our client in New York filed a claim against its own insurers, who had written fidelity and casualty policy covering its employees and agents.... The insurer balked at paying the claim, arguing that the Hong Kong office was an independent branch, not an agency. Fact-finding was in order, so I volunteered to go to Hong Kong to interview witnesses and review whatever paper trail that still existed. The senior partner in charge gladly agreed, as it was in the heat of August and he was probably a little too elderly to make such a trip.

So I flew out to the Far East. In those days there were no non-stop flights to Hong Kong, and a stopover in Tokyo was necessary. Planes could not reach Japan from the West Coast, so flights refueled in Hawaii. As the Japan Airlines DC-8 came over the south coast of Oahu, I could easily make out Waikiki and soon after Pearl Harbor and Ford Island which had been Battleship Row. The plane banked for its final approach, and I noticed the large bright red disk painted on the wing, the same disk as the Japanese planes had shown that December morning. It gave me an odd feeling to be arriving over Pearl Harbor in the same insignia as the former enemy "Jap" torpedo fighters and bombers.

We continued on to Tokyo where another associate from my firm and his Japanese wife, who were on vacation visiting her family, met me at Haneda airport. I was now in the heart of the capital;

of the country we had all been taught to hate, even though the war had ended twenty-one years before. It was not what I expected. The buildings were mostly new, low-rise except for one skyscraper and the Tokyo Tower, an inelegant copy of the Eiffel Tower. The then-new Hotel Okura was beautifully restrained and tasteful with exotic burnished woods, and kimono-clad hostesses welcoming me with bows at every elevator door.

Next day my friends gave me a quick tour of the highlights of Tokyo, including the impressive venues of the 1964 Olympics, the Meiji shrine, the department stores in the Ginza, where again hostesses would bow deeply to every customer who passed by. The following day my host and his wife took me out to the country by electric train, about an hour from the central city, for lunch at her mother's house. She in turn prepared an enormous meal, serving several courses but not sitting with us, each time bowing as she backed out of the room. I was getting a sense of extraordinary hospitality combined with a somewhat embarrassing class-consciousness together with a real show of deference to a gaijin (foreigner) guest.

Several years were to pass before I had further chances to change my mind about Japan. In 1970 I left my law firm to join the international legal department of a major oil company. The lawyer in charge who interviewed me warned me that if I took the job, I would have to be ready to travel worldwide several times a year, on short notice; to have a bag packed at all times; and sometimes to visit troubled or distressed countries. I could barely hide my excitement in accepting his offer, for I had developed a serious case of the travel bug as a result of my 1966 round-the-world vacation.

In December of 1970, I was sent to Tokyo to get acquainted with our business there (not suspecting that in two short years, I would be assigned to our subsidiary there). Again, to the Hotel Okura, where our local office kept several rooms for visitors from the home office. And on an excursion to a beautiful golf course near Mount Fuji, which in winter had a lot of snow on it. I did not play, but watched several rituals, the female "caddy-sans" with their nunlike headdresses pulling the golfers' carts, always finding the ball, not suggesting the club to use, but always helpful and cheerful no matter how bad the player was. The ritual bath where the bathers sat on little stools on the outside rim of the pool-size tub and washed themselves off before getting into the bath. Then a good dinner and back to the city. Experience later taught me that golf courses and national parks were the most beautiful areas in Japan.

That 1970 visit was only a week, but I was getting very relaxed and appreciative of the politeness and attention I received from everyone—hotel hostesses to Japanese office counterparts. In the next two years I made a couple of visits on specific contracts we had with independent Japanese oil companies, once going down to Taiwan to visit a customer.

In the late fall of 1972, having vowed to leave the country if Nixon were reelected, I was delighted to accept an offer to become general counsel of our Japanese affiliate and to reside full-time in Tokyo. In December I made an orientation visit, and picked out (from several offerings) an apartment in a new building where there were already three other company families from New York. It had three bedrooms, a pool, and views on one side of Mount Fuji (when it was clear, sixty miles away) and on the other of Tokyo Tower. It was a fifteen-minute drive from our office, or a ten-minute subway commute. Because the general counsel then was also one of twelve directors, I was entitled to a car and driver, a perk which I had never had, and which never repeated itself. It alone made the assignment an easy one to take on.

Each workday my driver, Aoki-san, would arrive under the portal of my building no later than 7:55 a.m., with the heat on in the winter and the AC in the summer, the car's radio tuned to the Armed Forces Network for the 8:00 a.m. newscast, a thorough review of the day's international and US news. I had the *Japan Times* delivered to my apartment, so by the time I got to the office I was reasonably current on what was happening around the world. Aoki-san and I never shook hands, he bowed, opened the back door with his white-gloved hands, and we were off. He did not speak much English and at first I knew no Japanese.

This problem was addressed but not cured by the supposedly private Japanese lessons I received as often as three times a week from a young Buddhist instructor, who was often traveling to various religious retreats. The lessons were first thing in the morning, but my boss seemed to think that was a good time to barge through my closed office door to discuss whatever cables had come in overnight, and to ask me to draft responses to those with some arguable relationship to my lawyer's skills. So the lessons did not go well, I was lazy at evening homework, and there was no attempt at learning the Chinese characters, 2,000 of which were considered only the basic foundation for reading texts in Japanese.

In my little legal department there were three young Japanese lawyers; one probably my age (thirty-eight), the others younger. Their English was acceptable in oral speech but wanting in written drafts. I had to review everything they prepared to send out, even within the office. But I was saved from meltdown by the arrival, only a month or so after my own, of a young Yale Law School graduate who had been a dual Japanese and economics major at Yale College. He had interviewed at our head office for a position in the international division, but he imposed one important condition: that he be posted to Japan right away without any preliminary work in the New York office. Smart hiring officers agreed, he showed up in Tokyo for his first time, and came to the rescue in our legal department, speaking fluent Japanese, reading some material, and acting as a go-between with the three Japanese lawyers and myself.

I was blessed to have his help and his backup on some of my assignments, mainly joint-venture price-formula negotiations with another American oil company, and our Japanese partners. My other work was fairly routine, involving some antitrust, contract, and tax issues. On complex matters or litigation, we relied on multilingual outside Japanese firms.

Our Japanese affiliate was a major enterprise in its own right, with about nine hundred workers in the head office in Tokyo, roughly the same number of independent "agents" who owned the gas stations, and over $2 billion in sales in the mid-1970s, with roughly 15 percent of the market. When a joint venture with some potential Korean partners was proposed to market lubricants, I asked my young Yale associate to handle it from the start, which he did very enthusiastically and with little review from me.

As the months sped by, we moved into brand-new offices and I had a good view of downtown. The opening ceremony was attended by a prince, Hirohito's younger brother. I shook his hand and chatted briefly at the luncheon, but that was as close as I ever got to the royal family. I was becoming more and more satisfied with my assignment and more and more enthusiastic about the life of an expatriate in Tokyo. I had a secretary who followed the classical music scene, and who ordered tickets for me when I chose to go. She also arranged for trips out of town, roughly once a month, to spas and historic towns within easy reach of Tokyo by train. I had conquered the quaint procedures for obtaining a Japanese driver's license, and sometimes Aoki-san would leave the company car at my apartment for me to explore the city; this was complicated at first since I could not read the Japanese street signs, but by dint of memorizing routes which Aoki-san drove, and with a good English map at my side, I explored many sections of the huge city. I also bought a Raleigh bicycle and rode in the evenings and on weekends around my neighborhood, which was quite hilly.

My driver and secretary soon learned my habits, my favorite restaurants and bars, and let me know of other possible entertainments. I became a devotee of sumo, and followed several favorite wrestlers closely. There were six grand tournaments a year, three in Tokyo, and I managed to get invited a few times, otherwise I could slip down to the drivers' room to watch important matches on their television. I grew to like sushi, sashimi, sukiyaki, tempura, and other local dishes, and often would invite my assistant and some other staff for lunch at favorite places, all of which Aoki-san grew to know. In the spring, we would go as a group to see the cherry blossoms, with box lunches (*obento*) and beer in a park or shrine, once even going to a Yasukuni shrine. To this day Japanese prime ministers are challenged whether they go or not, since the shrine honors the dead from World War II, and is said to have interred war criminals.

Never did I discuss the war, Pearl Harbor, war crimes, or other sensitive issues. I flew down to Sasebo for a ship launching, and went by bus the short distance to Nagasaki. We spent time at the central memorial featuring a seated male figure with one open hand, the other pointing to the sky. That was as close to the war as I ever got. Some of our Japanese partners' officers had been naval or air officers in the war, we were told in advance of meeting them, but the subject never came up. The overwhelming politeness and warm hospitality eventually erased any lingering dislike of the country or its citizens.

Business cocktail parties, and dinners within our office came up often, sometimes weekly. There the talk was mostly about work, or world affairs, Watergate was big news. There was a monthly directors' lunch prepared and served in the office by Mogi-san, a jack of all trades cook, bartender, and a man who tended the six or seven bonsai trees at my apartment. The other maintenance came in the form of Tokiko-san, world's most dutiful and devoted cleaning woman, who would wash and iron anything not nailed down. Between her, my driver, my secretary, Mogi-san, and a caterer who was the wife of another driver, there was little I had to do for myself.

As my interest in things Japanese grew, I began to collect various objects, a favorite pastime of the expats. I developed two specialties, antique wooden chests (tansu) and original woodblock prints. In my three-and-a-half years there, I acquired seven Japanese chests of all sorts in which I could store clothes, tapes and records, dining room mats, and all other kinds of essential and useful artifacts. My assistant bought a Korean chest for me, sight unseen by me. These chests are all in my house in New Milford, Connecticut, where the walls are covered with over 30 woodblock prints, including some by Hiroshige & Eisen. I also collected ancient pottery, some of the traditional blue and white Imari, others with colorful animal patterns. Some were wedding presents, with three stacked bowls each of which had a different hot dish for the reception. Others were purely ornamental, and they are all now stored in two glass-shelved breakfronts I designed and had made for me in a shop in Hong Kong. My shipment going home was a lot bigger and heavier than the contents of my Brooklyn Heights apartment, which had been sent to me in Japan back in January of 1973.

There were only two reminders of World War II that brought back thoughts of Pearl Harbor. One was the reappearance in 1974 of a forlorn Japanese soldier who had spent the years since 1945 hiding out in the hills of Guam, claiming to be unaware that the war was over. This despite daily planeloads of Japanese honeymooners at the beach resorts that had been developed over thirty years. The soldier was welcomed back to the mainland as a hero, complete with military decorations and a reception by the emperor.

The other reminder of the war occurred a year later, when my parents came for a three-week visit in the spring, my father having been retired by Yale after forty years, because he had reached the then old age of sixty-eight. Golden Week is a series of four holidays at the end of April and in the first week of May. Business effectively stops during a ten-day period. One of those holidays in 1975 was the emperor's birthday, on April 30 as I recall. Suitably dressed up for the occasion, my parents and I went to the Imperial Palace grounds to watch Hirohito take the salute of huge crowds. We were handed out good-size paper or plastic flags, the red disk on the white background, not the military version with a rising sun casting its rays outward. When Hirohito dutifully appeared on the palace balcony, though he did not speak, we heard the crowd shouting "banzai" three times. It all seemed a bit surreal, us joining in a salute to the man we had been taught to hate, and with the words we associated with Japanese soldiers' atrocities on our men and civilians of the occupied lands.

As my assignment drew to a close in the spring of 1976, I had had visits from each of my two sisters, as well as a few American friends from home. We had a directors' meeting where I got to know all the higher-ups in the parent company and their wives (there were at least one or two women in their group). We had achieved success in the main price negotiations with our joint venture partners. The purely legal office work went smoothly, thanks in large part to my young Yale assistant. I had visited three of the main islands, seen countless temples, and the Winter Snow Festival in Sapporo, a frigid outdoor museum of ice sculptures. I had made friends with a few Japanese-American couples, and found my Yale Yamamoto friend and his wife. My monthly out-of-town weekends had mostly been interesting, staying at ryokan (Japanese inns) visiting temples, photographing new and ancient architecture. I had mastered the protocol of the Japanese bathhouse, occasionally trying out the local public house. I had learned enough Japanese to direct taxi drivers when Aoki-san was off, I had learned enough cooking to be able to shop knowledgeably, though my repertoire remained slim. I had conquered the hills on my bike, though one day a taxi driver opened his back door just as I was passing, causing some painful bruises and a somewhat bewildered taxi driver. I had played squash at the British embassy court, a stand-alone building on their grounds. I had sampled enough restaurants to be able to take my parents and sisters to different ones every evening. And I had even managed to host an elegant dinner for about thirty people in my apartment, to honor my parents.

When it came time to ship out for home, my favorite couple, a Japanese banker and his American wife who ran a Blue & White antiques and fabrics shop, gave me a farewell April Fool's costumed dinner, though I was the only one to show up costumed, dressed as a samurai fencer. The courses were served backwards, nuts to soup. It was a fitting farewell, uniting Japanese and Americans in a sort of salute to transpacific understanding. As I boarded the plane to go home I realized I had been totally captured by the kindness of the Japanese people and the good taste of their culture. I had surely overcome and forgotten any thoughts of Pearl Harbor.

Looking back now from the perspective of the forty-one years since I left my Tokyo posting (exactly half my life), I still ask myself when, how, and why my feelings and beliefs about Japan changed from strongly negative to very favorable. One factor was surely the passage of time, the twenty-one years after the surrender on the *Missouri* to my quick first visit in 1966, and then my residence in 1973. The demonizing of the "Japs" which accompanied my grade-school years both in school and in print (cartoons and articles about their atrocities) faded over time. It all stopped very quickly and a couple of college courses focused much more on the miracles of Westernization initiated by the Meiji Restoration in the mid-nineteenth century. In a few decades Japan had been transformed from what we would consider a backward agricultural society run by an oligarchy to an industrial power that routed Russia and adopted railroads and cars and electricity with remarkable speed.

Some prejudices learned in childhood tend to disappear when confronted with the reality of the people and their culture. False impressions can be rapidly countered. When I came to live there, I was determined to enjoy my stay and to accommodate myself to a very different lifestyle. Certainly the material benefits, large apartment, car and driver, exploration of new cuisine, kindness and hospitality of strangers, ease of living where so much was done for me, all made it much easier to forget old animosities and welcome with an open mind the new challenges posed by any overseas posting. I would say now that within months, if not weeks, of my taking up residence, I had lost any remaining hostility, which was minimal in any event, and succumbed to the delights and curiosities which were so close and so available.

Certainly this transformation was made even easier when I met mixed Japanese-American couples who became good friends, when I talked to their children, and when I was invited by all-Japanese couples to dinner or to go out to try new restaurants. I was exposed through my weekend excursions (seven visits to Kyoto alone) to the best of ancient Japanese culture—graceful, tasteful temples fashioned out of woods that were new to me, the various chests I bought with elaborate fixtures, woodblock prints I began to collect which show samurai warriors, kabuki actors, sumo wrestlers, and everyday rice farmers and tradespeople, all were impressive. The bonsai trees I cultivated, the manicured gardens of bamboo, chestnut, azalea. cherry, and plum added to the visual appeal. And of course modern Japan, with its *shinkansen* (bullet trains), its superb subways and commuter networks, its hi-tech wizardry persuaded me that the Japanese were ahead of the US in many respects.

There was little mention of the war, and few reminders. On weekends, loud sound trucks circled my neighborhood with right-wing signs urging rearmament and slogans broadcast to uncomprehending ears, but in election after election the right-wing militarist parties lost badly. The political demonstrations that took place from time to time showed me that the postwar Constitution, largely written by MacArthur, had transformed Japan into a modern democracy with a totally free and often critical press, many TV outlets, independent courts (we had some successes in litigation), labor unions (we outwaited some strikers in our office building).

My three and half years in Japan were the highlight of my professional life. I had come to look forward to my work and my leisure pastimes. I had acquired several tastes for the artifacts of their culture, I had even broken 100 in my required golf outings. I returned to Japan many times on business and then after retirement on pleasure trips, the most recent in 2013. It remains a very special place in my thoughts and in my life.

PETER O. CLAUSS

In the City of Brotherly Love

I GRADUATED WITH MY YALE LAW SCHOOL CLASS IN the late spring of 1958, and after successfully passing the Pennsylvania bar exam that summer, I joined a Philadelphia law firm in the early fall at the age of twenty-one. In those days, Philadelphia still clung to its traditions. Many, including a number of law firm hiring partners, considered family connections very important. Most of the larger firms were largely composed of white Anglo Saxon Protestant (WASP) partners. Firms tended to concentrate along ethnic divisions. There were the WASP firms, as well as Jewish, Irish, and Italian firms, and so on. In 1958 even the largest firms were small by today's standards. The three largest had no more than forty to forty-five lawyers, and except for one, had no branch offices in other cities. The starting salary level between the medium and larger sized firms was also consistent. In 1958 the "standard" was $3,500 per year before one passed the bar exam and increased to between $4,500 and $4,800 afterwards. My firm was midsize, and I became its sixteenth lawyer. I was the first Yale Law School graduate the firm ever hired. All of the other lawyers, except one who had graduated from Duke Law School, had gone to Harvard, the University of Pennsylvania, or the University of Virginia. The firm was founded in 1902 by a Penn graduate who was invited by the patriarch of the Pew clan, which then controlled Sun Oil, to become its inside general counsel. He declined the offer, once telling me that in those days no self-respecting lawyer would take an inside counsel position. He believed it would compromise that lawyer's independence. Of the four name partners in the firm, he was completely retired and another, who had been a justice on the Pennsylvania Supreme Court, was deceased. The retired partner made it a habit to take me to lunch at his club several times a month, recounting much about the firm's history. Although he never expressly requested it, I believe he expected me to write a firm history. I never got around to it, although I still have copious notes. One of the other name partners, who over time became my primary mentor, did write that history in time for the firm's gala eightieth birthday celebration.

The city mirrored the ethnic divisions of the law firms, and local politics on the Republican side was controlled by two machines, one in the city proper run by Boss Meehan, and the other, known as the War Board of the McClure machine, controlled neighboring Delaware County. The éminence grise behind the War Board happened to be my family's nearby neighbor. He kept a very low profile, while exerting immense influence, single handedly picking most of the county judges and officials. Shortly after graduation I paid him a visit. He was tending to his orchids in his greenhouse when I arrived and told him what I was doing. He wanted to know where I had studied law. I told him. He exploded with the words "bunch of Commies in that place!" I placated him by explaining I had been the cochairman of the Conservative Society. His attitude probably mirrored that of many other Philadelphia lawyers of his generation. The machine in the city was soon to have much of its power reigned in by the progressive team of Mayor Joseph Clark and District Attorney Richardson Dilworth, a Yale Law School graduate. It was Dilworth, whom my father knew from architectural projects that he had designed, who sent a letter recommending me for admission to the Law School. The War Board continued its influence for many years thereafter.

During "practice" interviews with New York firms the question of my military obligation came up frequently. Oddly, the Philadelphia firm that hired me never asked about this, even though most of its partners had served in World War II or Korea. Predictably, soon after graduation I received a notice from my local draft board to report for a physical and was told to expect a draft notice within the next several months. I weighed a two-year commitment as an enlisted man against a three year or longer commitment as an officer. I decided to apply to the Judge Advocate General Corps and as part of the required paperwork asked the same name partner who later became my mentor if he would write a letter supporting my application. This partner was a tall and lean man of reserved and aristocratic demeanor with a wry sense of humor. He looked at me and drily informed me that the firm had not hired me a few months previously to then have me immediately leave for three years. He stated that I would join his military unit, which was then part of the US Army National Guard, and only serve active duty for six months, but with a long-term reserve commitment. His unit was the oldest military unit in continuous existence in the country, and was a cavalry troop founded in 1774, which fought in every war since then (as it still does). I knew of the unit, and expressed doubt that they would take me. Members had to be elected and it consisted primarily of men descended from old Philadelphia families, which I was not. He assured me this would not be a problem because one of my fellow associates was currently the executive officer of the unit and would be my sponsor. I was accepted and the first order of business was to learn to ride. We received excellent equestrian instruction, and in a few months I was able to ride in an escort to President Eisenhower. I left for six months active duty in March of 1959, and spent a number of nights in the first month of basic training in the latrine, which was then the only lighted area in the barracks after lights out, finishing a brief in a patent case to the Sixth Circuit which I had been preparing for one of the senior partners to argue.

It would be a number of years before the firm hired its first woman or minority lawyer, although the firm did hire an associate of Italian heritage about the time I started. He left the firm while I was on active military duty. When I returned I took over the firm's tax practice, which had been his specialty. Many of the lawyers then in the firm remained until their retirement. In my first few years lateral hires were rare, although the firm did recruit a number of federal law clerks.

Philadelphia, then and now, has a downtown area in which most law firms, corporate headquarters, and other service providers are concentrated in a small area of perhaps twelve blocks east to west and six or seven, blocks north and south, and most of the city's private clubs are located within this area. I knew that if a lawyer was to be successful he or she must control meaningful clients. Thus, within a few months of returning from active military service I joined a number of these private clubs, several for dining and others for squash, swimming, rowing, and tennis. My military unit had its own armory and provided an active social life. In addition to having places to professionally entertain, it seemed reasonable to expect to make contacts which hopefully would develop into clients. This actually was the case, but today I expect that a young lawyer joining one of these clubs would be surprised to discover that he will run into far more lawyers than prospective clients.

There were other professional activities in which young lawyers engaged, and in those early years I became involved with the Philadelphia Bar Association, the oldest in the country, and the tax section of the American Bar Association. In the local association I joined the public service and public relations committees. I soon found myself succeeding a local football legend as chair of the Unpopular Causes Committee, originally formed to help those indicted under the Smith Act find counsel. That purpose was pretty much moot when I took over, and I soon realized that most of my referrals would be to seek pro bono counsel willing to help seriously mentally deranged people. After a few years I became vice chair of the Public Service Committee when Community Legal Services was being established. At that time this was an early stepping stone to a future run for Chancellor of the Association. The Public Relations Committee was obsessed with improving the image of the term "a Philadelphia lawyer," which, since the founding of the republic, had at times been a term of great praise for excellent legal ability, but at others a term of great disparagement, as in a scheming and conniving shyster. I ended my involvement abruptly during the Vietnam War, when the association got involved in political issues that I felt were outside its charter.

For a long time Philadelphia has been in the shadow of New York City, but there were some crucial differences between then and now. Then, many corporations headquartered in Philadelphia or the surrounding areas within its orbit had no problem using a Philadelphia law firm as their principal legal resource. Today, that is less the case, with larger companies sending their more substantial work to firms in the Big Apple. When I began the practice of law, the Philadelphia area had a large number of corporate headquarters, including such companies as Sun Oil (now Sunoco), Baldwin Lima Locomotive Works, Scott Paper; Budd Company; Insurance Company of North America; Bethlehem Steel; Smith, Kline & French; Vanity Fair (now VF); Pennwalt; Food Machinery Corporation (now FMC); Lavino Shipping Company; Holt Marine (now Holt Logistics); Philadelphia Electric; Pennsylvania Power & Light (now PPL); Girard Trust Company (now Girard Bank); Fidelity Bank; Provident Bank (now PNC); and Philadelphia National Bank. In years not long after that, new companies were organized or moved to this area, including Alco Standard, Safeguard Scientifics, Norcross Greeting Cards, and Commodore Computers. These companies provided much of the legal work for the larger law firms in this city. Today, most of those companies are gone or have been absorbed as components of larger entities headquartered elsewhere. A few, such as Sunoco, Holt Logistics, PPL, FMC, and VF have survived as independent entities, although VF has relocated its headquarters to North Carolina, and Budd to Michigan before it ceased operating in 2014. Fortunately, other companies now maintain their headquarters here, including Comcast and Aramark.

Another difference between the two cities in my early days of practice centered on the degree of trust between lawyers on different sides of a matter, be it litigation or a business transaction. For example, I recall an early acquisition where my opposite number in a very large firm took me aside to recommend a certain tax structure which would benefit my client (I was well aware of the structure, but it was most kind of him to make the suggestion). Sadly, a number of years later the chairman of that same firm used a tactic in a larger acquisition which bordered on the unethical and was employed only to delay paying deferred portions of the purchase price. As another example, it was common then to trust in a handshake, whereas if a New York lawyer was on the other side in a litigation matter we almost always insisted on a written stipulation, sometimes approved by the court.

I had been elected a partner effective January 1, 1965. Less than a year later the partners selected me to be the managing partner. This had little to do with any particular skills I might have had. None of the others wanted to do it. I believe their reluctance was derived primarily from our compensation system. We had a very precise formula that weighed only two components—origination of work and participation in the form of billable hours. In those days we did not have a compensation committee. Instead, the partners met on a Sunday afternoon in January to hash out partnership compensation retroactively for the year just finished when the net profits to the firm had been determined. The origination and participation credits each counted for half. Origination credits belonged to the originator indefinitely and were not shared (unless divided between two or more when the first file for a new client was opened) and could not be transferred (it was unclear if they could be inherited because no partner had died while active for a long time). However, the originator of one major client had left the firm before I arrived and one of the name partners assumed the origination credit for that client which stayed with the firm. On another occasion a client belonging to the other name partner had sent some major matters to another firm and he told me if I could get the client back (which I did) the origination would be mine. Nevertheless, for a number of years after I became a partner most of the significant (defined by fees received) clients of the firm were originations of the two name partners, and two senior admiralty partners. Moreover, participation credits were determined by multiplying hours worked on billable matters by one's hourly rate that progressed in a fairly linear manner reflecting seniority with the firm. Thus, strict application of the formula would result in most of the firm's profits going to the two name partners, with another portion attributable to the two senior admiralty partners going to them. Not surprisingly, the Sunday meeting's primary purpose was to even things out with old-fashioned horse trading. For example, one of these four partners might say, "Well, you are being very generous to me, but so and so were very helpful, so I will give each some of my share." Then another would likewise do something similar. In some magic way, rough equity was achieved, but each partner left the room knowing exactly where the power in the firm rested.

I believe the primary reason my seniors did not want the role of managing partner was that it would deplete the available time which might otherwise have been spent in accruing participation hours or in various forms of entertainment and socializing that might lead to the origination of new clients. No credit for administration of the firm was included in the formula. Nevertheless, it seemed to me a wonderful opportunity. I felt that I could use this platform to modernize some of the equipment and systems used by most Philadelphia firms at that time. Younger readers will be astonished to learn that when I started there were no reliable copy machines (instead the secretaries manually typed and made multiple copies with messy carbon paper); there were no computers so changes and editing required retyping; even calculators were very bulky machines the size of a hardback book; and dictating machines were only in limited use. One of my first acts was to decree that all lawyers would henceforth dictate to a machine instead of a stenographer, and she (most were women) would then listen to the transcription with headphones and type what had been dictated. I was convinced that one could dictate to a machine several times faster than to a stenographer. The secretaries resented the change, and I suspect in addition to the discomfort of the earphones they worried they would lose their shorthand skills. Without my mentor's strong support this initiative and many others would surely have failed.

A few other observations are in order. Origination credits

lasted indefinitely, almost always belonging to the one who had brought the client in. In at least one respect the process was democratic. Unlike some firms where only partners could receive origination credits, in our firm an associate who brought in a client retained the origination credit. The complaints about the system started with a group of young Turks who wanted to change the system. They felt that a team often contributed to the retention of a client. They were concerned that as older partners retired the origination credit might be handed down to a successor, and they were particularly concerned that the credit related to the identity of the client, rather than the matter for which a new case file was opened. For instance, if a corporate lawyer who had never tried a case opened a litigation matter on which he would probably not work, why should he get the full credit? The first attempts to deal with these issues led to a gradual tweaking of the compensation formula to add a third component called "retention." Even this modification did not satisfy some, and admittedly it was very difficult to determine relative retention credits.

As a result, over a period of many years with what seemed like endless partner meetings, we finally arrived at a complete restatement of how origination credits would be determined. In essence, all clients would become "firm originated" after a period of years during which the originator of the client would receive a declining credit. We agreed to a seven-year period of full credit and then a second seven-year period during which the credit would be decreased. This was to apply to all clients then with the firm, which required the buy-in of all those with significant originations, and all future clients. Somehow, we were able to achieve this and the new rules became effective. There was one significant exception which bent the rules—if one could prove under an extremely strict set of guidelines that the client would not remain with the firm were it not for the sole efforts of the one claiming the exception. This exception, as we shall see, led to serious problems in the future.

The second important development emerged over many years as the firm grew in size from the sixteen lawyers when I started to over 125 at the time of our eightieth anniversary in 1982. This growth was not just measured by numbers, but by the addition of many new areas of practice that did not exist when I started, together with the concurrent trend toward greater specialization. This latter development greatly troubled me. I had the benefit in my early years of being exposed to a wide range of different areas of the law, which I felt gave me a great advantage since I was better able to see the forest and not just the trees. New areas of practice came about in unexpected ways. For example, when I started we had only three de facto practice groups: commercial law, fiduciary and estates, and a large admiralty practice. Litigation was handled by lawyers in these groups, most in the admirably section and none in the fiduciary section. Increased litigation in the commercial area necessitated that a separate litigation group be formed. For example, in my first year with the firm I was assigned the defense of a major claim involving a fatal defect in the prototype of the nose cone of the B-1 supersonic bomber, brought by a very skilled plaintiff's lawyer on behalf of a major defense contractor, and yet I had never even seen a jury trial, let alone assisted or otherwise participated in one. Fortunately the case settled in our favor prior to trial and I learned more about metallurgical engineering than I did of trial practice. A strong bankruptcy group emerged when the firm was chosen in 1970 as cocounsel to represent the Committee of Interline Railroads in the Penn Central bankruptcy proceedings. The expansion continued as our longtime representation of one of the largest coal mining companies in the country necessitated building an environmental practice. A small lateral group was added which brought in the governing organization in Pennsylvania regulating credit unions, creating expertise in that area.

A third area proved significant in what was to come. For years the firm favored growth from the bottom up. We mostly hired recent law school graduates, preferably those near the top of their class, including federal law clerks. Over the years I firmly believe that with very few exceptions we hired extremely bright and capable lawyers. However, as we grew, we added new specialties when we found holes in our own practice groups, and from time to time would bring in lateral hires. In the early years of my time with the firm this was fairly limited. We added the tax manager of a major electronics manufacturer, but he was gone a few years later as a result of his penchant for working as little as possible and a lack of expertise that became evident to even his staunchest supporter. It was not until years later that the firm's growth was fueled by a large number of lateral hires of individual lawyers or groups of lawyers, a few of whom proved to be a mistake, although in different ways. Two examples here will suffice. A lawyer with good credentials approached us with his two associates and convinced us that his unique practice involving environmental insurance claims would prove beneficial. We agreed and his group grew rapidly to twenty-two lawyers. However, his demands on firm resources were great and he insisted that several in his group become partners. We declined, pointing out that we were losing money on his practice group. He pointed to the upward spiral of revenues from his group, but even though he was a graduate of an Ivy League college and law school, he seemed unable to understand the difference between gross revenue and net profit. Another lateral hire caused us unbelievable problems, ranging from refusing to follow department guidelines to taking cases with obvious conflicts of interest. A third lateral hire proved to be extremely disruptive to the firm culture.

Another significant issue concerned a lively debate between two groups of partners over election to partnership. One group wanted to have only equity partners and the other wanted to create the categories of contract partners and of counsel. Over the years we developed something of a hodgepodge, which contributed to chronic friction. Finally, we faced the issue of opening branch offices. We ended up with two. One was in a suburban county bordering Philadelphia on the west, which was the logical direction in which the metropolitan area could grow. The other was across the Delaware River in New Jersey. However, each created a bonding of the lawyers in them, a feeling of separateness from the mother ship, and somewhat of a tendency to view their issues and identity as more important than creating an integrated firm.

Unlike many other firms where the partners' votes are weighted by length of service and relative compensation, every partner in our firm was entitled to an equal vote with every other partner on all matters. This created numerous problems, although not all of them were recognized in time. Second, although the matter was discussed and rejected a number of times, the firm remained a general partnership and never converted to a limited liability partnership.

We need now to fast forward almost forty years from the time I joined the firm, and particularly to 1995 and 1996. The firm's eightieth anniversary had been celebrated just thirteen years before and all of my partners who had started with the firm before me were gone, either retired or deceased. I was now the senior partner by reason of length of time with the firm and because I controlled a large group of clients. The origination, participation, and retention factors in the compensation formula had been supplanted by the more common method of annually electing a compensation committee which would determine shares prospectively. The quaint practice of listing all lawyers on a masthead and on letterhead used for correspondence (partners on the left and associates and counsel on the right) had been replaced by listing only partners in the order of their admissions to the bar. I was amused by the practice of one New York firm which changed the order of listing their partners frequently as their relative power shifted. It reminded me of the annual May Day parade in the Kremlin where the relative positions of the Soviet leaders were watched intently and analyzed.

Unfortunately trouble was brewing within the firm. The relations among many of the partners did not reflect the brotherly love supposed to reside in Philadelphia. Long festering disputes and outright antagonisms or perceived slights began to bubble up to the surface. This was particularly true between factions of homegrown and lateral partners. What may have begun as personality differences or as opposing viewpoints on firm practice and culture became far more acute when focused on compensation matters, or who should manage the firm or various departments and practice groups. Central to compensation disputes was the overhaul of the definition of origination described above. First, there were definitional issues. Was the sole exception to the declining percentage to be construed so strictly that one would only get the full credit if it could be proved that if that partner left the firm the client would also leave. Short of actual departure how could that be proved? Should origination be determined on a client-wide or a specific-matter basis? The greatest inequities and friction developed between the homegrown partners whose efforts were constrained by the new rules, and the increasing number of lateral partners admitted to the firm who argued that everything they brought with them had to be their origination because they obviously fell within the reach of the exception. The compensation committee tried to arbitrate these conflicting claims by applying a common sense approach. However, as the firm grew larger it became impossible for the members of that committee to really know why a particular client stayed and continued to send more work to the firm. Too often they had to rely on the self-serving "brag sheets" that each partner submitted to the committee. Some partners who believed that they had been slighted or unfairly treated then engaged in ad hominem attacks on those they felt had unfairly benefitted. One particularly disruptive partner took this even further, claiming he was discriminated against on ethnic grounds. Another, newly elected to the compensation committee, engaged in threats and coercion, stating in public that he was going to "slam" certain other partners whom he felt were "deadwood." For years the firm had been a very collegial place to practice law, but this was disintegrating rapidly. Several partners told me they dreaded even being in the office at certain times of the year, especially when partnership shares were awarded.

In addition to these serious divisions, there were deep-seated cultural differences among many of the partners, as well as some basic policy differences. Should the firm, for example, retain an admiralty practice? Should we pursue more public corporate clients or more privately held companies? Should we hold ourselves out as being capable of handling all things or be more restrictive in the types of work we could offer? Should we adopt strict minimum entry requirements where the firm would not accept a matter unless it was likely to result in a certain minimum fee?

To add to the troubles we had to remove one managing partner who had abused his position in various ways. A different partner breached the partnership agreement and the trust expected between partners, all to a very large financial benefit to himself. One of our largest clients, a public company, had a block of stock representing practical control owned by a trust set up by the company's founder. There were three trustees, one of whom was designated by the company, another by the company's principal bank, and the third by our firm. Each trustee also had to be a company director. Each served until a set retirement age. Two of our partners had served until that retirement age. When it was time to choose a replacement, a few of us more senior corporate partners chose a younger partner we felt had the requisite social connections and demeanor to fit well with the client. The senior admiralty partner and I had personally recruited this individual years before when he left the navy after law school, primarily upon the recommendations of his brother in law (a good friend of mine) and his father in law (a good friend of the admiralty partner). The partnership agreement clearly required that director fees of a corporate client and fiduciary fees from an estate or trust that was a firm client were to be treated as fees and paid over to the firm. After serving for a few years and paying these amounts to the firm, this partner announced that henceforth he intended to keep them because he felt that he deserved them. When the breach of the partnership agreement was pointed out to him he abruptly resigned as a partner, but continued with the firm. Most of us felt totally betrayed, none less than I. A few of us wanted either to sue him or remove him from the firm, or both. However, a majority (remember that each partner had an equal vote) was worried that we would then lose a very valuable client. We probably would have if the client became aware of the issue, but two of us believed the mere threat of public litigation would have brought the offender around or at least resulted in a reasonable compromise. I know for a fact that he would not have wanted to be embarrassed in front of his friends. Moreover, our work for this client was already in decline as a result of a number of factors, including the move of its headquarters to the south, and its appointment of its first in house counsel, who rapidly expanded her department and had started to send a lot of the outside work to New York counsel. At any rate, the actions of these two partners created a depressing atmosphere within the firm.

Finally, by the early part of 1995 these problems and differences had reached the breaking point. Department heads were at each other's throats, and pods of lawyers were threatening to leave, and in at least one case, did so. Then individual lawyers polished their resumes and perhaps even circulated them. A few left. One lateral securities lawyer with a very myopic view centered on his clients only, and who refused to participate in departmental matters (my department), did abruptly leave for another firm with three associates who mostly worked on his matters. This was not a major financial loss to the firm, but we had to scramble to replace the collective time of two of those associates. More importantly, a small public company client of this partner was in the process of suing our firm and naming each individual partner as a defendant for an alleged drafting mistake in a shareholder-employment agreement. The only persons who had worked on this agreement, or even knew of its existence, were the departing partner and the most junior of the associates he took with him. The litigation was later expanded to join the firm to which he departed because of a second alleged erroneous advice he gave to the client once he was with the new firm. Happily the matter was settled with our exposure covered by insurance, but the other firm did not fare as well. Even so, dealing with this litigation consumed hundreds of hours of our time and of our wind down committee before it was resolved, and all without cooperation from the departing partner.

At this point I felt I had to intervene before things got any worse. I met with the current managing partner and we decided to contact the legal consulting firm then recognized as the leading national firm with this area of expertise. We asked them to find us a suitable merger partner, preferably a larger firm based in another city that would like to have a sizable Philadelphia presence.

After what seemed much too short an interval the senior person at the consulting group met with us to report that there was no such firm that he could find and he did not think a merger would work. With the benefit of hindsight I think we were poorly served in this respect. Within just a few years a number of out of town firms opened or acquired offices in the Philadelphia metropolitan area. The consultant then suggested a different approach, which was that we clean out the "deadwood" (partners or associates who were no longer productive or profitable). I responded that this would run against the grain of our firm's culture, and that even if we did that I doubted it would solve the problem. He disagreed, claiming he had helped many firms with this approach. The partners voted, and to my surprise supported his proposal. He then appointed his son, who had very little experience, as the person who would interview each partner in private to build a "deadwood" list. Again I protested, explaining that many would simply name people whom they didn't like or wanted to get rid of for other reasons. He responded that he had more experience than I with this approach. As I feared, his son totally lacked an ability to "read" some of those he interviewed, and it quickly turned into a witch hunt. Some groups then coalesced and held secret meetings to develop strategies to get rid of others on their "hit lists." I had to personally intervene several times to protect valuable partners.

A series of partnership meetings took place seeking to save the firm, but this resulted in more confusion than positive results because many in the room had no real understanding of practice areas or clients other than their own. Even worse, even while a real effort was at least made by a majority to save the firm, a few others were plotting its demise. The partner described earlier who was removed as managing partner was secretly negotiating with the firm which had taken the departing securities partner and his three associates to pull away a much larger group, and even promised that firm that others who did not even have knowledge of what he was doing would be in the group. In an act of supreme irony, when the other firm contacted people on his list with offers, he did not receive one. Thinking it must have been an oversight he contacted the person with whom he was negotiating, and was told they did not want him. I guess his reputation preceded him. Fortunately, all but one of our junior partners declined the offers from the other firm.

It became increasingly evident that the firm could not be saved when several of our most talented and promising younger partners approached me and stated that unless the firm could emerge much larger and stronger they too would seek their future elsewhere. These developments prompted the legal consultant to propose an orderly dissolution shepherded by his firm. I have to wonder if this was not his plan all along, because it promised far more in fees to his organization than simply arranging a firm merger or a slimmed down firm shorn of "deadwood."

Fortunately, with the most difficult partners gone (both less than unanimous lateral hires), the remaining partners retained enough of the earlier collegial firm culture to agree to an orderly dissolution. A target effective date was chosen and almost all agreed to remain even if they began to plan for their exit and even contact others with whom they might associate. We even authorized a newly formed "wind down committee" to issue notices to the associates and other employees under the federal and local WARN Acts. During these meetings it emerged that at least four groups would explore their options—my business and corporate group, the admiralty and maritime group, the group comprising our western suburban office, and the group comprising our New Jersey office.

As to my group, I spoke with a number of our stronger partners, young and old, to determine their interest. Then, with the younger partner who approached me, we drew up two lists. One list was of twenty or so lawyers (mostly partners, but a few associates as well, with a mixture of corporate, securities, litigation, tax, ERISA, and litigation expertise) who were capable, profitable, and who controlled significant clients. This would be the group we would try to take with us. The second list, which began with over a dozen firms in the city and ended with only four, were firms where there were strong fits, either based on firm culture, personal friendships, or mutual strengths. Before we knew the outcome of our search, the wind-down committee of three partners had begun the process of an orderly dissolution.

A month or so later, effective on November 30, 1996, the firm dissolved. Why did this happen? What were the causes? Could it have been prevented?

I periodically review these questions in my mind, turning over alternative scenarios, and reluctantly each time come to the conclusion that the stage was irrevocably set. Primary among these were the problems created by too rapid an absorption of lateral partners, exacerbated by the compensation issues, and a gradual pattern of distrust or dislike among some partners toward others. Had we preserved the collegial atmosphere that was a firm hallmark for the first half of my tenure of thirty-eight years, the outcome might have been different. Certainly the ineffective and dismissed managing partner and the partner who abused his fiduciary duty both poisoned the well. I also fault the legal consultant who led us down the wrong path. But most of all I fault myself for having abdicated my responsibility as the senior in disassociating myself from firm management for so many years in order to concentrate on a growing and demanding practice and for ignoring problems with the bland assumption that everything would take care of itself. The buck has to stop somewhere, but I let it slide by. By the time I finally decided to try to do something it was far too late, although possibly a more personal and earlier intervention, one on one with individual partners, might have helped. Perhaps it would have just deferred the inevitable.

Now, some may wonder why I picked such a depressing topic to address. I did so mostly because it is obvious that what happened to this firm is no different than what has happened to dozens of other firms across the country, many of them far larger than ours. I hope that by exploring the reasons for our situation other firms headed down the wrong path in the future might be spared a similar fate. We were neither the first nor the last Philadelphia firm to end our existence. The largest firm in the city to collapse did so precipitously and with very little warning, even to many of its partners who only learned of the collapse after the fact.

John Morley, a professor at the Yale Law School, has studied in detail the breakup of thirty-seven prominent law firms in different parts of the country from 1988 through 2014. He believes that there are a number of factors contributing to law firm collapse that were present in most or all of the cases he studied, and that such a collapse is often sudden and chaotic. Interestingly, most of these firms continued to service their debt and remained profitable until the time of dissolution. That was true of my firm as well. He believes the primary catalyst is the decline in relative profits (a change for the worse in historic profits) that triggers a self-reinforcing spiral of partner withdrawals, which he describes as a "run on the partnership." The motivation is often the fear of crushing liability to partners who remain until dissolution from fraudulent transfers or preferential payments to these partners immediately before or after the firm is deemed to be insolvent. Thus there is motivation to leave early and not be the last partner standing. The impact of such a mass exodus is usually harmful to the firm because it loses revenue from clients who leave with the departing partners, but fixed expenses for such things as rent, salaries, pensions, and loan payments are often not correspondingly reduced. An exception to this general rule would be where the compensation due the departed partners had they stayed is greater than the business they generated. The general impact is also exacerbated by Model Rule of Professional Conduct 5.6, which requires the firm to repay the departing partners their capital shares unless the partnership agreement waives this requirement. If enough partners leave, this may also trigger negative covenants in lease or loan agreements accelerating maturity or payment dates.

The typical firm facing these problems will usually try to find a merger partner, and if successful may survive. If not, the firm is probably doomed. If creditors believe they will not be paid they may force a bankruptcy or insolvency proceeding, in which case fraudulent transfers, preferential treatment, and unfinished business doctrines may be asserted.

My firm avoided many of these problems. Our borrowings

were modest and had express provisions denying recourse to the individual partners. Our partnership agreement expressly negated Model Rule 5.6 by permitting the firm discretion about when to repay capital. Our profits in the year of dissolution, which occurred near the end of the year (we were on a calendar year basis), were on track to reflect profits in an average year so that relative profits remained unchanged. Most importantly, most of the thirty or so equity partners agreed to remain with the firm until around the dissolution date, so we avoided the "run on the partnership" that Professor Morley describes. We also never had to face a bankruptcy proceeding because we quickly resolved all issues with our single local bank creditor and our three landlords. We paid our other lawyers (approximately seventy associates, contract partners, and counsel), paralegals, and secretarial and administrative employees sixty days of compensation as required by the WARN Acts, and almost all of them swiftly found other employment (often with the help of the partners). The one suit brought against us was resolved by our insurance carrier. Our rapid expansion of years before had leveled off. We also enjoyed significant client loyalty until the end: most clients followed their originators or retaining lawyers to their new firms. Moreover, we were smaller than most of the firms studied by Professor Morley. Finally, once we were rid of the few really disruptive partners, we scored high in "bonding capital" because of the efforts we had invested in relationships that inculcated feelings of friendship, loyalty, and trust. We would describe this as our traditional firm culture. I am glad the reservoir left in our residual "bonding capital" was deep enough to permit an orderly withdrawal and dissolution, but there was not enough left to reverse course. Some partners wanted to do that, but at that point the damage had been done and matters had progressed too far to resurrect the firm.

Now, some twenty plus years later, I can report something of a happy ending to this story. The younger partner and I, after a flurry of meetings with the four firms on the second list, picked one and that firm took most, but not all, of the lawyers on our first list. It was much larger than our firm. Even though I retired from that firm after a dozen years, many of the others are still there and one of the younger lawyers we brought with us is now the managing partner of that firm. All of the lawyers, and almost all of the administrative personnel, of the dissolved firm found employment elsewhere fairly quickly. Our New Jersey office of a dozen or so lawyers stayed together as a new firm and was eventually absorbed by a larger firm in a merger. The lawyers in our satellite office in the western suburbs also stayed together as a new firm and it has since doubled in size. The admiralty lawyers in our Philadelphia and New Jersey offices formed a new firm specializing in admiralty and maritime matters and has grown and prospered. All of our firm's creditors were paid in full and all outstanding litigation against the firm (of which there was very little) has been resolved favorably. The negative financial impact on the partners left in the firm when it dissolved was thankfully not very great. Although the dissolution left an empty spot in the hearts of many of my partners, it could have been far worse, and for that we are thankful.

Arthur J. LaFave Jr.

An Unexpected Career

WHEN I CAME TO THE YALE LAW SCHOOL, I wasn't sure that I wanted to practice law in the traditional sense, but I felt sure that a legal background would be important to me in any future career. Later, like many of my classmates, I was deeply affected by the assassination of John Kennedy, which snuffed out any thought I had of a career in public service.

I did practice with a firm for a few years after we graduated, learned a lot, and enjoyed it. But events soon drew me away from the traditional practice into a career where that legal training and experience was not only helpful: it was essential.

What happened? I got caught up in starting a new business . . . and, in many ways, an entirely new industry. While specializing in taxation with one of Cleveland's larger firms, I met Mark McCormack, another Yale lawyer who had graduated in 1955, the year before I arrived at the Law School.

Mark was a serious golfer who had thoughts of playing on what was then the professional tour, very different and not nearly as lucrative as it is today. Mark knew that he was not quite good enough to contend at the very top, and so he backed away and talked to some of the golfers about becoming his legal clients and letting him manage all of their business and financial affairs so they could focus on perfecting their skill in their sport. Some of them had brokers, lawyers, accountants, and other advisors, each of which competed for the athlete's attention often with inconsistent advice. Mark's idea was to provide a single focus source for such advice and to seek new, income-producing opportunities for our clients.

One golfer in particular, Arnold Palmer, took him up on it. Soon others followed.

Although I have always enjoyed sports, I was never a serious fan or a regular participant after I left high school and the winning football team on which I had played. I never played golf and tried tennis on very few occasions. So sports were not a motivator for me in the way that it was for many of my contemporaries. But I found the legal and business challenges of these clients completely fascinating.

Back in Cleveland at the law firm, Mark needed some help. Lots of it. But in the minds of some traditional thinkers of those days, professional golfers were just a step above greens keepers. A few of those traditionalists ran our firm. To them, representing a professional golfer certainly didn't have the glitter that they saw in representing a local steel mill or a shipping line that hauled iron ore and coal. So while a number of the younger lawyers might have thought it was cool to represent athletes, many of the senior lawyers to whom they reported were reluctant to relinquish any of their team's time to such a "frivolous" endeavor.

But I was new to the firm and looking for more work. I was interested in finding legitimate tax and corporate work, and, quite frankly, there weren't enough steel mills or ore haulers to go around. I began working with Mark, and what started as an hour or two a day went to 12–14 hours a day in no time flat.

One of the first problems handed to me was to find a way to get some of the earnings of one of our foreign clients down from the 91 percent US tax bracket that this guy had reached with just his US earnings. (Yes, in those days our tax code had a 91 percent bracket, and I can't recall that any of those in that bracket lacked the enthusiasm to pursue more income!) After rummaging through a bunch of our country's tax treaties, I managed to get a good chunk of that client's income down into the low single digits.

That sort of paved the way for my entry into the sports business. It also gave me a thrill of accomplishment that I hadn't felt before. It made me really excited about joining this new business.

Over the next few years, I worked for and spent a lot of time with golfers like Arnold Palmer, Gary Player, and Jack Nicklaus; with Rod Laver and John Newcombe in tennis; Jean-Claude Killy and Karl Schranz, the skiers; and with race car drivers like Jackie Stewart, Bruce McLaren, and Peter Revson. I even met old-time greats like boxer Max Schmeling (he famously took the title from Jack Sharkey and fought Joe Louis twice). I spent a half hour chatting with him on a wide-open and lonely mountainside in Sapporo, Japan. Three of us, Schmeling, Killy, and I, were heading for the slalom course during the 1972 Winter Olympics.

All of these men were highly successful in their own fields, and they were super competitive in their relentless pursuit of winning. They were likeable, friendly, and alert human beings who had traveled all over the world and were comfortable conversing with people in all walks of life . . . from blue collar workers to successful business leaders, presidents, earls and dukes, even queens and kings. These guys had a sophistication that I found very genuine.

Those traditional-thinking senior partners at the Cleveland firm may have been slightly uncomfortable with professional golfers as clients, but they were okay with corporations, and we formed a lot of them . . . one for each client at the beginning to maximize the benefits from the surtax exemption. And as our clients' businesses in other jurisdictions grew we formed entities and forged relationships in lots of distant places, including Japan, Britain, Australia, France, New Zealand, Brazil, Canada, and Hong Kong. And at home, of course, we weren't just in Cleveland but had multiple offices in New York, Los Angeles, and Florida.

Our business was growing abroad pretty fast, and even in those early days in the 1960s, we were aware that corporate earnings abroad were not taxed by the US until they were brought back to this country. Opening offices and adding staff all over the world (in more than thirty countries) provided a legitimate opportunity to deploy our offshore earnings outside of the US. We had to find a way to park those earnings in a low-tax environment until they were needed. That led to a further complication in our corporate structure as we sought a low tax billing location.

All that organizational bifurcation and diversity was okay while there were just a few of us. And for the first few years we were all still in our twenties. By that time we had broken away from the law firm. The corporations, which were the law firm's clients, were owned by Mark and me (but mostly Mark) and the athletes were clients of the corporations. Over the next few years, our business continued to grow in size, geographic dispersion, and in corporate complexity. We began representing tennis and golf events, at first in Europe but soon in many other places, where we would become responsible for sponsorship and television rights sales. When we did, we would typically open another office at or near the site of the event, and when we did that, we would usually form another subsidiary corporation in that country.

Each of those corporations had its own name and letterhead, and we all carried separate calling cards for many of them. One of the guys in our group might write to the same executive at, say, GM, several times in a day, each time on a different letterhead reflecting the nature of the business he was discussing. This wasn't very smart!

The time had come to reconfigure our corporate structure into a single business. But by that time many of these entities, particularly those that were geographically distant, were like separate silos which the managers had become accustomed to operating with a great deal of independence. They all had separate bank accounts, for example, and separate caches of our money. At the same time, we were beginning to borrow money for the operation of the business as a whole, and we were sailing into an era of double-digit interest. When Mark asked me to function as the chief financial officer of our group, we didn't even have a single set of accounts. Our independent accountants prepared separate financial statements for each of the many corporations, but none that embraced our entire business. That wasn't very smart either!

We couldn't just wave a wand and collapse everything into

a streamlined and cohesive entity. People are seldom enthusiastic about giving up independence and authority that they have grown comfortable with, even proud of. It wasn't just a matter of issuing orders; there was a lot of cajoling and maneuvering. Things got very political. Factions developed and arguments were heated. "Why do we need just one computer system?" "It is a lot easier to use the computer language from my own region." "I don't need your computer just to pay my bills a little faster!" "It is a well-known fact that the best software is written in Britain." Well, it took a bit of time and a few bruises, but we ultimately came out with IMG as a well-recognized single business, using a single computer system and language, a single treasury, and a strong esprit de corps among its several thousand employees.

It was a fun career. Never boring. Filled with variety. Let mention a few of those experiences.

Beginning in 1965 until sometime in the 1990s, I would spend more than a thousand days in Japan and flew across the Pacific Ocean nearly 150 times. On my first full day in that exciting country I walked out of my hotel, turned right at the first opportunity and left at the next; and suddenly I was LOST. I did not know it then, but I had wandered into the Ginza. I couldn't read the signs, and nobody would answer my questions in English. The crowds were so thick and moving so frantically that it was hard to avoid being pushed off into the busy street. And there was a smell . . . not unpleasant, but definitely different from the smells I was accustomed to in American cities. It was a foreign smell. It was disconcerting. And it was also exciting!

A few trips later, without the experience of many more full days in Japan, we decided that it was necessary to find an office and hire a small staff. I had about six days, and all Mark had said to me was, "Don't spend too much"! I was on my own. I had never rented an office before. Tokyo was one of the largest cities in the world . . . it could take as much as eight hours to cross the entire area by taxi! Where should I look for an office? Furniture? Don't offices come with furniture? And walls—I guess we need them too. No, I don't want to have to take my shoes off. Carpeting: How much did you say that was! In addition to a security deposit, you want a full year's rent for key money? You have got to be kidding! And what is key money anyway?

This was long before smartphones and the easy and frequent flow of communication. It was before the use of office computers (or even memory typewriters), and before the fax machine. In those days, cutting-edge communication was done by telex, and each day through its annoying staccato, yards and yards of telexes traveled between IMG's Cleveland, Tokyo, and London offices, all in the stilted language and abbreviations of that medium.

I came back a month or two later to move into my comfortable new office suite occupying one upper floor in a small but brand-new building in Roppongi, only a short taxi ride from the Imperial Hotel, where I lived while I was in Japan (Room 1161), and within walking distance of the US Embassy, still an important landmark in post-occupation Japan in 1970.

I was sitting at my desk reviewing the morning's telex traffic, when the receptionist rang and said I had a visitor. It was our landlord, a pleasant looking Japanese man who lived on the top floor. He didn't speak any English, so I had one of the staff come in to act as an interpreter. After a few friendly words of welcome, he got down to the real reason for his visit. Because the elevator was rather small, he said he "hoped" we would not have too many Korean guests! What? I knew that there was some ugly discrimination by Japanese against Koreans, but I also knew that the two were physically indistinguishable and that much of Japan's large Korean population had lived there for generations, spoke perfect Japanese, and had all the native manners and mannerisms. It turned out that he was concerned about the garlic smell that he said many Koreans exude because of their fondness for their national pickled dish called kimchi. Of course I was shocked by his request, but that was not the time or place to deliver a lecture. I was a visitor in his country, and not a very experienced one at that. But I must say that I have never seen people consume as much garlic as Japanese themselves at their teppanyaki restaurants. Don't they exude a smell of garlic too? What if one of them came up on our elevator. Did you say you were a kamikaze? Does that mean what I think it does? What happened? How can you possibly be here now?

Yes, my very first Japanese employee had been training as a kamikaze pilot when the war ended. Although born in Japan, Mr. Kanda had been raised in Chosen (Korea) after it was annexed by Japan. His father had been in charge of some heavy industry there, and even during the early years of the war (before we were involved) an instructor would fly up from Japan to northern Korea each week for my friend Kanda-san's ski lesson. What an extravagant use of aviation fuel! I had read that the December 7, 1941, attack on our naval forces in Honolulu came as a result of Japan's critical shortage of oil!

Kanda-san was intelligent, well-educated, had a very westernized outlook, and yet was extremely well-connected. He could get a meeting with just about anyone in Japan. Kanda-san became my constant companion and a close friend. I learned a lot from him as he guided me through the Japanese business practices and culture.

Long after I stopped visiting Japan so often, I learned that my Yale classmate, Bud Klauser, had been there at the same time. We even engaged and became friends with the same Japanese attorney. Too bad—I would love to have compared notes with him.

Well, over its first four decades, the company grew in size and was very influential in changing and greatly enlarging the sports marketing industry. By the time Mark McCormack, its founder, primary owner, and CEO, died tragically of cardiac arrest in 2003, IMG had offices in more than thirty-five different countries and a staff of some 3,000 individuals. It was involved as an agent and/or a presenter in most sports. In addition to representing the sale of television rights to many of the world's most prestigious sporting events, IMG produced and sold more than 6,500 hours of television annually, ran the largest fashion model agency, and represented many of the best-known classical musicians on a worldwide basis.

In the aftermath of Mark's passing, it became clear that the time had come to sell the business, and it was sold to the private equity firm of Forstmann Little in the fall of 2004, with the help of Rothschild and Jones Day. That process, by the way was another fascinating, if concluding, step in my business education: shaping the company for sale, the auction process, the totally sleepless week leading up to signing, and then the collective holding of breath until closing.

III

PRO BONO PUBLICO

BILL FELSTINER

Helter-Shelter

THE LEVEES IN NEW ORLEANS COLLAPSED ON August 29, 2005. Three days later, at home in Santa Barbara, I received an email from the Red Cross:

1-SEPT-05. Hi folks, we are actively recruiting new volunteers who have a professional or demonstrated skill base. Basic qualifications: unflappable, outstanding interpersonal skills, infinite patience, flexible, multitask, good health ("sturdy"), personal and professional references, ability to live and function in high heat, high humidity, no running water, no electricity, no air conditioning, deal with challenging personalities and tragedy...and any of the following: folks with Class A drivers licenses, forklift license, warehouse mgmt, management experience, telecommunications (wired and wireless), computer networking, customer support/ training, accounting, vehicle maintenance/dispatching, refrigeration maintenance, electricians/facility maintenance, industrial safety/health/security, LVNs, RNs, public health, childcare, geriatrics, etc., Please call. We're not looking for "Ricky Rescues," drug/alcohol abusers, felons, mentally ill, etc.

Less than two weeks later I was the site manager of the community residential center in Monroe, Louisiana, one of the largest Red Cross shelters in the state. How the hell did that happen? What does this meteoric rise to the top of the heap say about the way that the Red Cross responds to disasters?

TRAINING

Reading the email and not being a refrigeration engineer or a Class A truck driver, I didn't think that the Red Cross would have much use for a seventy-five–year-old sociologist of law, but I called the chapter in Santa Barbara anyway, and was told to show up for an orientation course the following Saturday morning, September 3. The course was crowded, with over one hundred people. A significant portion of the program was by video. There was some history of the Red Cross, but most attention was paid to the range of its current activities locally, and to the principles that guide its efforts. There was an attempt to identify several high priority groups in the audience: doctors, nurses and mental health workers, city employees—who were being granted paid leave to go to New Orleans and work side by side with their counterparts there (perhaps naive except for police and firefighters since the New Orleans counterparts could hardly be in New Orleans)—and the hot numbers, truck drivers, and refrigeration engineers. We were all urged to attend the course on mass care.

That course was in two parts: an introduction to shelter operations and "simulated" problems in mass care. Although the speakers were experienced disaster workers, most of whom had responded to 9/11, Hurricane Andrew, and the La Conchita landslide, these courses were symbolic of the Red Cross's national dilemma, and in some way of its inadequacy in the face of the effects of Hurricane Katrina. What I mean is that the substantive portion of the course was exactly the same as had traditionally been organized for people who would be responding to small-scale disasters such as apartment house fires, localized floods, or wild fires, in which the number of victims was low and the duration of the Red Cross response was limited. In this portion of the course there was no effort to imagine what Katrina had wrought—very large numbers of evacuees destined to be displaced for very long periods of time. Nor was any attention paid to monetary issues, such as the relief available to evacuees from either the Red Cross or FEMA, matters that proved to be high on the evacuee agenda. The instructors did focus on Katrina in one way only. Although they never suggested that one's life would be in danger, they tried to alarm the audience, painting pictures of intense heat, nonexistent air conditioning, poor food, mosquitoes, fire ants, lovebugs, snakes, long hours, sleep deprivation, criminals, and the like. I guess the intent was to frighten away those who might have thought of Red Cross deployment as a form of paid vacation, or who knew themselves not to be up to a little hardship.

The Red Cross has been designated by Congress as the preferred provider of mass shelter in case of disasters and has a well-honed set of working rules designed to meet its responsibilities. First, volunteers are told that in a jam, if they were to focus on Red Cross values and principles, they would not be likely to make a bad decision or go down a wrong path. Second, they are continually told to remember, "it's not about me." Third, they are drilled about the importance of keeping track of shelter evacuees—knowing who goes out and when they return. Fourth, they are reminded that a shelter is "home" to its evacuees and that they are entitled to all the barriers to outside inquiry and interference that would ordinarily protect them in their residences. Fifth, volunteers are to remember that, if deployed, they will be involved in a chaotic situation, that that's the nature of disasters. And sixth, the Red Cross does not accept donations of used clothing and other stuff. In my case, attending to values and principles first proved helpful, "it's not about me" was crucial, keeping track of evacuees and not accepting donations were ridiculous notions, the shelter as home became problematic on a grand scale, and the chaotic nature of disasters, although accurate, was too often an excuse for failure, inattention, or callousness.

Then there were some more focused rules—no pets, weapons, alcohol, illegal drugs, or smoking in shelters; communications with clients are to be confidential; and local disaster volunteers, those who have not been trained or vetted in the usual manner, could be utilized or not depending on the inclination of the shelter manager. In addition, members of the media are not allowed beyond the front desk without permission of the evacuees, no contacts between people outside the shelter and evacuees are to be arranged without a resident's permission, and overestimating needs is better than underestimating them. Further, everyone ought to be prepared to do any job (that must have been intended in a downward direction—no job is too menial—not that everybody was to be prepared to run the Red Cross relief effort from Baton Rouge). In an effort to introduce some semblance of normalcy into evacuees' lives, rules should be posted, lights turned out and phones turned off on a schedule, and shelter meetings should be held daily at dinnertime and bulletin boards should be utilized to share information.

Having set up and run thousands of emergency shelters for over a hundred years, the Red Cross has developed protocols for just about everything, although many of us first-time volunteers remained ignorant of most of them during our few weeks on the job. We were to encourage clients to make decisions. We were not to have secrets. When we were not the leader, volunteers were to defer to leadership. We were not to be a resource "constrictor" (someone who gets in the way of deliveries). Red Cross personnel never transport clients. No matter the emotional pull, we were not to provide benefits to one client that we could not provide to all. In the event, this turned out to be a hard rule to follow if it was obvious that a ride or a few dollars would be easy to arrange and would do good service.

Apparently, shelter admissions criteria were problematic. The biggest problems would concern alcoholics and other substance abusers, former prisoners, and people with infectious diseases such as tuberculosis. The general policy favored admittance unless the person in question appeared likely to disrupt or endanger the larger community.

There were four important issues that were never raised in training: the entrepreneurial nature of shelter work, the issue of privacy as it affects prisoners in the shelter population, Southern culture, and the role of religion in Red Cross operations. All four turned out to be important when I was actually in the field.

In practice, Red Cross activities are the virtual opposite of military operations. In the Red Cross, assignment to jobs is not the norm: volunteers frequently and often repeatedly have to figure out on their own what needs to be done that they might be able to do. If a volunteer does not energetically seek work, he or she might well stand around bored and useless for hours, even days.

The Red Cross routinely encounters people seeking admittance to a shelter who have just been released from prison. No problem. Unless there are other issues, they are as welcome as anyone else. But what is to be done in a Katrina-type situation in which people currently serving sentences, many for felonies, are inadvertently released from incarceration and, together with registered sex offenders, disappear, perhaps into a general shelter population? How rigid are the Red Cross's usual rules about the privacy of information about shelter evacuees, and who can bend those rules and to what extent?

Volunteers responding to Katrina came from all over the country, but a disproportionate number came from California to the Deep South, to Alabama, Louisiana, Mississippi, and east Texas. As many a volunteer realized only after they had been summarily sent home by a shelter manager or local Red Cross chapter, there is behavior that is acceptable in California, but not in the Bible Belt.

The Red Cross is stridently secular. Some veterans say its "Cross" is not even a cross, but an *x* on its side. What is a volunteer to do when local staff and other volunteers drag religion, usually of the "Thank You Jesus" variety, into day-to-day activities? And what if the introduction of faith actually seems to suit the evacuees to whom it is directed?

Before deployment, volunteers went through two interviews; one to evaluate medical fitness, and the other a kind of background check and career analysis. Was one fit to go, and to go where to do what? Two nurses conducted the medical interviews. One asked questions, the other watched. The questions covered what one might have expected—medical history, medications, general health. The observer seemed to be trying to figure out who was weird, faking something or a substance abuser. The career interviews, frequently conducted by volunteers as new to the Red Cross as those they were interviewing, were a bit thin. In my case, the interviewer made a note on some piece of paper that I was qualified for a supervisory position. Like all other notes to such effect in my travel from Santa Barbara to Baton Rouge to Monroe, that one managed to disappear. This perfunctory prescreening—as a mental health worker in Monroe described it, "if you have breath on a mirror, you're in"—had consequences.

The call came late the next day, September 9th. I was to be deployed on Disaster 865 (Katrina), told to go to Baton Rouge, provided with a travel authorization code and a telephone number to call. I was introduced to Fred, the head of disaster services in Santa Barbara three times that morning. The poor chap was so exhausted that for him each introduction was a new experience.

WORKING IN SECURITY

The scene at the Baton Rouge airport was a bit confusing. There was an unmanned Red Cross sign saying that a shuttle was operating to headquarters, but it had the look of ancient history about it. Headquarters was an abandoned Kmart warehouse. There was an outside secure area in which one dumped one's gear. Inside, it was not at all obvious where to go or what to do. Other volunteers who came to Baton Rouge for assignment were also surprised that no one was stationed at the door to give directions to new arrivals. Eventually I found a sign that indicated the initial move was to take the orientation class, held every hour or so. The orientation was useless: just more information about hardships to come—heat, hydration, no water, no power, snakes, lovebugs, and other creatures.

After lunch I found an assignment desk, and was sent to sit in a circle with four other volunteers, all of whom ended up as colleagues in Monroe. Hank did most of the talking. A big, gap-toothed man from Michigan, he bragged about his experience running the Civil Air Patrol there, and seemed to assume he would play a big role wherever he went. Though he started out in Monroe as the night shelter manager, he soon embarked on a rapid downward spiral; the last I saw of him he was spending his days playing cards with a warehouse guard.

We were then told to report to the headquarters of the local Red Cross chapter in Monroe. Finding it with difficulty at about 9:00 p.m., we discovered that it had been closed since 4:30 p.m. In fact, it always closed at 4:30 yet, to the very end, Baton Rouge kept sending people there rather than to the shelter itself, several miles east on I-20. I've thought of three explanations for this pigheadedness. First, that it was just a thoughtless continuation of the situation as it existed when the local chapter was running an earlier shelter, which was cheek by jowl with chapter headquarters. Second, that it was an indirect acknowledgement that the chapter, rather than the shelter, was "in charge" of the shelter. And third, my favorite theory, that it reflected how totally divorced the Red Cross in Baton Rouge was from operations on the ground in Monroe.

The next morning we reported to the shelter, officially known as the CRC (Community Residential Center), but always referred to as the State Farm shelter, having been until recently regional headquarters for that insurance company. The building was one story, red brick, sort of corporate colonial. It stood at the intersection of I-20 and US 165, a major north-south route. From the main entrance one could see 18-wheelers rolling down the interstate. The shelter had two official entrances, one for volunteers, local officials, and security personnel, and the other for evacuees and visitors. The security at that entrance was as rigorous as at most airports—an x-ray machine manned by the National Guard, hand inspection of packages too big for the X-ray machine and Monroe police officers wielding wands for personal inspections while collecting overtime after doing their regular jobs. Since many evacuees arrived at the shelter with garbage sacks containing all that they had salvaged, this meant a lot of hand inspection. The evacuees had to go through this procedure every time they left the building, whether for a smoke or a weekend.

At the other entrance, manned by the National Guard, staff were required to sign in and out once a day. Otherwise, if you had a badge showing that you were a national volunteer, access was unencumbered. There were several exits that were not used as entrances, each guarded by a police officer. An informal arrangement between individual officers and some evacuees permitted smokers to go outside by the kitchen and return without passing through the main security checkpoint.

The staffing person to whom I was directed, a bouncy young woman, a junior at the University of California, Davis, gave me the choice of working in the warehouse or on the security detail. There was no exchange of paperwork, no inquiry into my background or experience, either with the Red Cross or in "civilian" life, and no question about what I had been told at my chapter or in Baton Rouge. I thought that the warehouse would be a better deal, but concerned that my septuagenarian back might not be up to heaving big boxes around for 12–14 hours a day, I enlisted in security.

Later in the morning I was introduced to Albert, the head of security, his deputy Mike, normally on the security detail at the American embassy in Lima, Peru, and Pam and Tom, the foot soldiers, a married couple from Indiana. Pam had been a prison guard; I never knew Tom's background. Pam gave me a tour of the shelter, an immense building, over 315,000 square feet, about seven-and-a-half acres, nearly half a mile in length. The shelter was so big and complicated that most volunteers spent lots of time, too much time, looking for some other volunteer. My duty that day was to see that all the locked rooms remained locked. It was not a bad way to become acclimated since all new volunteers had to spend many hours learning their way around this gigantic maze that had previously housed 1,200 State Farm employees.

The Path to the Top

Mid-afternoon of my first day at the shelter I was asked if I would be willing to accompany evacuees that night to the showers at

Wossman High School—the State Farm employees having had no on-the-job need for such facilities. So at 7:00 I rode the bus to Wossman with fifteen to twenty evacuees. My job, I guessed, was to make sure that the men stayed out of the women's showers. The evacuees showered; I hung around. They left; I stayed. The bus made another run. Same scenario. After the supply of bathers dried up, I spent several hours in the dark sitting on the tailgate of a pickup truck listening to two janitors discuss how far, by way of sexual adventures, it was proper for a family man to go. The consensus: not far.

The next day I checked my locked rooms. I tried to master the geography of the shelter. I hung around with Tom and Pam, who were not particularly friendly, probably because they had carved out a strategic position for themselves at the evacuee entrance, where they liked to gossip with whoever came along, to solve little problems if they could, and didn't want me encroaching on their routine.

Then, salvation. I had a chat with a woman who was in the cohort of Chris Barton, the deputy director of the whole shebang. These cohorts were an interesting social phenomenon. Volunteers seldom arrived in Monroe by themselves. Rather, they came in groups of about five (the capacity of most of the rented cars), originally from Houston, later from Baton Rouge. These rides to Monroe took many hours, so there was plenty of time to coalesce as a group. Of course, on arrival no one in the group was likely to know anyone else working in the shelter, so there was a natural inclination for the group to stick together, particularly for meals and such other activities, like boozing, as could be squeezed into very long days. Barton's pal told me that Barton had only a few days to go and did not have, was perhaps looking for, a replacement. True or not, the word on the floor seemed to be that everybody was responsible for finding her own replacement, although how high up in the Red Cross hierarchy this went was not clear.

I told Barton that I had heard that he did not have an obvious successor and that I had had a lot of administrative experience. He seemed interested and, either then or a short time later, told me to stick with him from dawn to dark.

Barton is a landscape contractor from La Verne, California, and has had lots of disaster experience. A direct descendant of Clara Barton, the founder of the American Red Cross, he always wore a green jumpsuit sporting a prominent name badge of his own design (the rest of us wore two rather less conspicuous badges, one identifying each of us as a "national" volunteer and the other, in red, meaning that we were volunteers at the CRC). Barton is a jovial fellow with a big laugh. He related well to evacuees and most of the volunteers liked him.

I now think that personality is a key to volunteer effectiveness in a Katrina-type situation. The basic needs of shelter evacuees are met. They have an air-conditioned place to sleep, the shelter is safe, and reasonable food and good health care are provided. Beyond that, most of what the evacuees need, want, or demand cannot be provided by the Red Cross—where is the FEMA money, how can I get through on the Red Cross 800 telephone number, where is my grandmother who was last seen under the I-10 bridge, why can't the showers be open all day and night, why can't I bring food into the living areas. Since there are no answers that will easily satisfy the evacuees, the tone and warmth of the response is crucial. Although this is the classic move of "cooling out the mark," a response that acknowledges the worth of the person in distress and appears to share her frustration will go a long way toward altering their mood. Barton was a master of this type of interaction.

As Barton's assistant, and possible successor as deputy director (he always used the qualifier in telling people who I was), I attended the daily 8:00 a.m. senior staff meeting. The meetings were held in a conference room too small to provide seating for all who were supposed to be there (the heads of functional divisions, the day and night shelter managers, the police and National Guard, a representative from the local Red Cross chapter), not to mention those who just came along. The meetings were chaired by the boss—variously called the director or site manager. Site manager, I suppose, because the responsibility extended beyond the shelter to include the emergency response vehicles, the outdoor food and supplies distribution tents, and the separate warehouse in what used to be a Kmart facility. But the site manager was also called the director, and that was the title on the organization chart, I think because in local parlance each disaster involved a job and jobs have directors.

ADMINISTRATION

The meetings were supposed to call attention to developments of general interest and to discuss problems or issues requiring input from different areas of shelter operations. The impending arrival of new evacuees might be announced and inquiries made to assure that we were prepared to receive them. Or a concern about "looting" at the outdoor distribution site might be noted, and suggestions sought about how to respond. However, all too often the meetings degenerated into squabbles between a small number of people that should have been handled privately or drawn-out tales about minor difficulties in which most people had no interest. At the end of the meeting, which took about an hour, Aimee, a local lawyer, would generally produce trays of vegetable casserole or monkey bread that she had cooked long before sunrise.

The boss was Tom Earl, a big, white-haired glib businessman from Minneapolis who always wore white shorts and a white Red Cross T-shirt, looking like a minor British official in colonial Calcutta. Earl originally was from Philadelphia where he went to Saint Joe's College. After a stint in the army during the Vietnam era, he worked for the FBI, the American Legion, and the Veterans Administration. After moving to Minnesota in the mid-'80s, he oversaw the Midwestern area for the VA's National Disaster Medical System. That job involved extensive interaction with disaster response agencies such as FEMA, the Air Force, and VA hospitals. In June 2001 he and a friend from the FBI started a company that focused on emergency management, terrorism, and counterterrorism. His career is a bit hard to track because he threw off remarks suggesting some kind of "dark" or "undercover" activities:

"I'm a good people watcher; I've done this for a long, long time. I have a very interesting background that I never go into, but you can almost read between the lines with some of the places where I used to work, okay?" A bit like Robert De Niro in *Meet the Parents*.

Earl liked to talk, in public and in private. He often recited his non-Red Cross disaster experience, the "seamless" way that he ran the CRC operation and the various growth stages the CRC would go through in its semipermanent existence as a "model shelter." I never knew whether the shelter had such extensive facilities because it was "a model shelter" or we were a model shelter because we had the facilities. Earl delighted in visits from dignitaries, such as Secretary Leavitt of Health and Human Services, Governor Blanco, Mayor Moyer of Monroe, and state legislators, visits which most of the volunteers on the shelter floor viewed as roadblocks to getting the day's work done.

So I stuck close to Barton for a day or two. His job seemed more to be putting out small fires than tackling big problems. The shelter already had a line of credit of $50,000 at Sam's Club. Barton and I made a visit to Home Depot to arrange credit there of $100,000. I never knew where these astronomical figures came from or what kind of Red Cross purchases they were supposed to underwrite. Earl later told me in one of his many expansive moods that the shelter had bought an ATV for the Monroe police when theirs collapsed. I was impressed, but I found out later that this grand gesture never actually took place.

Over the next several days I handled a shower crisis, oversaw a visit from the local hairdressing school, talked to Corps of Engineer people who were in town to find sites for FEMA trailers, mollified clothing donors who wanted their pictures taken with evacuees who did not want to be photographed, and helped the shelter managers process new evacuees.

By this time I was known by a few people as Barton's putative successor, but neither Earl nor Barton had said anything definitive to me, I had not been introduced at the morning staff meeting as anybody in particular and I did not appear on the organization chart. So my appearance as deputy to Earl after Barton left must have come as a surprise, if not a shock, to many volunteers at the staff meeting. In fact, even after I had taken Earl's place as director, five days later, I was often met with blank stares or disbelief when I introduced myself as the site manager.

Shortly after Barton left, Earl and I were walking back to the office from an inspection of the warehouse when I asked him when he was leaving. He said the following Wednesday, three days away. Assuming that a successor would be sent from headquarters in Baton Rouge, I asked who was to take his place. He put his arm around my shoulder and said, "You are." This was not quite what we had been told in training: "Wherever you go and whatever you do, don't worry because the people there in charge will have had extensive Red Cross experience." I almost dropped to my knees. It was the only time that I was concerned that I might not be up to the job, particularly since my total Red Cross experience had lasted less than two weeks and I had no idea what, beside run the staff meeting, the director did or who he or she did it with. In the event, about the only transition information Earl gave me was a phone list, his business card in Minneapolis, and a plea to be nice to the head of the Children's Coalition in Monroe which had set up a day care facility in the shelter. Just jumping into the fire at a senior level was not so unusual in the Katrina era. A corporate executive from California who, though she had disaster response experience, had none as a Red Cross volunteer, arrived in Monroe one evening and by ten the next morning was the day shelter manager whose only instruction was to get out there on the floor and meet the people.

Then, or shortly afterwards, I asked Earl if there were plans for my successor as deputy. Later that day he introduced me to the candidate, a local resident, who had some experience in setting up a computer network for a community college somewhere in Arkansas, but none with the Red Cross. An hour or so later I learned that she was the part-time secretary to an assistant district attorney in Monroe. It was obvious to me, somewhat belatedly, that she was a poor choice as the number-two person for the whole operation and we found another job for her, working in the communications office, which she did for only a few days before disappearing.

What was Earl up to, choosing a blatantly inexperienced successor supported by a totally unqualified deputy? A colleague gave me the first hint. Earl had frequently talked in staff meetings about the possibility that he would return to run the shelter after a few weeks off (this was at a time when some, including Earl, thought the CRC was to be a semipermanent operation). The theory, then, was that Earl was deliberately setting up a succession likely to fail, to screw up so badly that there would be no choice but to call him back from Minneapolis to rescue a foundering operation. Of course, we had no direct evidence of this scenario, but months later a local board member told me that Earl had proposed to the chapter that he be brought back to Monroe after a brief hiatus in Minneapolis at an outlandish daily per diem, plus hotel, car, laptop, and transportation expenses, a proposal that flew directly in the face of the Red Cross ethic of volunteerism, its condemnation of "desire for gain." His proposal was given short shrift, though he might not have been told so, and although the CEO and the board thought he had done a creditable job as director, he was from that moment persona non grata in Monroe. So that may well be how I got my job as director. Picked to fail by a venal predecessor.

At one time I told the officer in charge of the National Guard unit in the center that I was fascinated by the way the guard did business; it was resourceful and efficient, with strict adherence to the chain of command. The guard officer replied that he was fascinated by the way the Red Cross did business. I got it that he did not intend this as a compliment. I didn't pursue it, but I suppose what he saw was inefficient process, inconsistent decision-making, overlapping areas of responsibility, some skylarking, turf battles, and inflated egos. Many of these problems were the consequence of unavoidable conditions—limited disaster experience, rapid turnover which prevented smooth coordination with colleagues as well as mastering the details of the job, and sleep deprivation while working in an unfamiliar culture among many angry and frustrated evacuees—but that did not make the Red Cross as an organization look any more efficient to an army officer recently returned from Iraq.

So, after a perfunctory interview with the chapter CEO who appeared inordinately impressed by a couple of Yale degrees, I was in charge of the shelter and its auxiliary operations for the next two weeks. My main concerns were staffing, communications, processing the large influx of evacuees fleeing Hurricane Rita, keeping track of evacuees, facilities maintenance, staff misbehavior, resident unrest, resident health, preparing to meet a tornado threat, allocating services to nonresident evacuees, cooperating effectively with the local chapter, getting an appropriate fix on the role of religion, and the threat posed to our large population of children by unregistered sex offenders who might be among our evacuees. This sounds like a lot of headaches, and it was. At the same time, and more important, was the simple fact that, despite the turmoil inside the shelter bureaucracy and at the chapter level, the Red Cross was doing its job in Monroe. It was housing many hundreds of people safely and in reasonable comfort, feeding them decent food and providing superior health care.

Some of the issues that I faced were local; others were common to many shelters. Given the number of trained Red Cross volunteers prior to Katrina compared to the needs to staff about 1,200 shelters providing for at least 400,000 people with little warning after New Orleans flooded, it is no wonder that staffing was a problem. In the two to three weeks after Katrina, the Red Cross sought and enlisted 40,000 new volunteers. Not only was the training, like mine, rather perfunctory and geared to small-scale, short-lived disasters, but there was no opportunity to check references or police records. The predictable result was a distressing number of volunteers who were immature, unstable, insensitive to local culture, faking credentials to inflate their resumes, or just gaming the system for the debit cards, free housing and food, cars, and laptops that it provided. Of course, these people were a small minority of the volunteers I knew who generally were sincere, dedicated, hardworking, and in many cases quite skilled in their jobs, whether they had previous Red Cross experience or not. Nevertheless, this minority annoyed evacuees, interfered with the work of committed volunteers, and ate up an inordinate amount of supervisory time.

Even more salient to the staffing problem was the rapid turnover of volunteers. In theory, volunteers were to serve for three weeks. Even if this standard were met, once travel time and acclimatization were subtracted, there generally were only about two weeks left to be of real use. In a smaller, short-term shelter such turnover might have been manageable, but in the CRC, which was virtually an independent small town with its own government, security, and health and social services, it was frustrating and inefficient. Imagine trying to run an organization of some size with a third of your workforce replaced every week. Not that the Red Cross could do much about it since many volunteers were using up vacation or unpaid time, which had definite limits. On the other hand, these short terms did enable some volunteers to go all out, to work long shifts without days off, though others, according to the chief of health services, stayed too long, wore out, and became insensitive to the needs of the people they were there to assist. In any event, the volunteer nature of disaster relief in the US necessarily means dependence on short-term help and on retirees, who are disproportionately represented, and the unemployed. Unfortunately, this workforce is much less heterogeneous than the American population. In Monroe, among the over 200 volunteers present during my service, only two were African-American, and one of them was from the Virgin Islands.

Other staff difficulties arose from immaturity or naïveté. Generally, the most problematic volunteers were young; in their late teens or early twenties. Unfortunately some of them would get drunk in public, go swimming nude in motel pools, buy drugs, hire prostitutes, or make sexual advances to soldiers on duty, behaviors that would not cause consternation in many parts of the country, but were taboo in Monroe. When such behavior was called to our attention, we had no choice but to send the offending volunteers packing to Baton Rouge for reassignment.

Problematic volunteers were not just a Monroe problem. Months after the shelter was closed, the local CEO told me that in focus groups of chapter executives held by the Red Cross, the unanimous conclusion was that the number one mistake in the response to Katrina was the urgent request nationally for 40,000 that produced a mass of volunteers too many of whom were untrained, unqualified, and unfamiliar with Red Cross values, unvetted as to background, and in many cases of questionable caliber. The personnel problems that followed consumed an inordinate amount of management time.

RELIGION

The Red Cross declares, "It makes no discrimination as to nationality, race, religious beliefs, class or political opinions." It is a secular, not a Christian, organization. In most parts of the country any attempt to introduce any religious practice or expression into Red Cross activities would be condemned and rejected. But Monroe, Louisiana, is not most parts of the country. It is an intensely religious area. It is an intensely Christian area, Baptist and evangelical. It is not uncommon to hear someone say that though raised a Catholic, she became a Christian at this or that age. Churches are everywhere. The *Monroe News Star*, a Gannett paper, reports that interest in religion is higher in Monroe than in any of the other 91 cities in which it has papers.

There seem to be three levels of religion in Monroe. One is made up of the super-believers, in whose lives religion and church are so crucial that they pop up in conversation and behavior (informal prayer sessions at the drop of a hat) all the time. The second group is the ordinary believers who attend church regularly (though this may be as much social as religious), but whose ordinary discourse is not peppered with religious references. The third group is the casual or indifferent believers who join a church because not to do so would interfere with their social, economic, or political ambitions. My guess is that this group is rather small. A fourth tier, one common in my native California, the nonbelievers, is apparently a rarity.

Religion in Monroe creeps into the Red Cross regime in three ways. First, it becomes part of the ritual. Chapter board meetings are begun with an extended invocation by a local minister, and then launched into business by a rousing chorus of "Thank You Jesus." At the very beginning of the relief effort, the chapter CEO introduced herself to the first sprinkling of national volunteers to arrive with the words: "I want to tell you that I have received help from the Lord. The Lord is my strength and my guidance, and I just want you to know that the Lord will see me through all this."

Second, there appear to be instances in which private beliefs creep into organizational positions. The CEO remonstrated with the general counsel's office in Washington for hiring a local lawyer for the chapter about whom, she said, aghast: "Why he's a member of the ACLU; he's an atheist." No wonder that an excellent shelter manager from San Francisco, a lesbian, had no intention of making her sexual orientation public while in Monroe.

Third, and more important, religion can become part of the Red Cross program. This deviation from Red Cross values and rules did not seem to occur in the shelter where anyone so inclined was brought to heel by other volunteers, most of whom were not from the South and were quick to protect the secular posture of the national organization. But away from the shelter, where ERV (emergency response vehicle) drivers operated in twosomes, the picture was different. In the boondocks, in campgrounds, trailer parks, in motels, some drivers would pray with the evacuees to whom they were bringing food, even initiate the prayers which definitely had a "Christian cast." I cannot make up my mind about this practice that clearly would be condemned by Red Cross central. It seemed to be important to the evacuees. They were comforted by it. One could say that this is the Bible Belt and "when in Rome…." On the other hand, perhaps the Red Cross should stick to its secular mission and urge local clergy to go into the countryside to do the praying.

THE EVACUEES

How did the evacuees, the residents of the shelter, view the experience? I went back to Monroe twice after the shelter closed at the end of October, after fifty-three days of operation, and interviewed as many ex-residents as I could find. There are two extreme views. To many, the place was hell. Almost anyone could take it for a few days. But to do so for the foreseeable future was a different story. The hardest hit were the elderly, the infirm, the substance abusers, and the desperately poor. But their lot was just worse than that of the majority whose lives ranged from tolerable to difficult to unmanageable. This was mass living, hundreds of cots (particularly hard on those with problematic backs) side by side in vast rooms, noisy, untidy, with hardly anything to look forward to day by day or in the future, surrounded by high-energy children, many beyond parental control, patrolled by local police and National Guard, catered to by Red Cross volunteers who might or might not be there for altruistic reasons, for the gigantic recruitment effort that the Red Cross had had to make had brought in not only people with the best of intentions, but scoundrels of many stripes anxious to feather their nests or exploit the vulnerable.

It was hard to imagine, to really trade places with the evacuees, even for the Red Cross people on the spot who after a few weeks service returned home to normal life and expectations, and for whom the continual frustration of dealing with large and overwhelmed bureaucracies was short-lived. This was coupled to a tremendous loss of freedom. Want to smoke, take a walk in the heat and humidity of a Louisiana summer? Want to go back inside, face a security check as rigorous as any airport? Want to eat what you want to eat when you want to eat it, go out to a restaurant that you can't reach or afford? Want a beer with dinner, forget it. Want to throw a football around, try the parking lot. Want to go to school, risk a fight with the local kids who don't want you there. Want to take a bath rather than a shower, forget that too. Want to protect your belongings, better watch them day and night. Want to have some intimate time with your spouse, don't ask. Want to live in a place with consistent rules and unchanging faces, not possible with a turnover of Red Cross people every few weeks. Care about your self-respect, try being surrounded day and night by armed and suspicious police and soldiers. Want some social stimulation, try sitting around all day and night grousing with other people as miserable as you and equally at wit's end.

On the other hand, many evacuees were self-reliant, enterprising, and determined to bounce back. They had amazing strength just to be upbeat in spite of all that they had suffered. They found jobs in Monroe or they pitched in to help with the operation of the shelter. They worked hard to keep their families intact and optimistic. They transformed corners of the mass space into their own little areas. They organized daily activities for children. They made new friends, searched the Internet for residential and employment opportunities, and took advantage of the shelter's extraordinary array of first-rate health and mental health services, eye and dental clinics, pharmacy, clothing dispensary, and legal advice from the bar association. They exploited the center's outstanding physical and social resources for small and adolescent children, in part financed by the country singers Tim McGraw and Faith Hill. They befriended soldiers who were not only deployed a long way from home, but in many instances had just returned from Iraq. It is not that these evacuees liked the regimented life or the experience of mass living, but that they recognized the limits of what the Red Cross could do and they saw the need for the restrictions that so annoyed others.

Between these two extremes, or swinging back from one to the other, may have been the bulk of the evacuees. How one reacted to shelter life was close to how one took on life in general, but also probably reflected one's starting point. If you came to the shelter homeless, from jail, or from a bad situation on the streets or in the projects, the shelter was in some ways an improvement and could be viewed that way. If you came to the shelter from adequate housing, a decent social situation, and a job, the shelter was an awful tumble.

THE TOWN

The life histories of the people that I knew in Monroe suggested that it was an extraordinarily insular community. Even its most highly educated and successful citizens had lived most of their lives in or around the city. Very few had lived anywhere else. If they had gone to college it was likely to have been to what is now the University of Louisiana at Monroe. They did not know New Orleans, and did not like what they did know of it. They thought that big-city Mardi Gras celebrations were dangerous rather than frivolous and, except for those who skied, their most popular getaway was likely to be a weekend at a casino in Biloxi, Mississippi, only sixty miles away. They were different from the Catholic, high-living south of the state, and rejoiced in the difference.

But there is an upside to this insularity. Many people in Monroe are fiercely loyal to and proud of their community. They are accustomed to providing short-term disaster hospitality. When Monroe looked to be on the frontlines of the response to Katrina, they rallied to the relief effort in a way hardly imaginable to those who live in the midst of highly mobile populations. The initial steps taken to organize resources for the thousands of evacuees that were obviously on their way, and the sheltering facilities provided at short notice at the Civic Center, local churches, and in private families were extraordinary. A small number of those who first responded to the needs of the Red Cross, especially in health and mental health services, stayed with the relief effort from start to finish. Moreover, there were many other local organizations in addition to those represented at the Emergency Operations Center that played important roles in providing assistance to hurricane victims. In fact, the whole 211 effort (information other than police matters) for the State of Louisiana was run from the offices of the Monroe United Way, a local agency nationally known for its ability to raise funds out of proportion to the size of the community it serves. Finally, religion may explain in part the unusual generosity and determination to help of Monroe as a community. As I was frequently reminded, people in Monroe do not just talk their faith, they live it.

Obviously these volunteers, numbering in the hundreds, maybe even thousands, were sympathetic to the strangers in their midst. But what of the rest of the community, of the greater number of people who were uninvolved with disaster relief?

My information is anecdotal, but it is not positive. Many people were not concerned with the shelter: from the outside its fences, checkpoints, and patrol vehicles had the appearance of a prison, a world completely outside their daily experience. To others in the community, an influx of poor African-Americans from tough New Orleans neighborhoods seemed to spell drugs, gang wars, and violent crime. They spoke of the notorious Desire Street project; they heard rumors that the CRC was being trashed like the Superdome. The sheriff may or may not have tried to order that buses carrying evacuees from New Orleans should be turned away from the parish, but many people believed that he did and was right to do so. The editor of *The News Star* told me that it was commonly believed that the sheriff had successfully made it clear to evacuees with criminal records that they not stay in Monroe. A lawyer representing the Louisiana Bar Association told me that the reactions he saw in Monroe were about race and class. The people that he knew in Monroe referred to shelter evacuees as thugs, which he perceived to be code for what he called the "N-bomb." They believed that the shelter was a frightening place and that guards should be posted to keep its evacuees out of town. A common complaint was that more was being offered to evacuees by way of services than to homegrown chronically poor people. Attitudes probably hardened as time passed, hospitality fatigue set in, arrests of shelter evacuees were reported in the local paper, the flap over the sheriff's access to information was repeated day after day in the media, and what many had at first perceived to be a short-lived emergency had developed the potential to become a permanent change in the makeup of the community. Legally restricting FEMA trailers to already existing trailer parks certainly could be read along these lines.

Race relations were probably at the heart of resistance to integrating evacuees into the community. In Monroe, many important political posts are held by blacks who, after years of white flight, represent about 60 percent of the population. But real power, economic power, remains in the hands of whites, and the races not only do not mix below the surface, but neither seems to want real social integration. Some high schools are totally black, and most neighborhoods are segregated. The white head of mental health at the shelter, a retired local therapist, told me that the one black family living in her neighborhood "just takes up space." Confederate flags and singing Dixie were de rigueur at high school football games in West Monroe, the "red neck," and dominantly white community across the Ouachita River from Monroe. Monroe itself was faced with a dying downtown, a diminishing tax base, and an increasing demand for social services—not a context in which thousands of poor evacuees would be welcome for the long term. Whether or not the federal government response in New Orleans was laced with racial overtones, it is likely that the reception of New Orleans evacuees in Monroe was significantly affected by race.

It would be a mistake to confound the negative experiences of evacuees and local residents with those of the volunteers. Shortly after I returned to Santa Barbara, the Red Cross held a daylong debriefing session for locals who had responded to Katrina. The theory of the session, I think, was that we volunteers, having witnessed what for us would have been an inordinate amount of human suffering, would be depressed and could use some counsel to come to terms with our experiences. The opposite was true: we were all coming down from a terrific "high," from an experience which was intense, connected, satisfying, and fulfilling; an episode in life where we knew that we were needed, were doing "good," and that we recognized would be hard to duplicate in ordinary life. And it has proved to be just that.

HUGH G. MOULTON

Saving Erdenheim Farm

MANY OF US NEVER RETIRE. WE SIMPLY transition from being paid to work, to working as a volunteer, and usually having the privilege of "paying" to do so. This transition for me occurred after twelve years in private practice with a firm in Philadelphia and thirty years with a NYSE company, first in a legal capacity and then in general management.

Erdenheim Farm was a 500-acre farm adjacent to the City of Philadelphia, which had been in continuous agricultural use since the days of William Penn. It was the largest tract of privately owned undeveloped land in the five-county Philadelphia area. It was purchased by George Widener Jr. (Widener University, and Harvard's Widener Library), after his father, a patriarch of the family, made the unfortunate decision to sail on the *Titanic* on his return from Europe in 1912.

Nationally known for raising champion racehorses, Black Angus cattle, and cheviot sheep, the farm, with iconic views reminiscent of nineteenth-century rural America, had been enjoyed by generations of area residents traveling on roads that passed through the property. In 1971 Fitz Eugene Dixon Jr., Widener's nephew, acquired the farm and continued, at considerable expense, the agricultural operations and the exceptional stewardship of the estate. Of the property acquired by Dixon, a 115-acre parcel bisected by the Wissahickon Creek had been bequeathed to a leading local land trust, subject to a life estate in favor of Dixon. Although the farm was located in an upscale suburban area and consisted of prime developable land, Dixon, much to his credit, consistently refused to sell any portion of it for residential development.

However, in 2001 Dixon did agree to sell fifty acres for a Continuing Care Retirement Community (where Katie, my wife of sixty two years and I now live). With the remainder of Erdenheim Farm, in the view of many, now "in play," a community-wide effort was launched to preserve the remaining 450 acres of the farm. Dixon made clear that he would not entertain an offer to purchase any additional parts of the farm or protect it with conservative easements as long as he lived. He also indicated that his estate would expect to realize fair market value on any disposition of the farm following his death.

Because of my prior volunteer experience with conservation organizations including the Pennsylvania chapter of the Nature Conservancy, and several local land trusts, I was asked to lead the effort and became chair and president of the newly formed Whitemarsh Foundation, a 501(c) public charity. So began a decade-long effort to preserve the farm.

The foundation commenced operations early in 2002, with a threefold mission: preserve the farm from development; maintain the exceptional views of the farm from area roads; and continue some form of agricultural use after Mr. Dixon's death. At the first meeting of the foundation board we estimated that the cost to acquire and preserve the farm would be at least $50 million. This huge funding need was daunting and appeared completely beyond the capability of the foundation, which had with no track record, no staff, and no money. The initial question on everyone's mind was: "How can the foundation possibly raise the funds needed to protect the farm?" But since Mr. Dixon was in good health it appeared we had time to develop funding strategies and cultivate funders. One significant factor in our favor was widespread public support for preservation of the farm. Mr. Dixon viewed the efforts of the foundation with considerable skepticism.

Because of many uncertainties concerning the availability of the property and the amounts involved, our fund-raising consultant recommended that the foundation first concentrate on raising public money for preserving the farm and later from private donors for stewardship. For the next four years we laid the groundwork with the Commonwealth of Pennsylvania, Montgomery County, Whitemarsh Township (where the farm is located), and the local school district, as well as area foundations and conservationists. And the question which initially concerned us became: "How can we possibly not afford to preserve the Farm?"

Funding success depended on creativity, timing, salesmanship, and good old-fashioned luck. Fortunately, we had an abundance of all four. The funding effort was largely completed before the Great Recession effectively terminated public sources of open-space funding in Pennsylvania. Opportunistically, we were able to convert an environmental disaster into funding for the farm. And Mr. Dixon's untimely death assured the success of a referendum for a dedicated open space tax.

Among the more innovative funding strategies identified was Tax Increment Financing. The Continuing Care Retirement Community was expected to generate at least $1 million in additional real estate taxes above the preferential agricultural rate paid by Dixon. The site also included a forty-five acre, failing psychiatric hospital that consultants deemed "blighted." Why not use the tax increments to help fund the purchase of the adjacent open space instead of helping fund the construction of the CCRC? By the end of 2003 we had persuaded the taxing authorities, whose approval was required, that the TIF made sense and was in the public interest. Montgomery County, Whitemarsh Township, and the school district then took the necessary actions to approve the TIF, so that the tax increments (which were expected to be generated on completion of the CCRC construction in 2007) would be put aside for twenty years to provide debt service on a subsequent municipal bond issue to help pay for purchase of portions of the farm if and when the opportunity arose. The support of the school district was of critical importance since 75 percent of the tax revenue went to the district. The school board recognized that preservation of the farm would avoid a spike in school age population and the need to build additional capacity, and therefore was willing to defer receipt of the additional taxes until the expiration of the twenty-year term of the TIF. This was the first time, to our knowledge, that tax increment financing had been used to fund protection of open space anywhere in the country.

In August 2006, Dixon died after a short illness. He left one hundred acres to a daughter and the rest of the farm to a trust, of which there were charitable remaindermen, obligating the trustees to realize fair market value on any disposition of the property. Pennsylvania law allows municipalities to impose special real estate or income taxes to be used exclusively for preservation of open space, subject, however, to approval by the voters. At the foundation's urging, the Whitemarsh Township governing board authorized holding of a referendum at the November 2006 election for a 1/4 percent earned income tax, which would generate an estimated $1.2 million annually. We formed a political action committee, and with the help of local community groups conducted a campaign to approve the referendum. Although the farm was not identified as the object of the tax, the voters recognized that preservation of the farm was the intended beneficiary. When the dust settled, 62 percent of those voting approved, and the tax became effective in January 2007. This would enable the township to pay debt service on borrowings to fund open space without burdening the real estate tax rate.

In June 2006, there was a toxic discharge from a Merck plant into the Wissahickon Creek, killing thousands of fish and threatening the Philadelphia water supply. The federal EPA and the Pennsylvania Department of Environmental Protection brought suit for an injunction and other relief. The consent decree settling the litigation obligated Merck to fund $9 million of "Supplemental Environmental Projects" benefiting the Wissahickon watershed. With the political support of the state agencies we had been cultivating, the Pennsylvania DEP allocated half of the fund, or $4.5 million to the purchase of a portion of the farm, on the theory that preserving the property would prevent the storm water and pollutant runoff that otherwise was likely to occur from residential development.

The Dixon trustees, although fully mindful of their fiduciary duties, were supportive of the foundation's mission. They were hopeful that a conservation-minded buyer of the property could be found who would be willing to take over stewardship of the farm. Several were identified, but it was not until the fall of 2008 that the founder and CEO of a local public company and his family expressed willingness to consider the project. By 2008 the foundation had secured funding to purchase nearly 200 acres of the farm at the appraised value of just under $150,000 per acre.

The outline of a deal shortly took form:

The land trust owning the remainder interest in the property bequeathed by Widener would sell its property to the conservation buyer subject to easements preventing development on its parcel but also on other portions of the farm being acquired by the buyer.

The Dixon daughter would donate a conservation easement to the land trust on her one hundred acres of the farm and sell the fee to the conservation buyer subject to the easement, at a reduced price.

The foundation would purchase 190 acres from the trust at its appraised value of $26 million, subject to deed restrictions preventing development. The foundation would enter into a long-term agreement allowing the buyer to use the property for agricultural purposes, and pay the buyer $100,000 annually to maintain the property. By doing so, the foundation in effect was subsidizing the buyer by helping reduce the operating loss that would be incurred in farming operations.

The buyer would purchase the remaining forty acres of the farm from the trust, including the estate mansion, at fair market value.

In closings held in December 2008 and June 2009, the transactions were completed. Funding for the foundation's purchase came from ten separate sources, each with differing interests to serve and separate counsel. Bringing all to the table at the same time to achieve the agreed upon objectives was, as one observer noted, like "herding cats." During my professional life, I had participated in many challenging M&A transactions, but none of them compared with the complexity of the deal for Erdenheim Farm.

For the last eight years the conservation buyer has continued to raise black angus cattle, cheviot sheep, and thoroughbred horses; the iconic views have been preserved; and the farm has been protected from development by conservation easements and deed restrictions, in perpetuity, the rule to the contrary notwithstanding. The foundation has established a storm-water retention facility and nature preserve on fourteen acres; provided for public access on portions of the farm in the form of trails around portions of the perimeter; and restored a nineteenth-century farmhouse which today is serving as an environmental education center.

The foundation has operated in the black each year since its founding. Fund-raising has included $26 million for acquisition and $1 million in transaction costs, as well as covering operating expenses. The foundation has also raised a small endowment to help fund future operating expenses. I stepped down as chairman and president in 2015, but continue as an officer and active member of the board.

I consider myself to have been extremely fortunate to have participated in this extremely challenging project and to have contributed to its favorable conclusion. The largest privately owned tract in the five-county Philadelphia area has been preserved; generations of area residents will continue to enjoy the iconic views and now have access to portions of the farm; and the education programs conducted by the foundation will benefit future generations of school children.

The many hundreds of volunteer hours devoted to this decade-long project have been amply compensated. So much for retirement!

David Schimmel

A Peace Corps Detour:
Adventures and Misadventures in Ethiopia

THE YEAR WAS 1963. I WAS AT A FEAST IN A VILLAGE in Ethiopia sponsored by a local elder to celebrate his eightieth birthday. In addition to traditional foods—*wat* (a thick stew) and injera (a large sourdough flatbread)—there was a special delicacy: a huge platter piled high with cubes of raw meat. My host proudly explained that it was the blood of animals that makes men strong, and he urged me to fill my plate—especially with the red meat.

The issue was diplomacy versus health, and I was the associate director of the Peace Corps in Ethiopia. Our Peace Corps doctors had told us that the only safe food was what you could boil, cook, or peel. And it was clear that this food, which had been baking in the sun for hours, failed that test. While I watched a boy with a fly whisk occasionally swatting the swarming insects that were feasting on the food, I tried to think whether there was a way I could refuse my host's hospitality without insulting him and embarrassing the local volunteers who brought me there. Seeing no way to escape, I make a show of eating and "enjoying" the food. Diplomacy won and I lost. I soon developed a severe case of dysentery that kept me in bed for four days, and lasted for two weeks.

How did I get there? In 1957–58, my law school classmate Tom Headrick and I developed a proposal for an alternative to military service. We called it the American Overseas Assistance

Corps: it would send volunteers to third-world countries to serve as teachers and health workers. The idea took shape as my time in the army approached since I was getting an ROTC commission at the same time as a law degree.

We submitted the proposal to several senators including Hubert Humphrey. His staff combined our idea with others, and Humphrey introduced the Peace Corps proposal in the Senate when he was running against Senator Kennedy for the Democratic nomination in 1959. Humphrey's proposal never got to a committee hearing. But after the primary, Kennedy tested the idea in the presidential campaign. It received an enthusiastic response, and after he won, he established the Peace Corps in 1961 through an executive order.

Fast forward two years. After directing Yale's Hillel program, serving as an infantry officer in a basic combat training unit, and briefly practicing law, I was invited by Harris Wofford, a fellow Yale Law School graduate, to join his staff in Ethiopia. At that time, Ethiopia was one of the poorest countries in the world with a high infant mortality rate and an illiteracy rate of more than 90 percent. The hundreds of volunteers that the emperor invited to help modernize his semifeudal, isolated country served mainly as teachers and preventive health workers.

The ruler of Ethiopia was His Imperial Majesty (HIM) Haile Selassie I. His titles included King of Kings of Ethiopia and Conquering Lion of the Tribe of Judah. His bodyguards wore the Star of David on their uniforms, and lions roamed his palace grounds. Tradition and the Ethiopian Constitution proclaimed that he was a direct descendent of King Solomon and the Queen of Sheba. Furthermore, Haile Selassie (might of the Trinity) was the head of the Coptic Church, Ethiopia's official religion, and was considered the biblical messiah by the Rastafarian people. HIM was a slim, energetic and shrewd emperor who embodied authoritarian, one-man rule. He appointed and fired all-important executive, judicial, and military officials and was reluctant to delegate or decentralize power. He was a tough and stern monarch. Once when he was out of the country, his son seemed to collaborate with leaders of a coup that collapsed when the emperor returned. The story is told that when his son greeted his father at the airport, the Emperor is reported to have said: "I am pleased to see you alive, my son; but I would have been prouder to have returned to your funeral."

One of my assignments was to be the liaison between the Peace Corps staff and the Peace Corps lawyers who were on the faculty of Ethiopia's new law school. Therefore, my first challenge was to try to understand the country's legal system. What I discovered is that there were three legal systems. First was customary law where the elder councils resolved disputes based on traditional norms. These councils and their norms varied among Ethiopia's geographic regions and the many ethnic and linguistic groups that comprised the diverse nation. This was the legal system that governed over 90 percent of the population. Second was the formal or official legal system. To help with his modernization effort, the Emperor hired a Franco-Swiss team of legal specialists to draft a modern criminal and civil code based on European models. However, procedural provisions were imported from England, India, and the United States with little regard to coherence of the system as a whole. To further complicate matters, there was no competent legal structure to implement these laws. Moreover, there were no published records of court decisions, so precedent had little weight. Third was the Emperor's law. On special occasions, HIM drove slowly through the streets of Addis Ababa in his convertible Rolls-Royce, wearing his splendid imperial, medal-decorated uniform. On some of these occasions, he would benevolently allow citizens to hand him personal requests or petitions about a legal dispute. If anyone dared to approach him after he signaled that he wanted no more petitions, his bodyguards casually bashed them over the head with nightsticks. According to tradition, the Emperor personally considered some of the petitions while sitting on his throne and would render a verdict without regard to the written law, as his ancestor King Solomon was reported to have done in biblical times. In addition, the Emperor could add, amend, or delete any law he wished since he controlled the parliament.

Ethiopia's first law school was established in 1962, and its faculty consisted primarily of Peace Corps volunteers who were recent law school graduates. A few Ethiopian lawyers had studied abroad; but very few, if any, were judges. As a result, the first law school class consisted of Ethiopian judges who spoke some English. As the law school liaison, I had many long, sometimes agonizing, conversations with our Peace Corps law teachers, who faced the daunting task of teaching judges about their complex legal system influenced by European, Anglo-American, and Ethiopian laws, customs, and procedures. Meanwhile, my wife, who wrote her Yale dissertation on an American Supreme Court justice, was the law school librarian.

In addition to working with Peace Corps volunteers, I taught a world history course at Haile Selassie University. My best students were bright, ambitious Ethiopian Air Force officers who were eager to get a university degree. The most intense and memorable class discussions were about the French revolution. During these years, some university students and young military officers were talking secretly about the need for Ethiopia to move towards democracy, to modify the Emperor's one-man rule, and whether it would take a revolution to achieve these goals. But in 1963 it was highly dangerous to publicly criticize the Emperor, his policies, or his decisions. His Majesty was eager to modernize; but promoting democracy was seen as subversive. That is why class debates about the causes, justifications, and consequences of the French revolution were so intense: they were relatively safe proxies for prohibited criticism of imperial rule. During the next decade, criticism of the Emperor became increasingly widespread until he was deposed by a revolution in 1974 that replaced his rule with a ruthless communist dictatorship.

Cross-cultural communications in Ethiopia were problematic. I was in a small town to check on Tom, a volunteer who was furious with Tafari, his headmaster, who was not happy with Tom's teaching. Before my last visit, Tom had asked Tafari if he had any concerns about his teaching. The headmaster said, "No, you're doing just fine." But in private, Tafari shared a series of problems with me about Tom's repeated failure strictly to enforce the school rules and to follow the curriculum. When I shared this criticism with Tom, he asked me how I expected him to work under a "devious, hypocritical, lying SOB." When I told the headmaster that Tom would welcome direct criticism, Tafari explained that he would never humiliate and insult a teacher by criticizing him directly if this could be done indirectly. Then, he explained, "everyone can save face."

At a decrepit middle school, several volunteers decided that they could improve the school's appearance with a coat of paint. So they bought the sandpaper, brushes, and paint, and asked their Ethiopian co-teachers to join them one Saturday for a "paint party." The Ethiopian teachers said they would come, but never showed up. Assuming there was a misunderstanding, the volunteers rescheduled the painting and clarified the invitation, and again the Ethiopians failed to join them. The Peace Corps teachers told me what happened and concluded that the Ethiopian teachers were undependable, uncooperative, or lazy. The volunteers could not understand why their colleagues had lied to them and were unwilling to help. When I discussed this with the headmaster, he explained that the volunteers were asking the Ethiopian teachers to demean themselves by publicly doing manual labor that would undermine their professional status and reputation in the eyes of their students, parents, and neighbors.

Were the volunteers, missionaries, spies, or exploiters? Trying to explain why we were in Ethiopia was sometimes a challenge for both volunteers and staff. Most volunteers joined the Peace Corps in response to Kennedy's call to service. But in the historic experience of Ethiopia, foreigners came to their country to missionize or exploit. Most Ethiopians assumed that our volunteers were there for similar reasons. To Ethiopians in small towns and villages, it made no sense that American university graduates would volunteer to spend two years without pay in places where Ethiopian graduates were unwilling to live. So when volunteers said that the reason they came was to help meet the needs of Ethiopia, these unselfish motives seemed unbelievable and often increased suspicion. This suspicion frustrated some of the volunteers. So I suggested that they give a selfish secondary reason for being there (e.g., to help them get a job teaching about Africa, to be able to work with the US government or with an international company). These explanations usually satisfied suspicious villagers and made them more comfortable with a foreigner in their community.

Many university students and government workers assumed that the Peace Corps was a covert part of the CIA. They believed that volunteers were also spies that the United States placed in communities throughout their nation to collect intelligence about Ethiopia. When I tried to explain to Ethiopian officials that Peace Corps policy strictly prohibited collaboration with the CIA, I was often met with cynical smiles. To overcome these suspicions, we asked the Ethiopian government to provide our staff with a bilingual driver and office assistant. They agreed. In this way the government was able to place their agents in a position to monitor our activities. By inviting them to spy on us, Ethiopian officials would know that we weren't running a spy operation. In addition, we worked closely with our drivers and office assistant, shared our plans and problems with them, and listened to their advice. As a result, the Ethiopian government agents became our allies in countering some of the myths that often swirled about our foreign operation.

In 1963, there were no paved roads connecting any of Ethiopia's major cities. Therefore, to visit volunteers beyond two hour's drive over badly rutted roads, I flew in Ethiopian Airline's domestic aircraft—the World War II DC-3 two-engine prop planes. These planes carried fourteen passengers on one side and removable benches on the other side for seriously ill passengers traveling to and from hospitals in Addis Ababa. The DC-3s flew low over mountainous terrain, and the strong, intermittent air currents caused the planes to bounce uncontrollably. Hence, the nickname for these planes, the "vomit comet."

Outside of Addis and Asmara (the second largest city which the Italians occupied in the 1930s), there were no paved runways. Planes landed on grass fields. Before they landed, a man would emerge from a hut at the edge of the field to chase away the kids who usually played soccer on the landing fields.

On several occasions, I visited volunteers who worked with the Falashas (also known as Beta Israel or the black Jews of Ethiopia). The Falashas lived in dozens of small, isolated villages in the Gondar area of northern Ethiopia. I rented a donkey cart to get to the villages from the airfield. The Falashas speak Amharic and are physically indistinguishable from their Christian and Muslim neighbors. Their origins are obscure, and they practice something like Biblical Judaism. Most were flown to Israel in airlifts between 1979 and 1990. Today visitors to Israel are told that they have come to a biblical land. Historically perhaps. But Moses would be as mystified in Tel Aviv as he would be in New York City. In contrast, he would have felt right at home in a Falasha village. The Falashas were subsistence farmers who lived by themselves in tight-knit communities. They plowed with oxen, got their water from the village well, milked their goats, made their own cloths and pottery, and lived in thatch huts with no electricity. For me, walking into a Falasha village was like walking into the pages of the Bible.

Did the Peace Corps make a difference? For Ethiopians, our volunteers clearly helped their impoverished country meet some of its educational and public health goals. The population was divided into dozens of tribal languages, and most people did not speak Amharic, the official language. Because the Emperor wanted to modernize Ethiopia, he ruled that English would be the language of instruction in all high schools and the university so that educated Ethiopians could communicate with the rest of the world. Therefore, the scarcity of English teachers was a severe problem. That's why our few hundred volunteers were so important to meet this critical need by doubling the number of competent English teachers. Furthermore, since most Ethiopians did not understand that germs cause disease, volunteers who helped dig safe wells, build sanitary latrines, and teach about preventive health helped decrease Ethiopia's many endemic diseases.

For volunteers, Peace Corps service was a powerful experiential education. First, it gave them a special appreciation for America's constitutional values and democratic institutions that most of us take for granted. Second, for many volunteers, it changed their lives. This was the case for Paul Tsongas who was a volunteer in Ethiopia from 1962–64, years before he graduated from the Yale Law School. One day I drove to visit Paul who was a teacher in a village near Addis. We talked about how he overcame most of the challenges of teaching in a run-down school without adequate books, supplies, or support. He also talked about the satisfactions of working after school with both his students and village elders on community projects that improved the life of the village. Years later, as a US senator from Massachusetts, Paul said that it was his Peace Corps experience that changed the direction of his life towards a career in public service. On my way back from visiting Paul, I stopped at a rural gas station for a Coke. (I avoided local bottled waters despite their promotional labels that claimed that they helped cure malaria, dysentery, cancer, headaches, and other ills.) Knowing that foreigners drink from glasses, the station attendant reached under his counter and put a filthy glass next to the Coke. I signaled that I wanted him to open the bottle and that I did not want to drink from the glass. When he realized that the dirty glass was a problem for me, he smiled and took a greasy rag out of his pocket that he used to check engine oil. He then made a show of carefully wiping the glass and proudly holding it up to the light so that it almost sparkled. Again the choice of diplomacy versus health. When I insisted on drinking from the bottle and not from his "clean" glass, the attendant was clearly insulted and crestfallen. This time diplomacy lost. But I was able to return to work the next day.

THEODORE M. VESTAL

The Incident in Gambella

THE ORTHODOX EASTER WEEKEND WAS approaching, and the long fast in Ethiopia would be broken at the stroke of midnight Saturday night. Devout Coptics remained in church until the bells announced the beginning of the new day, and then returned home to feast on raw meat, injera, and a variety of *wat*. The spirit of the Ethiopian was resurrected with nourishment; short tempers of the fasting period were replaced with tolerance, and the highlands seemed to glow with a contentment found only at this time. For the American Peace Corps Volunteer (PCV) teachers, Easter was the sign that they had reached the home stretch (according to the universal inner clock of teachers who reckon how much longer they need deal with students before the next long vacation). The worst was behind, and the academic year continued for only another two and a half months. This was the last long holiday until the rainy season break, and for many it would be the final opportunity to travel to other parts of the empire for a change of scenery and a week of diversion.

I looked forward to playing host to some of my PCV friends from the provinces since many of them came into Addis Ababa during their travels, but with 600 mainly young Americans on the road simultaneously, the Peace Corps staff was in high alert until every volunteer was safely back home at the end of the week. Driving accidents especially were the bane of Peace Corps operations worldwide. Driving in a third world country is always challenging, and the Peace Corps/Ethiopia staff did all it could to keep PCVs from operating any type of motorized vehicle. There had been a close call at the beginning of the holiday when a Land Rover full of volunteers from Dire Dawa had collided with a Fiat on the mountain road to Harar. None of the Peace Corps people had been injured, but the Ethiopian driver of the other car had been killed and one of his passengers was in critical condition. In another incident in the same area, a Peace Corps staff driver had backed into a herd of camels and was perilously ushered out of town by a fusillade of spears tossed by the animals' enraged Somali owners. A few months earlier, I had a close call driving back from the movies in Addis when a taxi driver speeding down a steep hill totaled my crowded VW beetle. None of my four passengers were hurt, although I suffered a concussion and had no memory of the cabbie holding us at gunpoint until the police arrived and disarmed him, breaking his arm in the process.

At Peace Corps headquarters, the new deputy director, Norm Nailor, discussing the upcoming holidays, noted there had been no fatalities during the four years (1962–66) the Peace Corps had been working in Ethiopia. Twenty-four PCVs had died worldwide by that time. Just then, Nailor's phone rang. "Yes, Sheldon." I knew Norm was talking to the US embassy's chargé d'affaires. "What? A volunteer was drowned? Who was it?" Norm's relaxed mood had changed to high alert. "Right. We'll get someone out there right away." "Do you know which volunteers went to Illubabor for the holidays?" Norm asked me. "Sheldon says the Embassy received a radio message from Gambella, near the Sudanese border, that a volunteer is missing and presumed drowned. Can you fly out there to investigate? I'll get a doctor to go with you."

An hour later, Fuller Torrey, a Peace Corps physician, and I were flying westward in a chartered Cessna with a French pilot, Captain Adrian Gris. Illubabor Province was in Ethiopia's southwest and jutted well into the Sudan. The Baro River ran through it on its way to merge with the White Nile.

In the Spring of 1966, Gambella was a favorite holiday destination for PCV teachers. Many had found the highland's winter months chilly, damp, and uninviting for outdoor activities. At 1,500 feet altitude, Gambella, one of the lowest towns in Ethiopia, offered a warm, dry climate, swimming from sandy river beaches, and an opportunity to glimpse wild game. Its attributes were fresh on many Americans' minds. A few months before, *National Geographic* had published an article, "Ethiopian Adventure," that included photos of the Baro River area and mentioned swimming in the river to avoid sunstroke. The article's author, joined by some Yugoslav expatriates who lived in Gambella and hunted crocodiles for a living, swam in the river.

More than a dozen PCVs flew to Gambella during the Easter break. Ethiopian Airlines had a regular C-47 service from Addis Ababa to the meadow landing field. The last group of PCVs to arrive had a brief visit with other PCVs who were leaving Gambella on the same plane. With the temperature in the nineties, the six new arrivals decided to go for an early afternoon swim. On the drive into town they passed large numbers of Anuaks, the tall Nilotic tribal people of Illubabor. The PCVs were aware that there were crocodiles in the Baro, but they assumed they were all upstream. They saw nothing in the vicinity of the river to indicate that there was any danger. There were townspeople bathing and filling water containers on the beach near the Fasil Hotel. The danger from crocs seemed remote and unrealistic to the PCVs who had never before seen them in African waters. Likewise, the fear of schistosomiasis, the crippling disease feared by the Peace Corps in Africa caused by contact with freshwater parasitic worms, was discounted by the PCVs because of the Baro's swift current.

The four men and two women in the group plunged in on the town side of the stream and enjoyed the bracing effect of the cool water. A large sandbar and some sizeable rocks on the other side of the river were an attractive destination and resting place after a relatively short, crosscurrent swim. Unfortunately, one of the women, barely five feet tall, who thought she could float and dogpaddle across, really was a nonswimmer and found herself being pulled downstream when she was about halfway across. Two of the men, athletic six-footers, were able to get her to the other side where she could stand on a small boulder.

After a brief rest on the rocks, the PCVs returned to the town side beach, with the men assisting the nonswimmer across. Back on the strand, she told her rescuers she had almost drowned. Four of the group swam back to the sandbar and decided to drift down the current one-by-one to the next rock downstream. Hansen, the tallest of the group, went first and swam to the "second rock" from which he could walk to the adjacent sandbar. He had just gotten to his feet in water about thigh-deep when he suddenly fell forward almost as if he were diving back in the river. The three other PCVs had glimpsed a part of a crocodile's snout at the moment of the attack. Hansen's body was held under water for approximately five minutes, when it reemerged briefly before going down again.

The PCVs were stunned but managed to organize a search along the riverbank and in the Baro using dugout canoes. Soon, many townspeople joined the search in their boats and on shore. Some of the Ethiopians spotted the body emerging a few times during the next two hours. One of the PCVs did his best to get cables sent to Addis Ababa and to the Peace Corps office. Eventually, the messages were delivered to Peace Corps/Ethiopia after 11:30 a.m. the following morning.

In the early evening of the tragedy, the crocodile was spotted in the river, and a US Air Force colonel, Hugh Hart, who was hunting big game in the area fired several shots at it. The crocodile submerged, and although many people continued the search after dark using flashlights and auto headlights, the croc was not seen again until the following morning. Early Friday, the crocodile was located at the "second rock" just under the water. Colonel Hart firing a .375 Magnum elephant rifle shot the beast several times, and the crocodile floated in the current, coming to rest in shallow water by an island downstream from the beach. The croc's body, just under fourteen feet long, was pulled ashore. One of the PCVs had the gruesome task of searching for Hansen's remains in the croc's carcass. It was evident that Hansen had been killed and consumed by the predator. The district health officer prepared relevant remains for shipment back to Addis Ababa and stored them in a wooden box. The local Ethiopian Airlines agent was able to divert a regularly scheduled C-47 from Asosa to Gambella to pick up Hansen's remains and the five other PCVs. That plane left Gambella for Addis Ababa ten minutes before Fuller and I touched down there at 3:30 p.m. in our Cessna.

We immediately felt the heat and stripped off our coats and ties before unloading our bags and walking to the airline shack just as a police jeep pulled up. Police Colonel Hailu Gebru introduced himself and drove us into town. He expressed his sympathy about the death of Mr. Hansen who had been attacked by a crocodile while he was swimming. That was the first that Fuller and I had heard of the crocodile. Colonel Hailu further explained that two other PCVs from Addis Ababa, Steve Buff and Evelyn Ashkenaze, whom I knew, were at the hotel and could give us more details of the tragedy.

We found Buff and Ashkenaze on the veranda of the Fasil, and heard a thorough narrative of the events preceding our arrival. Buff had drawn a map of the river where Hansen had been lost, which he gave to me. Evelyn seemed somewhat distraught by what had happened, and we asked her to fly back to Addis Ababa with us the next day. Then Dr. Torrey and I set out to interview the Ethiopians whom the PCVs had mentioned. Colonel Hart and his Swiss white hunter were still on the other side of the Baro where their Land Rover was bogged in the soft mud of the bank, and we decided to visit them the next morning.

The Ethiopian officials were polite, well-educated highlanders who confirmed the details of Hansen's death. They maintained that the PCVs had been warned of the danger of crocodiles in the areas where they swam. For whatever reasons, the young Americans had not heeded their warnings.

After a sleepless night in the hotel, Fuller and I walked down to the beach where Colonel Hailu had a dugout with three oarsmen awaiting us. We climbed in as the Anuaks shoved off. We were in midstream when I glanced upriver and saw two pairs of evil-looking knots, the heads of crocs, fifty yards away and moving toward us. Then something struck the bark a tremendous blow. Water came cascading over the side of the dugout. I grabbed both sides and thought for a moment we might be swamped. To our right a crocodile was swiftly swimming away. We had rammed into him just as he was surfacing. I looked back to our left. The two *Crocodylus niloticus* I had seen earlier were passing behind our stern unaware that they had barely missed having some helpless prey thrashing about them.

We pulled up on the bank not far from the mired Land Rover. Stout ropes had been secured to the front bumper, and six Ethiopians were wading in the loblolly getting in position to push the vehicle. Up an embankment a dozen men held the rope, and Fuller and I joined them in tugging as the driver put the four-wheel drive Rover in first gear. Anuak began a work chant and Fuller and I joined in pulling on the rope in time to the rhythm. The Rover moved laterally and then slowly forward. It started up the hill and gathered speed as it reached the top. The work party gave a shout of triumph, and Ethiopian Safari's Land Rover was again ready for action.

Colonel Hart came from his camp and after introductions were made, he reiterated his version of the Hansen affair, which jibed with the PCVs' accounts. We then set off in the dugout for the island where the croc had been killed. We took photographs of the beast's skin stretched and lying in the sun before we were paddled back to our hotel.

The airline agent had arranged for a jeep to take us to the landing strip. Captain Gris had already gone out to check the Cessna, and we were soon in flight back to Addis Ababa. Evelyn and I sat in the back of the four-seater while Dr. Torrey sat in front with Captain Gris. Our plane soon left the flat river valley for the more familiar mountain scenery of the highlands. We flew northeast on a straight line for the capital. In an hour we had passed out of Illubabor into Welega Province. To the north we could see Mount Tuka, not really looking 10,200 feet in altitude, beyond the town of Lekemt. It was a clear day and the terraced hills and the round thatched roof huts were distinct below. I dozed off only to be awakened by the voices of Fuller and Captain Gris.

The oil pressure gauge which had reacted normally when we took off, had plummeted down to the left as if it were not working. This meant the Cessna was out of oil, and the engine would catch fire if the plane did not land quickly. We were too far beyond Lekemt to turn back, and Addis was forty-five minutes away. We all looked below to locate a landing site. We thought of the highway meandering through the mountains, but it was serpentine and there was no straight section long enough. The fields were risky because many were divided by stone fences which could not be seen until you were on top of them. Most plots were small rectangles which the Shewan peasants plowed with oxen just as their ancestors on the Amhara Plateau had been doing for centuries. There was no good place to land.

The French captain was not too upset. He had been in tough situations in Indochina and Algeria, so he accepted danger with grace. He told us there had been a landing strip that had not been used for ten years at Ambo, which was fifteen minutes away. If we could get there, he would set us down.

We flew on in silence. Death had been on our minds during the past day but none of us had expected to face it then. Risks were the companions of Peace Corps personnel in Africa. Strange tropical diseases, reckless drivers on mountain roads, and airplanes skimming the escarpment were all potential life terminators. I looked down at the paperback book I had been reading: *Honest to God*, at that time, a best-selling theological thesis by Bishop John A. T. Robinson. That might have been an appropriate final reading, but the good bishop's prose couldn't hold my attention.

Ambo came into sight and familiar landmarks in miniature jumped up at me: the highway I had driven down several times with my family in our Volkswagen; the big Italian hotel where we had spent a rainy night; and the main attraction of the area, the hot spring Olympic-size swimming pool. To the east of the town was a flat meadow overgrown with tall grass and slender trees, to the side of which sat a single structure, Ethiopian Airlines' storage shack, the size of an American outhouse.

We all assumed the emergency landing position—crossed arms over the forehead. The Cessna touched down hard, bumped along roughly and came to a quick stop. Captain Gris had made a spectacular landing. We all looked up in happy surprise. Gris confessed that the last time he set down on a strange field, he had broken the landing gear. Eight feet in front of our propeller was a coppice of young juniper trees standing four to six feet tall. They were not thick but still they were big enough to snap the landing gear or tear off a wing. A few yards beyond the trees rose the mud miniature skyscrapers of the African ant, which would have effectively braked anything that got by the first obstacles.

Gris said he would phone the airline's Addis office to send a mechanic to Ambo to troubleshoot our oil system. Meanwhile we would have time for a swim and a leisurely lunch. If repairs were successful, the flight to Addis would be about thirty minutes. We hiked the two miles into town, enjoying the bright sun and pleasant temperature of the plateau. At the hotel, Gris made his telephone call and was told that EAL would have a ground crew driven out to him right away.

Dr. Torrey, a very conscientious medic, was anxious to get back to Addis, and with some doubt about how soon the EAL mechanic would arrive and how long it might take him to repair the plane if he could repair it, he decided to catch the next bus for the capital. Evelyn and I walked him to the bus stop where he took the last seat in a 1938 Fiat bus filled with Ethiopians, bundles, and goats. We wished Fuller bon voyage in Amharic and returned to the hotel pool where Gris had already befriended the best-looking girl at the poolside. After an hour's swim, we changed and had an excellent European lunch in the restaurant. We walked back to the landing field where a VW painted in the green, yellow, and red of Ethiopian Airlines was parked. Three Ethiopian mechanics had gone over the plane and found nothing wrong with it other than a lack of oil. The oil pressure now registered correctly. Had we known it, there had been sufficient oil in the shed to give the Cessna an oil change, and we could have filled up and flown on to

Addis without waiting.

We thanked the mechanics and climbed back into the Cessna. The short taxi area was no problem for Gris who turned us around and took off with room to spare over the barbed-wire fence along the highway. In thirty minutes we were standing on the paved runway of the Addis Ababa International Airport. Evelyn and I drove in my Land Rover to the Peace Corps office in Casa Inces, where we chatted with Norm Nailor, the deputy director. He had met the five PCVs who had flown in earlier from Gambella with Hansen's remains. Arrangements already had been made for the return of Hansen's body to the United States for burial, and a memorial service had been scheduled at the Lutheran Mission in Addis. After reporting all we knew about the Gambella episode, Evelyn and I started out the office door. A taxi pulled into the drive and out hopped Dr. Torrey, covered from head to foot with dust. The bus from Ambo had just arrived in Addis.

In the days that followed I had opportunity to ponder my two-year overseas assignment that was rapidly coming to a close. As an associate director of Peace Crops/Ethiopia, I had fulfilled an ambition to be a part of "a peace corps of talented young men and women, willing and able to serve their country … as an alternative or as a supplement to peacetime selective service… to be ambassadors of peace" that presidential candidate Senator John F. Kennedy had proposed in a ringing and inspiring campaign speech at the Cow Palace in San Francisco on November 2, 1960. It had been my good fortune to serve in Peace Corps/Washington and in Peace Corps/Ethiopia when the organization was in its nascent days and to work with a cohort of patriotic and adventurous Americans, "Kennedy's Children," who asked not what their country could do for them but what they could do for their country. We did indeed carry out the mission of the Peace Corps in promoting world peace and friendship by helping the people of Ethiopia in meeting their need for trained men and women; in helping promote a better understanding of Americans on the part of the people served; and, after returning to the United States, in helping promote a better understanding of other people on the part of Americans.

Of course difficult problems had to be ironed out when we first set up the PCV program in Ethiopia. A local staff had to be hired. Then, how to decide on "duty" locations? How will PCVs be housed? What equipment will they require? Will they be given local currency and wished good luck in taking care of themselves? What will be their relationship with the US embassy, USAID, US military in country, and the local bureaucracy? How to get PCVs out to their assignments? How to get them to do more than carry out their primary assignment (usually teaching)? What projects might they carry out during summer "breaks?" What should be the vacation policy? What to do when PCV letters or other communications are judged to be insulting to local communities? What to do with "problem PCVs?" Who and how to evaluate the PCVs and staff? How to correct shortcomings found by evaluators? What in-country training ought to be provided? What testing of PCV and staff language skills ought to be conducted? What completion of service conferences ought to be held? Run by whom? How should PCVs respond to US military actions in the host country and worldwide? Working through these issues was a challenge, but getting them right was a reward.

The Peace Corps' aspirations were high, as was the altitude in the highlands, the roof of Africa, where we mainly served. The country was at peace, and the Peace Corps was appreciated for what it was accomplishing. There was no job description of what I was doing as a Peace Corps executive. As it developed over time, what I did was to strive to facilitate the PCVs doing their best in their work and to help them be happy in their assignments. Most of them had never held a full-time job before and had not traveled overseas, much less lived in a foreign land. Their dedication and perseverance were commendable, and many displayed the highest values associated with the Peace Corps: humility, generosity, kindness, empathy, and fidelity. I've been fortunate to maintain friendships with a number of these remarkable individuals over these many years since our time together in the Horn of Africa.

I journeyed throughout Ethiopia, a heaven-blessed land of natural beauty and potential abundance, meeting Ethiopians from all walks of life. I encountered a fascinating culture and a handsome people whose intelligence and courteous ways were beguiling. At that time, historian Arnold Toynbee said that in the Peace Corps, the world was seeing the Western tradition at is best. This frequently was the case with the volunteers in Ethiopia, especially in those naive days before the Vietnam War and Watergate scandals.

Since the Peace Corps began in 1961, nearly 200,000 Peace Corps Volunteers have served in 139 countries. Unbeknownst to most Americans, 302 PCVs have died while in service to their country. Incredibly, given the size of Peace Corps contingents in Ethiopia, there have been only four fatalities in Peace Corps/Ethiopia, and none since 1973.

In later years, I went on to other fulfilling labors in government service, the academic bar, international education, and higher education administration with extended residencies in New Delhi, Kyoto, and Hamburg. The Ethiopian experience set the standard for my studying other nations, people, and cultures, and for coping, in general, in a foreign land. And my fraught adventure in the very full twenty-four-hour period surrounding the Gambella episode was never matched in intensity or depth of thought about life and death.

Paul Zimmerman

Subterfuge Works

WHAT IS THE ROLE OF SUBTERFUGE, OF DOING things backwards in order to get them done at all? It seemed to be the order of the day in both India and Kenya. In August 1966, our family departed for India, where I served as Peace Corps director for the three southern states of India: Mysore, Kerala, and Madras, as they were then called. The job was challenging, difficult, and time-obsessive, but it was the high point of my professional life. I supervised the work of 150 Peace Corps volunteers in those states, assisted by a staff in my office in Bangalore, the largest city in Mysore. Volunteers were provided after a request from the central government of India in New Delhi. The requests came to the central government from the states that requested Peace Corps volunteers. If the central government approved a state request, it was then sent to the Peace Corps office in Bangalore for implementation.

A difficult part of the process was our office's consultation with senior officers in the three states whose duty it was to request the Peace Corps volunteers from the central office. These Indian officers often had an idea of what they wanted volunteers to do, but, most of the time they did not focus on the details: how the volunteers would accomplish their work, where they would be located, with whom they would work and the like. So, the requests from the states to the central government were actually written in the Peace Corps office, and then reviewed by the Indian officers. In effect the volunteer projects were often the creation of the Peace Corps, rather than local officials, and then "disguised" by the contrivance of a request being made to the central government from the states. In the absence of this subterfuge, volunteers might have been assigned to jobs which were nonexistent or to work with locals who did not want their assistance or under conditions that would have been difficult, maybe impossible, to tolerate.

As it was, the volunteers varied in ability and interest. Most were quite dedicated, but others joined the Peace Corps because they did not know what they wanted to do after graduating from college and often required extensive support. Dissatisfaction could exist on either the volunteer or the local side or both. Accommodation, discussion, and often action were required—changing the location of the volunteer, changing the volunteer's job (we preferred not to do that), or changing the volunteer's Indian supervisor. On occasion—fortunately not very often—the volunteer was not up to Peace Corps standards, and had to be removed from the program. But these difficulties would have been magnified over by many times but for the foresight and planning that went into the "original" requests. In fact it was generally believed in the expatriate community in India that there was a trade-off between American financing of development projects and that country's willingness to accept large numbers of Peace Corp volunteers—the more money Ambassador Bowles provided, the more volunteers Mrs. Gandhi would accept. In effect the ultimate reversal.

I encountered the same situation on a smaller scale in Kenya. My wife, Margot, had been sent to Nairobi to expand her nonprofit employer's program in Africa. While in Kenya. I did some work for the UN Development Programme, writing a proposal on how a UNDP grant would be used by the Kenyan government. Yes, the Kenyan government was supposed to write the proposal, but the UNDP knew this would not happen, so asked me to write it. The government thereafter "submitted" the proposal back to the UNDP, as its own. No one was hurt although the bureaucratic capacity of the Kenyan government was not augmented in any way.

Lest the reader think that formalism prevailing over reality is limited to third-world countries, I have a story from the heart of Dixie to tell. After ROTC training at Yale I was the legal officer of an infantry battalion stationed at Fort Benning Georgia. Fort Benning then had a rule that an accused could request as counsel any officer on the base who had a law degree. I was one of few such persons, so when that word got around I received a number of requests to be a defendant's lawyer. So I tried these cases without having had any prior trial experience. One of my clients, a career soldier, was accused of having filed false expense reports when he was transferred to Fort Benning from another army base. Three civilian army investigators came to his apartment, and in front of his wife and children, told him that if he did not sign the confession they had brought with them, he would probably not see his family again. Terrified, he signed the "confession." When the confession was introduced at trial by one of the investigators on the witness stand, I objected on the grounds that it was a false "confession" illegally extracted by the investigators, and later denied by the defendant. After private consultation among the judges—army officers from the same unit as the defendant—the written confession was disallowed. Whereupon, the chief judge turned to the investigator, still on the witness stand, and said: "OK, the written confession is not admissible; now tell us about your conversation with the defendant, and what was said back and forth with the defendant." So much for military "justice."

IV

POLITICS & PROFESSIONS

HOWARD FINK

A Political Interlude

IN THE SUMMER OF 1971 I HAD JUST COMPLETED
a year teaching at the University of Illinois and had returned to Columbus, Ohio, and my position at Ohio State. I
had been marginally active in Democratic politics since arriving there as a law professor in 1965. I received a call from Bob
McAlister, a fellow lawyer, Democratic activist and friend. He and
Tom Kaplin, another lawyer and Democratic activist, wanted to
start a McGovern for President committee prior to the 1972 Democratic convention. I immediately signed on and we got to work.

Nixon was president and the war in Vietnam had dragged
on and escalated after he had beaten Hubert Humphrey following the debacle of the 1968 Democratic convention. There were
fewer primaries in those days and the one in Ohio would turn out
to be pivotal to the nomination. But we knew little about running
a primary or organizing a delegation. We had to learn it all from
scratch with a little help from the Ohio Democratic Party and
the national McGovern for President organization. McGovern's
appeal to young people could be compared to Bernie Sanders's
today. After the 1968 Chicago disaster, the convention rules had
been changed, requiring that half the delegates be minorities or
women. So it was to be a unique convention.

McGovern for President organizations had sprung up in many
Ohio counties with little help from a central command center. On
a Saturday in May organizers from across the state met for the

first time in a large classroom at the Ohio State College of Law. I chaired the meeting and was elected to be the floor leader of the delegation to the 1972 Democratic convention, which was to meet in July in Miami, Florida. The number of delegate votes we would have at the convention would depend on the percentage that McGovern would win in state primary contests against Hubert Humphrey and, in some states, George Wallace. In the June Ohio primary, we did not win a majority of delegates, but the number that McGovern actually won seemed to point to a majority of the convention votes—so far, so good.

The four-day July national convention was a joyful gathering, but the seeds of disaster were there if then unrecognized. The first mistake was agreeing to the seven p.m. starting time. Instead of starting in the afternoon to get the minor business over, we started in prime time and went all night. McGovern's eventual acceptance speech was delivered at three in the morning eastern time. But in all the excitement of a crowd of delegates that had included many show business and movie stars, popular liberal political figures, and lots and lots of young men and women at their first political outing, we saw only the good.

The majority of our delegation was controlled by the Hubert Humphrey delegates led by an old-line union leader named Frank King. I was the floor leader of the McGovern forces. We fought over seating and recognition. At one point when Frank King refused to let me make a floor motion, I went next door to the California delegation led by Willy Brown, a charismatic African-American leader. I said, "Willy, I need to be heard." "No problem," he said, and got recognition for me.

At another point we had a dispute that was so potentially explosive that we retired to a back room and settled it, and agreed that no one would discuss it. Coming out, I refused an invitation to speak to Walter Cronkite. Later we got into a pushing contest that involved another CBS star.

We won the nomination and adopted a progressive platform that included winding down the Vietnam War. We believed we could do it. We not only defeated the Humphrey forces, led by major union figures, but also those delegates pledged to George Wallace. So it was four days of wonderful, hopeful unreality, with the nicest young people and older men and women imaginable. What could go wrong?

The convention had nominated Senator Thomas Eagleton of Missouri, who had strong labor backing, for vice president. While we were behind in the polls, we went home full of optimism. Then disaster struck. News reports, undenied, surfaced that Eagleton, a dynamic campaigner in election after election in which he would work himself to exhaustion, became depressed, even though he had won the nomination. Impatient with a counseling cure, he submitted voluntarily to the quick fix of electroshock treatments, which snapped him back in a flash. But when word of the treatment spread, in a day when mental illness was much more feared and misunderstood than today, he was forced to resign. A long, disheartening search for a replacement followed. Another cause of failure was that so anti-war were McGovern's young supporters that he hid his military record of twenty-five bombing missions over Germany during the World War II. President Johnson later urged him to emphasize it, not to hide it.

We returned from the convention full of hope and enthusiasm. But on the Monday following that great week, the politics of politics intervened. Bob McAlister was informed that he would not be leading the campaign in Ohio. A man named Ron Sklar, from Cleveland, known to none of us, was to take over. Bob McAlister and Tommy Kaplin quit the campaign. I stayed on in a minor role and watched the edifice collapse.

Looking back after forty-five years, my view of the failure has changed. Historians point to the Eagleton fiasco, the lack of control of the convention process, mistakes made by a young and eager staff and a clouded message. Surely there were mistakes. McGovern was portrayed as a bumbler, a novice, disloyal to his original running mate, and for failing to get a substitute quickly. But in fact, as time went on, the campaign improved, the crowds grew larger, and money started to pour in. But it was too late.

I now think there never was a chance for McGovern to win

on an anti-Vietnam War stance, led by college kids temporarily exempted from the draft, and by women who would never be drafted. The war was being fought not by the young, affluent, college kids, but by the poorer, less-educated boys who were then an even larger part of our country. Thousands had died or come home wounded or maimed. They were mocked and ignored. The McGovern movement was seen by many as a repudiation of those boys, sometimes even picturing them as war criminals. They were the boys of the voters who hated the "arrogant, self-righteous" college kids. And there were more of them than there were fervent McGovernites.

Much has changed in the intervening years, but much more has not changed in our country. Given the same circumstances, a draft army, thousands killed or maimed, even in a hopeless war, the same result would occur today. Looking at today's politics, the divisions in our society have perhaps grown even more drastic than they were in 1972.

I believed in McGovern. He was a fine man in a doomed campaign. I will always look back fondly on the adventure.

CARLA ANDERSON HILLS

Tough Times Can Beget Better Times

IN THE SPRING OF 1973, I WAS FOCUSED ON FEDERAL litigation at Munger, Tolles & Hills, a firm that my husband Rod and I along with four friends had founded eleven years earlier. Also that spring I was filling in as an adjunct professor to teach antitrust law at UCLA's law school in response to an urgent request from Dean Murray Schwartz. One morning as I was preparing for class, I received a call from Elliott Richardson, then attorney general, asking me to come to Washington to become his assistant attorney general in charge of the civil division. Rod and I thought very highly of Elliott. I said that because of my current commitments I could not come until the fall, and he said he could wait. I talked about the possibility with Rod, who was very supportive. After much debate, we decided to take the plunge. In October, Rod who was working on a matter in New York and I flying in from Los Angeles met in Washington DC to consider how we would reorganize our lives.

These were not tranquil times in Washington. On October 10, just prior to our October visit, Vice President Agnew pleaded no contest to charges that included tax evasion and bribery and resigned as vice president. I met with Elliott and his deputy, Bill Ruckelshaus, to talk about the many challenges facing the Justice Department. While we were in Washington, Rod and I had lunch with Elliott's wife, Anne, to talk about schools for our four children. Rod looked at houses and put a deposit down on one near the Richardson's. It was all set. We agreed to come at the beginning of the New Year. The next morning we flew out of Washington home to Los Angeles, excited about the future. When we arrived in L.A., we turned on the radio and were stunned by the announcement that Elliott Richardson had just resigned as attorney general along with his Deputy Bill Ruckelshaus over their refusal to carry out President Nixon's order to fire Special Prosecutor Archibald Cox. Solicitor General Robert Bork, a former Yale Law School professor, became acting attorney general. Rod and I decided that this was not the time for us to move to Washington.

It is an understatement to say these were tumultuous times. On December 6, 1973, the Democratic Congress appointed House Minority Leader Gerald R. Ford to be vice president. Widespread unhappiness ignited by the Agnew and Watergate scandals, fueled by the Vietnam War, gave rise to marching in the streets and riots that closed all bridges leading into Washington DC. Making matters worse, the economy was floundering, bludgeoned by an oil crisis. Labor costs were rising, federal revenues were falling, inflation was at double digits, and interest rates were soaring.

A few weeks later Bob Bork, in his role as acting attorney general, called me urging me to come. He said that he stayed on after the resignations of Richardson and Ruckelshaus to hold the Department of Justice together. In response to his urging, I did come to Washington in January to meet with Senator Saxbe, whom President Nixon had just appointed attorney general. I will never forget that meeting. After we spoke for about ten minutes about how he was managing the various divisions in the Department of Justice and the current political challenges, I asked him whether I would have the authority to hire people I thought best suited to work in the civil division. His response was "Mrs. Hills, is it your intention to hire only women?" I was amazed. I then asked him who was going to be his deputy attorney general, and he said Larry Silberman, a respected Washington lawyer. I asked if he would mind if I spoke with Larry before I firmly committed. He had no objection, so I contacted Larry. Looking back, it was Bob Bork and Larry Silverman who persuaded me to come to Washington.

I took over as assistant attorney general in charge of the civil division in February 1974. I brought in as my deputy Richard Lavine, who had headed the civil division in Los Angeles in 1959–61, when I was an assistant US attorney, which was my first job after graduating from Yale Law School. We had a superb team with plenty to do. The Department of Justice's civil division handles all the civil trial work involving the federal government, including the president, the cabinet, and all of the departments and agencies. Existing turmoil generated some profound constitutional questions, arising out of the Nixon tapes, the oil tariff litigation, legal actions arising out of the May Day Riots, and about 43,000 other fascinating lawsuits.

On August 8, 1974, roughly six months after I came to the civil division, President Nixon, under threat of impeachment, stepped down, and Vice President Ford, a distinguished graduate of the Yale Law School, became president. Early one Saturday morning in February 1975, as Rod and I were planning to take our children to the zoo, the telephone rang. I answered and was told that the president would like to see me that morning. When I walked into the Oval Office, President Ford said that he was rearranging his cabinet, and had asked Jim Lynn, then secretary of Housing and Urban Development, to head to the Office of Management and Budget. He said he would like me to become secretary of HUD. My response was "I am honored by your suggestion, Mr. President, but I am not an urbanologist." His response was "What I need most at HUD is a manager."

He mentioned that the first piece of legislation that he had signed as president was the Housing and Community Development Act of 1974 which created block grants to replace more costly and inefficient categorical grants. He recognized that communities across our nation, and their needs, differ. As he put it, "Often Washington does not know best; what Phoenix needs may not be what Newark needs." It is tough to decline a president's request, and I agreed to move to HUD whenever he said. The White House sent my nomination to the Senate promptly and the Finance Committee voted to confirm my appointment on March

5, 1975, with Chairman Proxmire recording a "nay" vote because I was not an urbanologist!

When I arrived at HUD, I knew I would have to testify in roughly ten days on its 1976 budget. At that time, the federal budget year ran from July 1 to June 30. I also knew that I would be asked to report on what had been accomplished under the new Housing and Community Development Act. I immediately called a senior staff meeting to bring me up to date. The questions I put to my assembled team was "How many units of housing have we supported under the new program in fiscal year 1974–1975, and how many units do we think we can support in fiscal year 1975–1976?"

There was silence. Pressing both questions, it was clear that the answer for the current fiscal year was zero. Why? Because the regulations for the Housing and Community Development Act of 1974 that President Ford signed the previous August had not been drafted, and here we were halfway through March. Even if we could draft the regulations quickly, we were required under the Administrative Procedures Act to put the draft out for a sixty-day public comment period. Then we had to assimilate and consider the comments before finalizing the regulations that would govern implementation of the act. Frankly, I was shocked. Suddenly it dawned on me that that I would have the "pleasure" of testifying in a matter of days before the Senate Finance Committee that contrary to the department's earlier projections of supporting 500,000 units of housing in the first year under the new act, we would not be supporting any. At the hearing, which was not easy, I did just that. However I was quick to add that in the upcoming fiscal year, members could count on the fact that HUD would support 500,000 units, which we did.

To ensure that we met our stated goal, I called in the ten regional managers from offices across the country to hear directly from them their respective projections. As we got into the conversation, I asked each to state how many employees they had and how many units did they think they could deliver. If a regional administrator in an office with fewer employees stated that he/she could deliver more units, I suggested that it might make sense to reallocate our resources to those that could do more with less. It worked. We not only met, but also exceeded our goal that next fiscal year.

That experience reminded me of my initial conversation with President Ford saying that he needed a manager at HUD. As a result of his twenty-four years in Congress, his long service on the House Appropriations Committee, and nearly a decade as House Minority leader, he knew what the federal government could do well, and what it could not do. He opposed federal spending that was ineffective, recognizing that inflation could destroy the American dream for average working Americans. In his first State of the Union address, he told Congress (controlled by Democratic majorities in both the Senate and the House) that he would veto bills promoting excessive spending. And this he did—sixty-six times. Remarkably, fifty-four of his vetoes were sustained, giving evidence not only of the correctness of his decision, but also of the respect and trust he had built over the years on both sides of the political aisle.

I recall one bill in particular—the Emergency Middle Income Housing Act—introduced in the House in March of 1975. The bill authorized the Secretary of Housing to make periodic interest reduction payments that would limit the homeowner's mortgage interest payments to 6 percent. The costs of this bill were huge— as was its popularity—for the benefits were spread broadly. President Ford immediately saw that the bill, which was not focused on our lowest income population, went much further than necessary and was wasteful. He wanted to help Americans in real need. But with the economy in bad shape he did not want to take action that would shrink the economy and thus their opportunities, under the guise of trying to help.

When it came to making the decision, he did not hesitate. He vetoed the bill on June 24. The motion to override the veto was defeated the very next day. Respected leaders like Lud Ashley, a Democrat, who called the bill that had been sent to the president "a turkey that will not fly," helped to draft a more realistic approach.

On July 1, 1975, one week after the veto, Congress presented, and the following day President Ford signed in a Rose Garden ceremony the Emergency Homeowners' Relief Act. This legislation, unlike its predecessor focused on the homeowners who had lost their jobs, authorized payments to stop foreclosures that were underway, and expressly provided for an end to the program in one year.

Time and time again President Ford, who believed that our nation must live within its means, took action to help stabilize the economy, and he brought Congress along. He did so not as a result of promises and oratory, but because of the confidence and trust he engendered in all members—Democratic as well as Republican. His knowledge of government and dedication to find the right answers was the foundation for that trust. I have vivid memories of his willingness and capacity to debate issues openly and to reach decisions expeditiously. He personally heard appeals of his cabinet secretaries seeking to reverse a budget recommendation of the Office of Management and Budget. Participating in those sessions on more than one occasion, I witnessed his extraordinary grasp of the substance of the issues—how one program related to another, the objectives, the trade-offs, and the costs.

I also watched him brief the press on the budget of every department and agency of government in January 1976. I believe he is the only president in modern times to have done so. He began by saying:

> The combination of tax and spending programs I propose will set us on a course that not only leads to a balanced budget within three years but also improves the prospects for the economy to stay on a growth path that we can sustain. This is not a quick fix. It does not hold out the hollow promises that we can wipe out inflation and unemployment overnight. Instead it is an honest realistic policy; a policy that says we can steadily reduce inflation and unemployment if we maintain a prudent, balanced approach.

He then took questions about every department and agency for more than an hour. My heart was in my mouth, but it needn't have been. He did a superb job—displaying a knowledge about our government that was breathtaking.

He constantly looked for ways to improve our nation's well-being not only domestically but also internationally, for he believed that opening commercial opportunities beyond our borders would contribute to our economic growth and that establishing economic bonds internationally would help resolve strategic issues. As he said in a speech in 1974: "We live in an interdependent world, and therefore, must work together to resolve common economic problems." He signed the Trade Act of 1974, which sought to promote an "open, nondiscriminatory, and fair world economic system ... to foster the economic growth of, and full employment in the United States." The act set forth procedures, initially called "fast track" and now called "Trade Promotion Authority," for approving trade agreements that exist today.

President Ford understood that under our Constitution where power is divided with the executive branch having authority to negotiate with foreign governments and Congress having authority over commercial matters like tariffs and taxes, we needed a compact between the two branches if we were to secure good trade agreements. Under Trade Promotion Authority, the president is required to give Congress notice of the intent to negotiate a particular trade agreement and the objectives sought. Congress can vote to prohibit the proposed negotiation, but once it agrees, when the agreement is presented, it must vote for or against it, without amendments. Without this compact, a single amendment could kill a deal struck after years of negotiation.

His decisions domestic and international were guided by principles—not polls or politics. Honest, open, unassuming and thoroughly competent, he restored balance to the executive branch and dignity to the office that had been labeled "the Imperial Presidency." He was willing to make unpopular decisions like:

- Granting amnesty to those who sought to escape service to Vietnam
- Pardoning Richard Nixon
- Signing the Helsinki Accords

He knew at the time, and said so, that these decisions were unpopular and would likely cost him politically, which turned out to be true. But his decisions were motivated by what he thought was right and just for our nation, not by what was popular at the time. He firmly believed that we must look forward focusing on current and future challenges, and not be distracted quarreling over past problems.

For an appointed president with a minority party serving the nation in such troubled times to set any policy in a twenty-nine-month period would have been remarkable. But he not only set policy, he put his mark on our government. He led us out of the worst recession our nation had suffered since the Great Depression, and as a result of his sound policy choices we were able to create three million jobs, cut inflation from double digits to below 5 percent, and increase our GDP by $200 billion.

A little more than a decade later another Yale graduate, Vice President George H. W. Bush, became president and was guided by those same principles. He brought to the Oval Office his rich experience in Congress, as ambassador to the United Nations, as our representative in China, as head of the CIA, and as vice president, accumulating knowledge and building relationships that he put to the service our country. His experience and wisdom helped to end the Cold War.

In November 1988, shortly after the election, I received a telephone call from Craig Fuller, chief of staff to Vice President and President-Elect Bush asking if I could stop by the vice president's office that afternoon. I agreed, having no idea what he had in mind. When I got there we had a great talk about world affairs in general, and then he said that he would like me to join his administration as US trade representative. I was surprised. I was practicing law focused on antitrust and some international issues. But as we talked about the challenges facing the world and our nation, I was intrigued and told him that I would be honored.

Shortly after our discussion and before his inauguration, he gave a reception at the vice president's house to which he invited those whom he had invited to take a role in his administration.

One guest was Clayton Yeutter, who was then serving as US trade representative. The vice president said to me as he laughed: "I want Clayton to take the position of secretary of agriculture, but he has not agreed to do so. See if you can talk him into it, and I will see how good a negotiator you are!" I went over to talk to Clayton, whom I did not know well. I told him I hoped he would take on the role of secretary of agriculture. He said he thought he would do so. Not only did that please the then vice president, it was a gift from heaven to me. Every department has responsibilities that affect the interests of specific groups and tries to respond to those groups' wishes to the extent possible. Commerce is concerned with heavy industry, Treasury is primarily concerned with the financial sector, and Agriculture with the farm community. To have Clayton, who was extremely well informed on trade issues and a stellar diplomat, head of the Department of Agriculture was an enormous plus. He came from Nebraska and was well liked by the farm community, which in those days was neither pro trade nor in favor of opening markets. We became solid partners and fast friends.

President Bush was strongly for opening global markets. He had a vision about how nations of the world could and should work more constructively together. He understood that our economic growth and prosperity were increasingly tied to commercial opportunities beyond our borders. In his words: "We don't want an America that is closed to the world. What we want is a world that is open to America." Since the end of World War II, the United States, whether under a Democratic or Republican administration, had been a leader seeking to open global markets in the belief that the free flow of goods and service, capital, and ideas would benefit all nations. America led in constructing the General Agreement and Tariffs and Trade (the GATT) signed by twenty-three nations in 1947. The steady opening of global markets over the next seventy years added substantially to our GDP. According to calculations by the Peterson Institute for International Economics, the opening of global markets since 1950 has increased America's GDP by more than $1 trillion. Our allies also benefited, and our trade helped create the economic bonds that contributed to global stability. But it is not only industrialized nations that benefited. According to studies conducted by Dr. William Cline, an economist at the Peterson Institute, a 1 percent increase in a poor country's trade reduces its poverty by an equivalent percentage. And helping poor countries advance economically through trade is not only an efficient development tool, it creates customers for tomorrow and enhances security, for too often countries in poverty cannot seal their borders or enforce their laws, and become havens for international crime.

The Bush administration had an ambitious trade agenda that included the Uruguay Round, the eighth round of trade talks that had been launched in 1986 to improve and update the GATT which then had 125 members. The GATT dealt primarily with tariffs. Our goal in the Uruguay Round was not only to further reduce tariffs but also to create global rules to govern trade involving agriculture, services, investment, and intellectual property. We also sought to pry open Japan's retail sector and to reduce its barriers covering procurement, telecommunications, semiconductors, construction, and computers using sections 301 and Special 301 of the US Trade Act of 1974 signed into law by President Ford. And we initiated a new approach called the Structural Impediments Initiative, which sought and succeeded in removing the oligopolistic measures that restricted outside parties from participating in a number of economic sectors. In addition, we signed a number of agreements covering investment, taxes, and specific sectors with the newly independent states of the former Soviet Union as well as with Russia. An integral part of our policy was to encourage the transition of command economic systems to market economies aimed at creating more normal trade and investment relationships.

Most remembered today is President Bush's launch of negotiations of the North American Free Trade Agreement. He had a long-term vision of free trade from "the tip of Alaska to the tip of Argentina," and he believed that President Carlos Salinas was courageously moving to improve Mexico's economy and could serve as a model for the rest of Latin America. Mexico had made substantial progress since joining the GATT in 1986. Serious conversations about the possibility began in 1990 at Davos when Jaime Serra Puche, Mexico's commerce minister, who was there with President Salinas, raised with me the possibility of initiating that spring formal negotiations of a bilateral free trade agreement. He said that his government's objective was to maintain the existing momentum for its economic reform. He wanted President Salinas to make a request to launch negotiations when our two presidents were scheduled to meet on June 11.

In my weekly report to President Bush, I stated that in my view the only viable means for securing congressional approval of such an agreement was to use the "fast track" provisions contained in the 1988 Trade Act which provided for an up or down vote without amendments. To use that process we needed first to receive a formal request from Mexico to begin negotiations and second to notify Congress of our intent to move forward. However, the Congressional notification triggered a period of sixty legislative days, during which either the Senate Finance or the House Ways and Means Committees could preclude use of fast track by a simple majority vote. Several groups including agriculture and labor among others had already indicated opposition to a trade agreement with Mexico. Other groups worried that it would take our eye off the Uruguay Round negotiations that had nearly collapsed. And I believed that Congress would resist unless the president and members of his cabinet engaged in intensive consultations with them and the private sector. My view was that we needed more time to consult and to lay the necessary groundwork for the negotiations, and I suggested that in June the two presidents simply issue a joint statement that both nations would benefit from a comprehensive bilateral free trade agreement and direct their trade minister to initiate the preparatory work and consultations and report back before the two presidents met again in December. President Bush agreed.

When the two presidents met June 10–11, in accordance with plan they strongly endorsed a comprehensive bilateral free trade agreement between Mexico and the United States, and directed their trade ministers to begin the "preparatory work." Jaime Serra and I met to talk about our "preparatory plans." I met with key members of Congress to figure out whether or not we might proceed in August. Chairman Rostenkowski and Representative Archer of the House Ways and Means Committee expressed concerns that an August notification would distract attention from the Uruguay Round during the crucial autumn months, but said they would leave the decision on timing up to the administration. Senator Bentsen, chairman of the Finance Committee, also said that he would leave the timing up to the administration, and Senator Packwood said he supported early initiation. All strongly agreed that notification should occur when both houses of Congress were back in session in September.

As soon as word started circulating regarding the possibilities of a negotiations, I was contacted by John Crosbie, then trade minister of Canada, stating that Canada wanted to join the negotiations. I was frankly surprised. Canada's Liberal Party and its New Democratic party had strongly opposed the US-Canada Free Trade Agreement that was signed January 2, 1988, and their opposition almost brought down Prime Minister Mulroney's Progressive government. I said: "John are you sure you want to go through that ordeal again?" He said "We do not want to be left out." Over the Labor Day holiday, Prime Minister Mulroney was a house guest of President Bush at Kennebunkport and made it clear that he wanted Canada to join the negotiations. After discussions with the president, I talked with Jaime Serra about Canada joining the negotiations. We were both concerned that politics could again erupt in Canada, forcing it to pull out with the possibility of killing ongoing negotiations. To cover that possibility in September 1990 we three trade ministers—John Crosbie, Jaime Serra, and I—arranged to have dinner in New York, after which we issued a press release acknowledging that the three governments were planning to move ahead with negotiations of free trade agreement for North America and stating without singling out Canada "that if any one of the three participants pulled out of the negotiations, the other two would proceed."

President Salinas in accordance with the plan delayed his formal letter proposing negotiations from June 11 until August 21 and President Bush responded on September 25 to his letter noting that Canada had expressed a desire to participate. That same day President Bush sent notice to the chairmen of the Senate Finance and the House Ways and Means Committees regarding President Salinas's request (at that time we did not have a formal request from Canada) which started the sixty legislative day fast-track clock ticking on the bilateral negotiation. We figured our September notification would not affect the timing of negotiations since there were relatively few legislative days remaining in the year. And we believed that it could be argued that the sixty-day clock needed to be restarted in January with the beginning of the new Congress. We did not want or need a debate on process. We knew we would face considerable debate on content.

On February 5, 1991, Presidents Bush and Salinas along with Canadian Prime Minister Brian Mulroney announced their joint intention to seek a North American Free Trade Agreement, and on that date President Bush advised the chairmen of the House Ways and Means and the Senate Finance Committees of his desire to begin trilateral negotiations with Mexico and Canada for a North American Free Trade Agreement (NAFTA). Both committees held public hearings on the proposed negotiations that February. On March 1, 1991, President Bush requested a two-year extension of fast-track procedures to cover the NAFTA. There was considerable debate, but the June 1, 1991, deadline for disapproval came and went, which guaranteed that fast-track procedures would be available. Later that month negotiations were formally launched in Toronto with a meeting of the three trade ministers along with members of the nineteen working groups.

Subsequent ministerial meetings were held in Seattle, Zacatecas, Chantilly, Montreal, Mexico City, Toronto, and Washington DC. In addition, a number of public hearings were held across the country. I led a delegation of twenty-six private sector representatives and eleven members of Congress to Mexico to meet with President Salinas and Jaime Serra. We were anxious to complete negotiations before our November 1992 elections. I provided President Bush with regular updates on our progress, often sharing key issues that he could raise with President Salinas when they met. Negotiations were intense. The final session took place in Washington DC with the three trade ministers, Jaime Serra, Michael Wilson who had replaced John Crosbie, and I, along with our deputies and key members of the various negotiating teams. We all committed not to leave until negotiations were completed, and at times they were heated. At one point Michael Wilson abruptly left the room upset about an issue, and from the window we saw him walking around the hotel grounds.

That persuaded me that we needed a break. I called my staff and asked whether it would be possible for me to buy tickets for that evening to whatever was playing at the Kennedy Center. The answer came back that "the Kennedy Center is dark this evening. I asked, "What is available? We need to cool things off." The response was "Why don't you consider going to Camden Yards, there is a great baseball game, and I am sure someone on one of our negotiating committees will gladly donate box seats?" The suggestion had little appeal to me, but I asked Michael and Jaime if they would like to take a break and drive up to Baltimore and see a baseball game. Michael was hugely enthusiastic; Jaime was willing. Turns out the Toronto Blue Jays, Michael's hometown team, were playing the Baltimore Orioles. So, we arranged to get the tickets. I drove up with Jaime. Michael came in a separate car. We arrived at the box, which offered an informal dinner as we watched the game. Around the fourth inning Jaime, who was a great soccer fan but definitely not a baseball fan, said to me, "Have we seen enough?" I looked at Michael who was transfixed. I said, "Jaime, absolutely not. We have not had dessert, and look, Michael is relaxed!"

So, we had dessert. As the sixth inning was underway, Jaime again asked if it was time to leave. I said, "We will go after this inning." I said to Michael, "Jaime is anxious to leave; are you ready?" Reluctantly, he said he was. We thanked our hosts, left the box, and were in the hallway when the crowd roared. People rush out screaming "Wow, a triple play! I have never seen one!" I thought Michael was going to cry. I was fearful that all the brownie points we had earned during "our break" had just then evaporated! But we returned to the negotiating table and very late on the night of August 12, following a total of fourteen days of continuous negotiations, we stood up, and shook hands having reached a deal!

President Bush signed the agreement on December 8, 1992, and President Clinton got it through Congress and signed the legislation December 8, 1993, and the agreement took effect in January 1994. The NAFTA was a first in so many ways.

- It was the first comprehensive free trade agreement to join a developing economy with highly developed economies.

- By linking the economies of Canada, Mexico, and the United States, it created a huge market, today accounting for roughly $19 trillion and 490 million consumers.

- It eliminated tariffs on all industrial products and almost all agricultural produces save for a handful with Canada.

- It was the first trade agreement to open up a broad range of services, including financial services and banking and to provide national treatment for cross-border service providers.

- It opened up the automotive, textile, and apparel markets between Mexico and the United States.

- It removed significant investment barriers, provided basic protections for North American investors, and created an effective dispute settlement mechanism to ensure investors had access to neutral, third-party arbitration in cases of disagreements with a host government.

- It was the first trade agreement to establish enforceable protection for copyright, patent, trademarks, and trade secrets.

All three economies have benefited. Today 80 percent of world trade is conducted through global supply chains, and NAF-TA has created one of the most vibrant. Specialization among the three NAFTA partners has boosted the region's productivity, making North America the most competitive region in the world. We do not simply sell to each other, we make things together. Forty percent of what the United States imports from Mexico consists of US content, and 25 percent of imports from Canada consist of US content. The equivalent figures with respect to China and Japan are 4 percent and 2 percent. Today one-third of America's global trade is with its two NAFTA partners. Canada is our top export destination and Mexico is our second. The United States sells more to Mexico than to all the rest of Latin America combined. Indeed, we sell more to Mexico than to Germany, France, the United Kingdom, and the Netherlands combined. Some 14 million US jobs depend on our commercial relationships with Canada and Mexico. In Mexico, NAFTA accelerated and locked in ongoing economic reforms that reduced its public debt, stabilized inflation, and built up its foreign reserves. Its economy is stronger. Intraregional trade is up five-fold since the NAFTA's implementation. It also incentivized new habits of cooperation to enable the three nations to take full advantage of the new economic opportunities. Today our three governments work closely together to improve security at our borders. We share intelligence to expedite the movement of legitimate travel and products so that we can concentrate on the illegitimate. Collaboration has made us more effective in responding to natural disasters and in reducing the reach of organized crime.

In addition to the substantial economic and strategic benefits the NAFTA generated for the three participants, it also set a powerful example globally, giving renewed momentum to the Uruguay Round of Multilateral Trade Negotiations that had collapsed in 1990. Within four months of the NAFTA taking effect, representatives of all of the then 125 members returned to the negotiating table, completed the Uruguay Round, incorporating many of the new provisions contained in the NAFTA, and created the World Trade Organization, our modern-day system governing international trade. President Bush 41 will be remembered for his many contributions, foreign and domestic, but the NAFTA will surely be near the top of the list.

Looking back, I was privileged to work for two presidents whose long experience in government and deep dedication to principle not only contributed greatly to the well-being of our people and globally but also provides a model for the kind of leadership America needs so it can continue to be the extraordinary nation that it has been for so many decades past.

Henry Monaghan

Equity Chow

OUR CLASS HAS BEEN VERY FORTUNATE IN having had such vigorous class agents as Joel Sprayregen and Bill Felstiner. Bill's recent invitation to us to do something for the reunion therefore came as no surprise. Nor did its content. Observing that most of us had "nonlinear" professional careers (of which he himself is a clear example), Bill invited us to describe one such "difficult, important and interesting" event in an effort to show the diversity of our careers. Perhaps, I thought, I could contribute along these lines. I could focus on some of the interesting litigation that I have had over the years, such as representing the musical *Hair* in various state and federal courts and in the Supreme Court, or in arguing before the Supreme Court against a Congressional effort to strip the court of some appellate habeas corpus jurisdiction. Or (heaven forbid!) I could describe in detail one of my law review articles that has a bearing on topics of current legal interest. But none of this would capture how I feel about my post law school career. I have been a professor almost all my life, teaching classes, writing articles, reading books and articles about law, history, philosophy, and English mysteries. With a satisfying regularity, the years have rolled along, one after the other. I go to my office every day and see my colleagues and students. I still enjoy reading judicial opinions and law review articles. My dear wife, Nancy, characterizes Columbia Law School as an "adult day care center." (Given the care I receive at the school and especially from my wonderful assistant/friend, that characterization has much to commend it.) My academic career has been an "indoors," sedentary, bookish, and linear one.

My career has also been very satisfying and one that I am happy to have lived. But I have no appetite—none—to write about that career. On the other hand, I wanted to contribute. So, for this essay (and with Bill's permission) I decided to do something different: to make some brief remarks about Yale Law School's role in placing me on my career path.

My admission to the Law School was, I am confident, the result of affirmative action. In the '50s, elite schools were very interested in first-generation immigrants, which explains the college placements of many of my high school classmates from Sacred Heart High School in Holyoke, Massachusetts. After high school, I went to the nearby and recently created junior (now community) college in Holyoke; my class was twenty-seven strong. Subsequently, I graduated from the University of Massachusetts at Amherst, which had only recently changed from an agricultural college to a budding university. My LSAT score was, shall we say, singularly undistinguished. When I arrived at Yale I had a reading vocabulary that considerably exceeded my speaking vocabulary; I had simply never heard pronounced many of the words I understood. I should also add that I had never traveled anywhere. There was neither a budget nor a culture to support such activity. My family never had a car.

This, however, is decidedly not a hardship story. Far from it. I never went hungry or lacked warm clothes. Holyoke was then a vibrant, blue-collar, heavily Catholic community; and it was the paper mill capital of America. While the quality of the education at Sacred Heart could hardly compare with that offered in the elite public and private schools, the nuns instilled in all of us a sense of self-worth not defined by the status of the colleges, if any, we would attend. And there I developed a passion for learning that exists to this moment. The parish priests were a particularly important inspiration in this respect, as were the Dominicans and Augustinians who would preach weeklong novenas to a packed church. Holyoke

Community College prepared me for further study. We met in the old wooden Holyoke High School building after the regular high school classes had ended in the early afternoon. With no faculty of its own, it was staffed by professors from Smith, Mount Holyoke, and Amherst. I got started on a pretty solid education, and I loved the time I spent there.

When I came to the Law School, I never felt any sense of alienation or of being disconnected. In retrospect, I attribute most of that to my classmates. I recall our class as being unpretentious, warm, helpful, and very supportive of one another. (I'm not sure that I would say the same for some of the current crop of Yale law students that I now encounter. They seem to possess far more sense of self-esteem.) I also think that having all or most of the unmarried students in the quad itself had a lot to do with the school's hospitable atmosphere.

Which brings me to Equity Chow! That was a little sandwich business operated by an entrepreneurial class member. It kept me in spare change and, more importantly, in all the sandwiches I could eat. I'm sure that those of you who lived in the quad will remember the basket full of sandwiches I brought around in the evening. I would arrive on each floor calling out "Equity chow! Equity chow!" And then I would proceed with a litanylike chant of "salami, bologna, ham and cheese, cream cheese and jelly, peanut butter and jelly, and tuna." I remind you that a tasty ham-and-cheese sandwich sold for twenty-five cents, and a thick P&J for twenty. I have particularly fond memories of the congenial atmosphere in the halls when I would arrive.

I came to the Law School blessed with a pretty good memory, which proved to be an important asset until the computer came along. But Yale drilled me in the indispensable supplements to memory. Begin with reading. Here, Joe Goldstein proved to be an important teacher. Joe taught me bankruptcy, which it seems fair to say, was very far from his first love. When I would ask him a question, his response would be, "What does the statute say?" What I didn't know but now suspect is that Joe's response was quite often because he didn't know what it said. Whatever the reality, however, I really learned to read statutes and other documents closely.

Next came thinking. What impressed me most and certainly made an indelible mark on me was what I learned on that subject from my classmates, particularly in the first semester contracts course. Nick Katzenbach taught the subject. When he would call on someone, the student would often begin with "I think." And I would say to myself, What does it matter what you think? Judge X of the … court said in an opinion …. Why, I thought, shouldn't we focus on that, rather than what you thought. But, of course, thinking is of overriding importance, and many of my classmates were long used to doing their own thinking. The school's emphasis on the importance of thinking for yourself was an important lesson for me.

Finally, I remember Fritz Kessler. He would ask in his German accent, "You agree with me, don't you, Mr. Moonohan," not expecting any response beyond the nod of the head. Kessler, in particular, impressed on me the importance of law. I can still remember being far more concerned about what Lord Mansfield thought than what even Justice Cardozo said about the same topic. I remain that way now.

Yale Law School provided a wonderful learning environment for me and it set me on my career path. When I started clerking, I quickly understood that I had been equipped to handle the legal problems that came to our court. The lessons I learned at Yale I try to impress on my own students. There are only five words that are important: I read and I think. And law is important, even if it is not the most important thing in the world.

Gloria Neuwirth

Life After Yale

A COMMON PHRASE I HEARD WHILE IN LAW school, from students and faculty, was, "Why are you in law school, taking the place of a man?" the implication being that I would get married, have children, become a housewife, and never practice law. This was the '50s, with its emphasis on families and domesticity. A woman's place was in the home and her role was to nurture the family, not to practice law. Well, here I am at age eighty-two, still practicing and going strong. I did get married and have a family, all of which affected my career path, but I was able to have a wonderful life and fulfilling career.

During my third year in law school, like my classmates I went to interviews for jobs with law firms, but I was greatly discouraged. I was told directly by several interviewers: "We don't hire women." One firm recruiter followed that by saying, "You're a pretty girl; come in if you would like to talk." But it was clear that no job offer would follow.

One job I wanted was working for the New York City Bar Association, but when I interviewed for it I was told they would not hire me because there were evening meetings. Others did not interview me at all. It was depressing to see my male classmates being offered their choice of jobs while I, who was open to any area, including public service, was not even considered for any job, although we had the same qualifications. The other women in my class were similarly affected. Only one woman, in the class before us, landed "a Wall Street job."

I finally obtained a position, working on a joint research project of Columbia University Law School and the New York City Bar Association dealing with the issue of court calendar congestion, especially as a result of automobile accident litigation. Roger Hunting, the man who hired me, was a great boss. He respected my ideas and contributions and gave me a lot of freedom in the work. Together we wrote a report which was published as a book: *Who Sues in New York City: A Study of Automobile Accident Claims.* This was a basis for the no-fault legislation in New York which is still in effect.

After this work was done, I concentrated on raising my family of four children, doing intermittent research work on a number of cases dealing with church mergers, some of which went up to the Supreme Court. I also became active in the community, my children's school, and charitable organizations. I saw the large pool of women who were smart and willing to work, and I tried in the 1960s to start a part-time legal agency to make use of all that talent, but it didn't get off the ground. The law firms weren't interested. I still think there could be more room for this kind of arrangement.

It is now sixty years later, and I still see the same pattern—lots of educated and talented women who want to be productive in the workforce but are handicapped because of the lack of "work-life balance." A person who wants to have a satisfying life cannot meet a firm's demand of recording 2,000 or more billable hours a year while at the same time having primary responsibility for raising a family. As we know from studies, women are still carrying the larger burdens of care for children and elderly parents and household work. There are some changes in the upcoming generations, but they are developing slowly.

Sheryl Sandberg, in her book *Lean In,* has a chapter titled "Make Your Partner A Real Partner." It is a nice concept in theory, but it is not the current practice for most couples, and it ignores the fact that many women do not have partners and are functioning alone.

Our society is way behind many other developed nations that provide varied opportunities for child care, so that women can work outside the home if they choose to do so or in many cases if they need to do so. If we would attend to childcare needs, it would be a positive contribution to society as well as to the legal profession.

When my youngest child was five years old I was able to find a part-time job, and that gradually became full time. I worked with a solo practitioner, who subsequently made me his partner. As is commonly known, partnership compensation is erratic, going up and down from year to year. When my divorce hit me, I needed a steady salary, so I joined a large New York firm. As the oldest associate, and as an attorney with not much business, I didn't fit in. Also, I was used to doing a lot of pro-bono work, which the firm did not appreciate. There was no way I could put in the number of billable hours the firm wanted, so they fired me.

In retrospect, being fired was a good thing because it enabled me to follow my own path. I went back to my old partner, and together we built a solid, profitable firm, working on our own terms. When my partner died, I continued on my own as a solo practitioner. I missed the synergy and sharing of knowledge as well the camaraderie of working with others, and I wanted to protect my clients in case I was not available, so I joined another firm.

In the new firm, which was male-dominated, I was treated like a junior associate, though I was as knowledgeable as most of my colleagues. I had published several articles, and I was a member of the Executive Committee of the New York State Bar Association Trusts and Estates Section. I often did not speak up when I should have. This was partly because of the firm culture, though I admit it was also because of my own background and training that inculcated in me that I should not be assertive. On two occasions elderly male clients turned me down because they wanted a male attorney. This was a blow to my ego, though I understood the culture these men were coming from. I am pleased to report that I now have no hesitation in speaking up and expressing my opinions. I believe that my generation of women have come around to this liberated stance, and I know that the younger women are much freer in their expressiveness, although they are also put down and dismissed in the ways that we were.

I went back out on my own, but eventually I joined my current firm, where I have now been for twenty-two years. I believe that this size (twenty lawyers) is perfect for me. We all know, like, and respect each other, and it is a pleasure to go in to work in the morning. We share a similar philosophical approach—we work hard and take our practice seriously; we also care about and spend time with and for our families and contribute to our community. The entire firm concentrates on trusts and estates and not-for-profit organizations, so we understand each other's work and are able to provide mutual support.

Practicing in trusts and estates is very special and extremely satisfying. There are two main components. First are the complications of working your way around the Internal Revenue code and regulations, solving problems and putting the pieces together like a jigsaw puzzle. Second, and even more fascinating, are the ways in which you learn of and get involved with the most intimate and personal issues that people face. Families are each unique and complex, and working through the issues to achieve optimal planning for varied individuals has been most rewarding. I believe it is among the most gratifying areas of law, and I am proud to have been the agent to achieve optimal results for many clients.

This work has carried into my personal life, in that I believe I have become more attuned to the trials and tribulations of friends and people in my family, close and extended, and become more positive, understanding, and empathetic.

In 2007 I took a leave of absence for several months and served as a senior lawyer of the Center for International Legal Studies. I was assigned to teach United States constitutional law at the University of Pecs, in Hungary. I had studied "con law" at Yale, but that had been almost forty years before, and much had changed. It was a challenge to get up to date, understand the complex issues. and prepare a series of lectures explaining the US constitutional structure and current cases. Unlike in the US, the law school classes in Hungary were almost exclusively presented by the professor, with minimal student participation. In the end, it was well worth the effort and I was rewarded with positive student feedback.

Over the years I have become increasingly involved in combating discrimination and oppression of women around the world. I do pro-bono work for Donor Direct Action (donordirectaction. org), an international organization that directly provides support of women's rights organizations in the Congo, Somalia, Afghanistan, and other countries around the world. Last year I had the opportunity to go and review the frontline work of MARTA, one of these organizations working to end violence against women in Latvia (donordirectaction.org/marta).

Here in the US I have become increasingly convinced of the need for passage and ratification of the Equal Rights Amendment to the Constitution and I am supporting efforts to that end as well (eracoalition.org). The ERA would strengthen protections against pregnancy discrimination, gender-based violence, and other forms of sex discrimination, and would provide the basis for a real guarantee of equal rights to women and men.

Yale Law School encouraged and empowered me to do all this, and I am extraordinarily grateful for having had the opportunity to make my small contributions.

BURTON RAFFEL

A Writer on Writing

OST WRITERS ARE NOT, AT AGE EIGHTY-FIVE, both creating and even sometimes publishing books at the rate of two and three a year. Most writers are not graced, even if they reach seventy-five, with the opportunity to reflect upon their lives and careers. To my knowledge, no writer has ever done what Stanley Kunitz did, namely, writing superbly at age ninety-five! But I am grateful for the opportunity to do what I am doing: as I say quite frequently, these days, "I intend to live forever—until further notice."

If I am at least somewhat calmer than I have been, and a good deal less anxious about literary reputation, it is in part because I have been fortunate enough to mellow with time. That is by no means inevitable: writers, like other people, can grow more rather than less harried as they age. My relative serenity is not, however, the symptom of a graceful decline toward the grave. I have been fortunate in a good many ways that go far beyond mere survival.

I have been blessed, in my third marriage, with a wonderfully unusual lifetime partner. Elizabeth has long since become my first reader and most trusted critic, as I was for her when she was still writing novels. Over the years, her judgments have become more complex and subtle, giving me a numerical ranking for poems in manuscript. When she says, "This is good," I immediately ask, "But is it a 1 [her highest ranking]?" If she hesitates, I know I have at best an incomplete poem, at worst a dead loser. By now, indeed, that happens less often. And I, for my part, write fewer poems destined for the trash. I make no future predictions. As a literary phenomenon—and if I am not literary, I am nothing whatever—a change in inner perspective has produced major changes in how I work, and in my focus. I have finally been able to acknowledge that there has to be some reason, even some good reason, why my translations (there will now be no more of them) have found a readier market than my original work.

Though I have recently ended my long teaching career, I had also discovered a new kind of "teaching," one that crystallizes aspects of my lifelong interest in languages, linguistics, and translation. This is a series of fourteen fully annotated editions of Shakespeare's major plays, aimed at—for, believe it or not, the first time—making Shakespeare's dramas fully accessible to a wide readership, from high school to graduate school levels. The process of annotation, in this extremely comprehensive fashion, involved a sustained effort to satisfy every conceivable textual need, from definitions of words to explications of syntax, metaphor, prosody, and (of course) every reference not immediately clear to the general reader. Preparing these volumes was an immense amount of work, but also great fun, in considerable part because this is Shakespeare, and other than Dante he is the greatest writer I (or you) have ever encountered (unless you can read Homer in his language). The series is called The Annotated Shakespeare; it is published by Yale University Press.

My literary ambitions have not, I think, seriously shifted. Their expressions may appear to register a change, but appearances can be deceiving. What has happened, it seems to me, is that I have become a good deal more accepting ("less anxious," as I phrased it at the start of this autobiographical update) of my literary reputation, whatever it is and whatever it is not. For far too long I thought in terms of what it "ought" to be. I now think much less about the whole question. A younger friend of ours, a visual artist, asked the other night what I felt, looking back at what has come to be rather a long life. Did I feel differently about what has been? Did I view events and people and myself differently, and in what ways? "I

see my life," I replied, "with a much greater sense of amplitude."
What I meant by that, I explained, was that I retrospectively see
my life, and of course, the literary career which is so basic to that
life, in larger blocks of both time and significance. "There comes
to be a visible pattern," I said. "You start to see that in a very real
way there are no 'accidents,' no aimless happenings. You see that
what you did was what you were meant to do, for either better or
worse—and in a realistic sense there is no 'better' and no 'worse.'
It was, it is, and you are, and that's that."

Thus, my flight from New York City, in the early 1960s, having
been astonished and horrified by the "literary life" as it was and
still is lived there, was not only what I ought to have expected of
myself, but also had consequences that I should have expected.
But I did not. Cutting myself off from a "scene" in which I had
begun to experience some "success," but for all that in a social
context which I seriously and quite properly feared for my inner
and as a result my artistic development, necessarily removed me
from much fundamental success-making machinery. In a word, I
wanted to have my "purity" and the "cake" I might have had, had
I stayed in New York to see it baked and then to eat it. Things simply don't work like that, and now I know it and am quite at peace
both with the knowledge and the fact.

Let me give a more concrete example of what I mean. I have
just finished reading a novel, published a dozen or so years ago,
by a reasonably well-known poet. It is a fascinating book, but
definitely not a good one; its interest lies in what seem to be the
authentic and probably autobiographical details of the writer's
life. No commercial (trade) publisher would touch such a book,
clumsily, at times ineptly written, with what would seem to most
readers a tedium of first-this-very-particular-stuff-happened and
then-that-very particular-stuff-happened. A small nonprofit publisher brought out the book, with the aid of many subsidies and
grants. I doubt that sales amounted to much. Now: I would have
read the book, once, with great vexation. "This is so much worse
than the novels I cannot get into print, which proves yet again
the utter corruption of the whole system," etc., etc. The book in

question is indeed worse than any of my outpourings of fiction. So what? Where is it inscribed, on the tablets of Literary (or any other) Destiny, that the sole and invariably determinative component of "success" is merit? And what in the hell is "success," anyway?

I remain ambitious. Nobody could work as I work, in what have always been extended bouts of intense frenzy, without being ambitious. Plenty of first-class writers come to nothing, not being able (or not having the sustaining determination, or even the interest) to drive themselves as I do and have always done. It does not make me better, to whip myself on. It just makes me, as it always has, a lot more productive.

Does being more productive make me happier? In some profound inner sense, obviously it must, or I would have stopped a long time ago. But in another perspective, the very question is irrelevant—as are whatever may be the results of my ambition. Again, I can see that irrelevance very clearly, today, but was wholly blind to it, before. What difference does it make, in the larger or smaller universe, whether I become, say, a Nobel Prize winner (as I will not) or a footnote (as I may very well, but only if I am lucky)? All we can do, we human beings, is live our lives, and live them as best we can. Some years ago, I told my students that if I learned I would die in six months, I would want to be living my life in such a fashion that I would nod, calmly, and continue doing what I was doing (probably writing). And, when it was all over, so be it. I like recognition; I relish applause. But I do not need either of them.

Since my formal retirement from teaching at seventy-five (caused by my physical problems: diabetes, severe hypoglycemia, and both rheumatoid and osteoarthritis), I have been able to maintain a more or less uninterrupted writing schedule. Now that I no longer have to expend enormous chunks of time on class preparation—reading, meeting with students, and grading and guiding graduate students—I spend half a dozen hours a day at the computer. For me, teaching itself was in large part a performance art, physically strenuous and even of the athletic. At the same time, South Louisiana's mainly beneficent climate lets me devote the later afternoon to creating what has become a kind of formal garden. It has an extended brick patio that I fashioned brick by brick. In addition to the plants, it has decorative vases, statues, and bas-reliefs. I find that sculpting shrubs and carting rocks not only deepens serenity but allows my mind to chew unobtrusively, even unconsciously, through possible new writing projects, which then "surface" in much clearer and more immediately workable form. I have always written novels this way, staging scenes, then restaging them, then restaging them again, sometimes a dozen times before I finally write them. I swim half an hour a day, every day, the year round, in my small heated pool. It enables me, very consciously, to work at anything from poems (which tend to write themselves in the rhythms of waterborne motion) to, not surprisingly, this autobiographical update, which you are now reading. Asked what I thought about this or that topic when I was younger, I would often say, "I don't know: I haven't said anything about it, and I never know what I think until I've spoken." But now I say, "It does not matter much what I think, but only what I do. And what I do, I can do better if I have been able to rehearse my approach to that 'doing.'" I can do that best, these days, when I am not at my computer, but mowing the lawn or replanting, or only sitting outside and watching squirrels and birds and the wonderfully tall trees all around me.

I am no longer even as social as I once was, which is not perhaps saying much. I have tended to be a loner and even at times a hermit of sorts. I maintained a fairly decent-size correspondence, until virtually all my friends, scattered all over, began turning up either dead or disconnected. I see very few friends, exchange emails with not many more, and with the best friends of all can a few times still exchange long telephone conversations—all of which are as sustaining as the books I read, the music I listen to. When my arthritis allows, and for the ten or twelve minutes it grants me, I make noises on the piano.

I lead a good life, I have led a good life. I have no interest in leaving it, as sooner or later I must. I most determinedly intend to write until there is nothing at all that I can do, which to me must be the state of nonbeing we call death. Not only does death not frighten me, but it also does not much concern me. I live for being alive, and for the writing I do. I will die when I die.

A NOTE FROM ELIZABETH RAFFEL

Burton wrote this reflection on his life in 2013, some months before he was diagnosed with a degenerative disease. He died September 29, 2015, at 87. This chapter addresses one of his greatest challenges: failing to achieve a literary reputation for his fiction and poetry, but his fiction in particular. He was proud of his success with the many translations for which he is known, and yet he believed the other would have meant more.

RICHARD RAVITCH

Becoming Lieutenant Governor

O N JULY 3, 2009, I WAS ON VACATION ON LONG Island with my family, preoccupied with nothing more momentous than the question of whether to go sailing or play golf, when I got a call from Charles O'Byrne. He had been David Paterson's chief of staff and remained the governor's closest political confidant. It was O'Byrne, at Paterson's behest, who had asked me to head the citizens' commission on the Metropolitan Transport Authority in 2008. O'Byrne arrived soon after the call and, without preliminaries, told me what the great urgency was: if Governor Paterson asked, would I take the job of lieutenant governor of the State of New York?

I was both flattered and flabbergasted; I hadn't held a major state government post in more than twenty-five years. During that time, Mario Cuomo had finished twelve years as governor. In 1994 he lost the governorship to a Republican, George Pataki, who served another twelve years. In the 2006, election, Democrats Eliot Spitzer and David Paterson were elected governor and lieutenant governor in the usual way; on the same ticket.

Spitzer had been the state's aggressive attorney general; with his election as governor, he began to be talked about as a contender for the Democratic presidential nomination. Paterson had

* An earlier version of this chapter was published in *R. Ravitch, So Much to Do,* PublicAffairs, New York, 2014.

been a state senator for twenty years, occupying the seat once held by his father, the legendary Harlem politician Basil Paterson. New York political observers looked forward to another long stretch of years marked by a governor who was a strong political force and a lieutenant governor who was marginal to the business of running the state.

But this more or less orderly pattern of New York gubernatorial politics was interrupted not much more than a year after Spitzer took office on March 17, 2007, when the governor resigned in disgrace after having been identified by federal investigators as a client of a prostitution ring. David Paterson succeeded to the governorship.

The post of New York lieutenant governor became vacant.

But that didn't explain why O'Byrne was asking whether I was willing to be appointed to the job. The New York lieutenant governor was an elected official. Normally, if the post was vacant, the majority leader of the State Senate would take over the lieutenant governor's duties until the position was filled by election again. But these weren't normal times in New York. For one thing, the state was in a fiscal meltdown stemming from a national economic downturn and years of imprudent budget practices. Even more explosively, since June 8 the State Senate had been deadlocked, evenly divided between Democrats and Republicans—which would have been bad enough—and paralyzed by lawsuits, lockdowns, and mutual accusations of double-dealing and corruption. The crisis was precipitated when four Democratic state senators temporarily defected to the Republican side. Three of them would later end up in jail, convicted of offenses ranging from assault to embezzlement.

One result of the crisis was that Governor Paterson was unable to travel outside New York State, because if he did so the president pro tem of the Senate was supposed to serve as acting governor. But the competing factions in the Senate were making different claims about just who the president pro tem was. The possible disasters in legislation and governance were limited only by the imagination.

O'Byrne said the governor's lawyers had concluded that while it wasn't a sure bet, Paterson probably had the authority to appoint someone to the lieutenant governor's post for the remaining year-and-a-half of his term. Moreover, there were reasons why Paterson wanted me to be that someone. First, people knew I didn't aspire to elective office, so I wasn't likely to be seen as a threat to any elected official beyond Paterson's term. Next, I was a Democrat but had a reputation for not being a down-the-line partisan. Finally, I had played a role in overcoming a succession of New York financial crises, and there was no doubt that the state was now facing one of them. Paterson said he needed my fiscal expertise.

I was intrigued, but some questions had to be answered. Did I have any conflicts of interest on account of my business dealings and board memberships? What would my colleagues in these enterprises, for-profit and nonprofit, say about the added burdens that would fall on them if I took the job? What would my wife, Kathy, think of my spending substantial amounts of time in Albany, 140 miles and a cultural world away from New York City?

O'Byrne said the governor's counsel, Peter Kiernan, was standing by to help answer at least some of those questions. He explained the issues that had to be addressed, adding that if I was seriously considering the governor's offer, I should retain my own counsel.

Kathy knew what it would mean to me to be able to serve in this situation; she was totally supportive. I called my business and nonbusiness colleagues. They, too, were encouraging. I asked my friend and neighbor Matthew Mallow, then a partner at Skadden Arps, to begin studying the conflict-of-interest issues. A few days later, Paterson himself called, and I told him that if I had no conflicts, I would take the job. With Matt and Peter's help, I concluded that there were none. On July 6, I told the governor I would accept.

The next evening, my birthday, Kathy and I were meeting Joe and Hilary Califano for dinner at Peter Luger, the famous Brooklyn steak house. Leaving Manhattan in the car, I heard that Paterson was on television announcing my appointment. I knew the press calls were about to start. But the first call wasn't from a journalist. Kiernan called to say he had learned that the Republicans were hunting for a state court judge who would grant an after-hours injunction against my taking office. Because of the deadlock in the Senate and the issues it raised about gubernatorial succession, the governor wanted me to be sworn in before the litigation began. Kiernan and I should sign the oath of office immediately. With any luck, the secretary of state in Albany could then certify it before a judge could act.

Matt arranged for a notary to get into a taxi to Brooklyn. By the time the notary arrived at Peter Luger, our dinner order was on the table. So I signed the oath amid the steak, tomatoes, and creamed spinach. The document was driven by taxi straight from the table to Albany, where it was duly certified and filed—just one hour before lawyers for the State Senate's Republican majority leader, joined by one of the defecting Democrats, found a Long Island judge and persuaded him to issue a temporary retaining order.

The governor got ready to appeal the court's order. Under normal circumstances, the state's attorney general would have argued the governor's case. But, as with so much else at this time, the circumstances were not normal. When the state's attorney general, Andrew Cuomo, son of the former governor, heard that Paterson might appoint his own lieutenant governor, Cuomo opined that the appointment would be unconstitutional, a "political ploy that would wind through the courts for many months."

Cuomo, it turned out, miscalculated the impact that the depth of New York's political and fiscal crises would have on the state's courts. With the attorney general unwilling to make the governor's argument, Paterson retained Kathleen Sullivan, a prominent constitutional litigator, to represent him. On the one hand, New York law generally permits the governor to fill vacancies by appointment. On the other hand, a section of the state constitution provides that the president pro tem of the Senate is to "perform all the duties of lieutenant governor" during a vacancy in the lieutenant governor's office. If the president of the Senate was to "perform all the duties" of the lieutenant governor, did this mean there was no vacancy that the governor could fill? Or did it just mean that the president pro tem was supposed to pinch-hit until the governor filled the vacancy in the same way he filled many other state vacancies?

There was also a broader question: if a governor appointed a lieutenant governor to serve until the next election, would the appointment violate the general principle that the lieutenant governor should be an elected official?

The issues were abstract, almost metaphysical; but the consequences of the courts' decision would be very concrete. The lower courts ruled against the governor but called the issue "one of great import" that "ought to be resolved finally and expeditiously" and allowed the governor to appeal directly to the state's highest court, the court of appeals. On September 22, in a four to three decision, the court of appeals upheld my appointment. The majority cited the need to "assure the structural integrity and efficacy of the executive branch." I could finally take the oath of office in person. By that time, though, I had learned enough about New York's fiscal problems so that they cast a pall over the fun of winning.

The job of lieutenant governor has its share of perks. I had offices in Albany and New York City, with a highly competent administrative assistant in each. The New York State Police provided me with security and drove me, at speeds not available to civilians, between New York and Albany, New York, and Washington, or wherever I had to go.

My New York City offices were nondescript, part of the quarters that the state owned in a big office building on Third Avenue near Grand Central, the southern terminus of the Albany–New York rail route. My Albany offices, in contrast, came—literally— from another century. They were in the state capitol, a strange and magnificent structure that housed both the state's legislative branch and the highest reaches of the executive branch. The capitol had taken more than thirty years to build. It was finished just before the turn of the twentieth century and was the most expensive government building of its time.

Because the lieutenant governor presides over the State Senate, my Albany offices adjoined the Senate floor. They featured extremely high ceilings, extremely elaborate carved-wood paneling, and extremely copious gold leaf. Over time, the rooms came to seem like a metaphor for the job I held, elaborate and empty. True, my sole official function, presiding over the Senate, included the power to cast tie-breaking votes. One might have thought that the power to break ties would have made me at least a potentially important part of the legislative process, but it didn't really amount to much. For one thing, the state constitution had been interpreted to permit the lieutenant governor to break ties only on procedural matters, not substantive ones. Also, I had decided that even where I did have a tie-breaking vote, the better course would be not to cast the vote but to convene the leaders of both parties and try to work out a compromise.

As things turned out, even the hypothetical tie-breaking situations soon became, in practical terms, nonexistent. At virtually the same time when I was appointed lieutenant governor, and perhaps because of the appointment, the last holdout among the defecting Democratic state senators who had brought the Senate to a standstill switched his allegiance again and returned to the Democratic fold. The Democrats regained a thirty-two-to-thirty margin of control and held it for the rest of 2009 and 2010.

The partisanship in the Senate remained bitter. Both sides were preoccupied with the coming 2010 legislative elections, because the party that held the majority in 2011 would control the legislative redistricting that was set to take place in 2012. The 2012 redistricting, in turn, would determine the future balance of power in the State Senate for a decade. But there was no way for me to have much effect on these issues.

I did what I could. I tried to reacquaint myself with the state legislators I already knew and make the acquaintance of those I hadn't met. I got to know people in the executive branch. I offered to help the governor's staffers in any way I could, while making clear that I wasn't going to interfere with their prerogatives. Not infrequently, state legislators or state commissioners in the executive branch faced policy issues that I knew something about. When they asked for my opinion or help, I gave it. I visited Washington often and stayed in regular touch with the staff of New York State's Washington office, which had the big and often thankless job of making sure that the New York congressional delegation understood the impact of federal legislation, enacted and proposed, on the interests of the state. I lobbied to the extent I could on behalf of federal funds for the state's education and Medicaid programs.

Still, I had no political relationship with any elected official and no political clout that would have flowed from such a relationship. I was allowed to hire only one staffer of my own, the talented Suzanne Garment, whom I had met more than thirty years before when she worked with Pat Moynihan at the United Nations and who became my special counsel. One more staffer was assigned to me by the governor's office. I was lucky that it turned out to be Michael Evans, an extraordinary young man who is now president of the Moynihan Station Development Corporation. I had help from Nora Fitzpatrick, an employee of the Federal Reserve Bank of New York, which was rightly concerned about the effect that the fiscal plight of states and their cities could have on the nation's municipal securities markets. Nora was assigned to me for a full year. Later on, when I got support for my work from several New York foundations, their funds paid for additional staff.

But I had no portfolio, no duties, no one in state government to whom I had to report or who had to report to me. In that sense, the eighteen months I spent in the lieutenant governor's office were the most professionally frustrating period of my life.

My absence of official responsibilities gave me a considerable amount of freedom, and my experience had given me a sense of the uses to which I could put this freedom. I thought a lot about how I could apply the lessons I had learned from the years when I had real functions and responsibilities. And over those years I had acquired relationships with journalists; the press had always been my sword and shield in public life.

At no time in my public career did I ever employ a press agent or public relations firm—not out of an excess of modesty but because I quickly understood that if you are seen as seeking self-interested publicity, the press will lump you together with all those politicians whom journalists view as manipulative supplicants. Instead, I was usually able to gain my objectives by establishing a different kind of relationship with the reporters who covered matters in which I was involved.

One night in 1975, when I was new to government, I was schmoozing in an Albany bar when a reporter asked me what I thought of Governor Rockefeller's legacy. Nelson Rockefeller, I began my answer, was a cross between Ponzi and Robin Hood. The next morning, I was mortified to see my remark on the front page of the local newspaper. So by the time I became lieutenant governor, I had learned, when in doubt, to say "off the record."

More important, I did not find it difficult to establish relationships of trust with reporters, because I shared many of the values with which most reporters approached public issues. A good number of these reporters were my friends. When I wasn't in government, I saw them socially. We came to have a fair amount of mutual confidence. As long as I never tried to mislead a journalist in order to get a favorable story published, I had an excellent chance of getting accurate, fair reporting.

Serious journalists also liked the opportunity to intellectualize the political events they were covering; I enjoyed the same process. I spoke to them with a candor that satisfied them and me. I would talk to them frankly about events in which I was involved, help them develop a story, and make sure they knew I had no interest in having my name mentioned.

By the time I arrived in Albany as lieutenant governor, I had also learned something about the role of editorials in politics, especially state politics. Many people in politics take positions on the basis of editorials because they don't have a strong internal compass that dictates their own opinions. If an editorial is written with some intelligence and expresses a clear point of view, it carries a surprising amount of political weight and can have a profound influence on political decisions.

More particularly, I had learned about the *New York Times*. Politicians who run for office pay close attention to any and all media outlets. But in New York, especially when I first entered public life and even now, there is no question that the *Times* was the dominant factor in the way the press mirrored government and politics. In the political culture in which I grew up, an event never really happened unless it was reported in the *Times*. Television news desks often got their stories from early editions of the *Times*. Getting praise from that newspaper or looking good in its pages was a valuable political asset. Candor requires me to acknowledge that a call from the *Times* never failed to get a rapid response. It often took a fair amount of time and effort to provide the information a reporter asked for and to explain, sometimes ad nauseam, the parts that he or she didn't have straight. But those efforts bore fruit in the way events were reported.

In the most general sense, my aims were usually congruent with those of the *Times* editors; it was not a stretch for me to make the arguments that I thought would get their support. But there is no denying that the values of those editors, actual and perceived, had the power to shape the positions of even public officials who might otherwise have acted differently. Once, during one of the many school-busing controversies that rattled the country, I remember being dumbfounded when Pat Moynihan, then a US senator, took a pro-busing stance that seemed to contradict decades of his past writings. I asked him why. He raised those famous eyebrows of his and said simply, "The *Times*, my boy, the *Times*."

So, while I was lieutenant governor, I had no real power but enjoyed the advantage of a sympathetic forum. Wanting to do something useful, I began to study and report on some of the fiscal issues I thought were particularly important to New York. They involved both the reasons why the state budget was in such crisis and the consequences of the crisis.

The chief reason for the crisis was Medicaid, which made up fully a third of the state's budget and, as I learned, was a case study in the costs of good intentions. Medicaid provides joint federal-state health-care coverage to low-income Americans. The federal government reimburses state governments for part of what they spend on Medicaid and sets rules for state Medicaid programs.

I found that New York has two large structural problems with

Medicaid. The first is that it simply does not get enough federal reimbursement. The federal government's Medicaid reimbursement rates to the states vary widely, from 74 percent down to 50 percent. The rate depends on the state's average income. New York has a high average income, so it gets a low reimbursement rate.

But two states with the same average income can have different Medicaid needs. One state may not have many rich people, but not many poor people either. Another state with the same average income may have more rich people, as well as more poor people, who put larger burdens on the state's Medicaid program. New York is the second kind of state, with large Medicaid needs. Its federal reimbursement rate did not reflect these needs.

The second structural problem with Medicaid was that federal reimbursement money was not free money; it is matching money. That is, a state had to spend its own funds in order to get the federal funds. From the beginning of the Medicaid program in 1965, New York, for generous reasons, designed its state program to attract the maximum number of matching federal dollars. For example, New York's was one of the few state Medicaid programs that covered low-income adults who have no children. New York thereby got more federal money but spent more state money to do so.

A mountain of lesser problems is piled on top of these structural problems. Some of the added problems are nationwide. For instance, states spend disproportionate amounts of their Medicaid money on people who are "dual-eligible," eligible for Medicaid because they are poor and for Medicare because they are old or disabled. Because these people receive Medicare as well as Medicaid, Medicare's "freedom of choice" rules keep states from being able to serve them better and more economically through managed care.

Other problems are New York problems. In New York, payment rates to health-care providers are set by the state legislature rather than by administrators, making costs harder to control. New York is one of the few sates that shares Medicaid administration and costs between the state and its counties; this, too, makes cost control more difficult. New York's medical malpractice system costs so much that it seriously distorts the allocation of health-care resources.

I prepared a report that recommended the enactment of a bill to reform the malpractice system, limiting awards so as to save the health-care system hundreds of millions of dollars. It urged a state takeover of Medicaid and eliminating the legislature's power to set reimbursement rates directly.

I had a lot of help from talented bureaucrats in the state's health-care agencies, health-care experts in the state Budget Division, think tanks like the Urban Institute, private foundations like the Kaiser Family Foundation, and, above all, from Jim Tallon, president of the United Hospital Fund and former chairman of the New York State Assembly's health committee. Though the report was never acknowledged by the governor or his chief of staff, Larry Schwartz, I was gratified by the reaction it received from the press. But the problem of Medicaid's high burden on state budgets continues. And since the Affordable Care Act relies on Medicaid to provide health-care coverage to more Americans, the problem may get worse.

I was born in the year when Franklin Roosevelt became president and have lived through a time marked by some of the country's greatest achievements. We emerged from the Great Depression. We won a world war. We overcame racial segregation. We survived at least one threat of Nuclear Armageddon and saw the demise of the Soviet system that produced it. Today we face challenges of similar weight. They too may be managed—if people will participate in the democratic political process. Politics remains the only way these problems can be solved in a democracy, but making the political process work depends on the willingness of good men and women to give a part of their lives to participating in it.

Joel J. Sprayregen

Big Noise in the West

AN ACLU STUDY MISSION TO THE SOVIET UNION in 1970 transformed my life by serendipitously elevating me to a leadership role in a worldwide movement to secure freedom of emigration for Soviet Jews. Becoming an advocate for Russians refused emigration inspired me to apply the force of the First Amendment, including filing—and winning—my "dream" free speech case, as well as arguing the cause before an international tribunal.

My first two years lawyering were spent as staff counsel for the ACLU, fulfilling aspirations that had motivated me to study law and honing litigation skills working alongside experienced lawyers. I then joined a respected corporate law firm. By dint of successes in my cases and departures of senior lawyers, I became chair of litigation. I simultaneously served as general counsel of the Illinois Division of the ACLU. Our ACLU team earned victories in what seemed like important cases, e.g., freeing an avant-garde literary journal from post office seizure, ending a program under which the federal government covertly destroyed tons of mail deemed "foreign political propaganda" and ordering a high school (located in the territory of which Senator Paul Douglas supposedly said, "They should beam the Voice of America to southern Illinois") to rehire African-American teachers fired en masse when students were integrated.

Mayor Daley the First and a series of corrupt Republican governors then ruled Illinois, not benignly. We achieved institutional change in a series of federal cases—ultimately upheld by the Supreme Court—abolishing the formidable self-enriching power of election officials to award ballot position to their cronies. Political scientists testified that first place on the ballot conferred a minimum 15 percent voter advantage, a dismal reflection on democracy. In 1970, my life path seemed clear. I would hopefully grow as a corporate litigator. And my pro bono activities—which I knew would be central to my life—would be rooted in the community of civil libertarians.

My reasons for quickly agreeing to join the mission to the Soviet Union were varied. Cold War bipolar enmity seemed to be evolving into détente, Russian *haute kultur* intrigued me (perhaps like the fictional young woman who tried to read *War and Peace* every summer), and I am addicted to educational wanderlust, as evidenced by eleven million documented airline miles. My father had emigrated from Russia fifty-seven years earlier, but—remembering anti-Semitism and poverty—he despised his country of origin and urged me not to go. "I can tell you it's bad," he said. I knew our contacts would be orchestrated by Soviet officialdom. We were promised a chance to meet Soviet lawyers. I did not anticipate that I would have opportunity to meet dissident Soviet Jews because the KGB (secret police) restricted, and sometimes punished, unapproved meetings.

Our ACLU mission consisted of about twenty people, mostly intelligent and well-educated (if you can thus generalize about lawyers and academics) and of course left-liberal politically. At this time a phenomenon unprecedented in six decades of Soviet rule was emerging: a few daring Soviet Jews were sending eloquent publicized letters demanding emigration to Israel. Almost all were refused, all lost their jobs, and several were imprisoned. I arranged on my own a briefing in New York with Israeli diplomats whose responsibilities included doing what they could—which was quite limited—to let Soviet Jews know they were not forgotten. The diplomats warned me not to contact the authors of those letters. This well-intentioned advice was mistaken because this new breed of activists believed their protection lay in becoming known through meetings with Western visitors.

Unbeknownst to most observers, notably—and disgracefully—including academic Sovietologists, the USSR was well advanced into the decline which led to its implosion in 1991. Leadership, from Brezhnev down, was sclerotic, the economy was misperforming, and once-unifying revolutionary ideals were widely mocked. Jewish education and culture had been virtually eradicated, leaving many in the West to wrongly conclude that Soviet Jews felt little kinship with Jews elsewhere. Israel's lightning victory in the 1967 Six-Day War had stirred feelings of pride in many Jews, all the more because USSR media had publicized boasts of Soviet-supplied Arab armies that they would annihilate Israel. Pro-Israeli beliefs were accelerated by the anti-Semitism which—as my father remembered—was endemic in the country. Many Soviet Jews were highly educated professionals. But they were subject to strict quotas and rarely filled top positions. These factors fueled the emigration movement, fortuitously beginning as I prepared for our trip.

The USSR was still a police state suppressing elementary human rights. The feared KGB could imprison anyone for "anti-Soviet conduct." I devised a simple signal to attract Jews seeking to confide. I went to the main synagogue (there were about fifty for three million Jews, the only surviving Jewish institutions). I conspicuously carried a bag from El Al, Israel's airline, its name emblazoned in Hebrew and Roman letters. Emigration-minded Jews were mostly secular nationalists rather than religiously observant, but they could meet foreigners at synagogues. I concluded that, so long as I did not act surreptitiously, the worst the KGB might do would be to expel me.

My signal worked like a magnet, leading to mind-expanding conversations in seven of eight Soviet cities visited. We conversed in English and Hebrew; my intermediate Hebrew was on a level with theirs. Conversations with emigration-minded Jews, mostly highly intelligent scientists and engineers, followed a pattern. They said they no longer identified with a failed anti-Semitic country; they demanded "repatriation" to Israel, which they regarded as a dynamic kindred country, with all its real-life dangers and failings. They said the Soviets were seeking détente in bad faith, not for peaceful purposes, but out of economic/military weakness. My new friends uniformly instructed: "Make a big noise in the West!" This meant publicizing both Soviet weakness as well as the demands of many Jews to emigrate, two points which they felt were obscured by well-meaning liberal advocates of détente in the West. They emphasized they were not trying to reform the USSR; they only wanted to leave. They added that the Soviets had no persuasive answer for denying emigration, which was guaranteed by several international conventions.

On our first Saturday in Moscow, three young men initiated conversation on the steps of the historic Choral Synagogue on Arkhipova Street. Scholarly looking Leonid Rigerman, a physicist, invited my wife and me to lunch at his apartment. When we alighted from the tram, our host knocked on the window, as he explained, to awaken the informer who had followed us. Rigerman and his American-born mother (his father had died) told me their story: His parents, both communists, were married in the US. They sought refuge from our Depression in the USSR and renounced their American citizenship. Rigerman was born in the USSR. He had once succeeded in gaining entrance to the US Embassy and was given a visa application. I told him he could plausibly claim that his parents had not effectively renounced US citizenship because they were acting under duress during the Great Terror, which meant he could argue that he was born the son of US citizens. After my departure, Rigerman tried to reenter the Embassy, with executed application in hand. He was severely beaten by Soviet guards, who explained that this five-foot-three-inch physicist "resembled a bank robber."

Another man I met at the synagogue was Mordecai Elbaum, an engineer in his late twenties. He had dropped his Russian name "Mikhail." He was a study in red; He had a fiery red beard, and wore a red shirt from which hung a large Jewish Star. He took us to Red Square, and insisted on being photographed with us in front of Lenin's tomb. When I asked if he didn't fear such brazenness would get him arrested, he answered with a phrase I was to hear countless times from dissidents: "You don't understand," adding: "living in this country is no different from prison. I will leave them with the choices of imprisoning me or kicking me out!"

Leningrad (now Saint Petersburg) was a different story because western media and diplomats were not proximate. My request at the Synagogue to recite prayers over the Torah was granted; I carefully chanted in a modern Israeli accent as a signal. As I descended from the altar, a man in his mid-thirties whispered urgently in English: "Meet me this afternoon!" I said yes, and he replied: "When and where" I said "two o'clock" and chose the place with deliberate irony but also because it was a landmark: "Kazan Cathedral," which the Soviets had converted into a Museum of Atheism. He walked away, insisting, "Don't wear your bright American clothing!" At age thirty-six, I was somewhat dapper. About three blocks from the synagogue, an elderly man approached me and asked in Yiddish-accented Hebrew: "What hotel are you at?" When I told him, he responded in Hebrew "Someone will come at 6:30 tonight" and started to walk away. I insisted: "Who will come?" His response: "A young man wearing glasses." I had thus agreed to two rather surreptitious meetings with dissidents. You never told one dissident about another, because you never knew who was an informer. At the cathedral, the young man introduced himself as Misha Korenblit, a dentist. He insisted that we chat while walking on side streets. He application to emigrate to Israel had been rejected. He said his real talent was journalism but, "If I wrote, the authorities would know how much I hate them." He denounced all things Soviet with such vehemence that I had a margin of suspicion he might be an agent provocateur seeking to entrap me into saying something for which I could be arrested; e.g. he said, "I bet they showed you beautiful model apartments. Up there (pointing), eight families share a kitchen and bathroom, living like pigs." He said no one from Leningrad was being allowed to emigrate.

At 6:30 p.m., a tall young man with glasses greeted me outside my hotel. His scholarly demeanor immediately put me at ease. Zev Mogilever, a mathematician, had unsuccessfully petitioned to teach Hebrew in his children's school because Soviet law supposedly allowed everyone instruction in his native language. When I told him I was attending the Kirov Ballet that evening, he asked if I would meet him during intermission. I agreed. He took me for a short walk and gave me, with irony, a Soviet book in English, supposedly authored by Lenin, predicting that in the year 1980, the entire world would be joyously communist. In the book was an envelope addressed to his friend in Jerusalem. Suddenly Misha darted out of an alley, flashing a wry smile. I momentarily feared he had come to arrest me. But then we embraced. Years later, he told me they had feared that—with my seemingly naive openness—I might be a spy. After long discussion, they concluded that I was kosher. Such was the paranoid atmosphere in the USSR of 1970.

For the remainder of our three-week mission, Marilyn and I lived a double life, adhering to the propagandizing agenda of our official Intourist guides while touring far-flung Soviet republics, including Georgia and Uzbekistan. We enjoyed art museums and walking in the footsteps of Russian history. Meetings with government-employed Soviet lawyers followed a pattern. They would begin by challenging us about the Vietnam War and the civil rights struggle. They would ask about the status of the Smith Act, aimed at outlawing the US Communist Party, as to which I enjoyed ending the discussion by informing them that the US Communist Party initially supported the Smith Act when it was used against Trotskyites. They justified restrictions on civil liberties by arguing that the USSR was in the early stages of its history—like the United States when we enacted the Alien and Sedition Acts in 1798. While the Soviet lawyers were intelligent and skilled, on occasion they lapsed into propagandistic absurdity, e.g., by relying on Depression-era statistics to ask if American lawyers still earned $25 per week.

Our guides—who we knew were required to report to the KGB—seemed sincere in wanting us to appreciate Soviet achievements, especially military, construction, and industrial. On occasion, they went too far. In Kiev, a young guide took the microphone on the bus and said: "We are passing Communist party headquarters. When we had our Revolution, the people decided that we should have only one political party, so the people smashed all the other parties." A chorus of guffaws erupted while the young guide stared in seeming disbelief. Our group consisted mainly of left-liberals mindful of the excesses of McCarthyite anti-communism. Once over drinks at night, I contrasted the drabness of the USSR with the sunniness of Spain. An academic lady from New York rebuked me: "You visit fascist Spain!" I answered that was quintessential knee-jerk liberalism, urging boycott of Spain "while visiting über-totalitarian USSR." Years later, I gave a speech in a mid-western city to young Jewish business leaders. A man came up and told me he was the son of that academic lady. I was impressed that he had apparently learned more than his mother.

While adhering to the prescribed itinerary (if we missed a tour, our guides would inquire petulantly: "Don't you want to learn about Soviet achievements?"), we met dissident Jews in seven cities. On a street in Tashkent, a middle-aged man slipped me a letter in Russian. It was a plea for an invitation to emigrate to Israel. He wrote that his father had been executed as an "enemy of the people," that he had never had a happy moment in his life, that his fellow workers taunted him to "get out to your Israel," and ended by saying "If I could, I would walk there."

In Tbilisi, Georgia, a crowd escorted us from Friday night synagogue services to a festive home dinner with the Buzukashvilis, a large clan. Georgian Jews, religiously observant, reminded us of Greeks in the demonstrative warmth of their hospitality. They were also hard-drinking, which enlivened our conversations. Their motivation to emigrate was religiously inspired. They said they had lived in exile in Georgia—a Christian enclave in the Caucasian Mountains—since the destruction of the First Temple in 587 BC, and that they wanted to participate in building Israel, which they called the Third Temple. When I gave them a tallit (prayer shawl), they said they would save it for the bar mitzvah in Jerusalem of their then nine-year old son. As it turned out, I attended that bar mitzvah in 1974 at Jerusalem's Western Wall. But that is getting ahead of the story. As we left their home to be escorted to our hotel, a vehicle with a bright official light on top raced toward us from a darkened side street. We trembled in momentary fear, but the vehicle passed us. Our hosts said, with relief, "Just an ambulance!" I later learned that "ambulances" were routinely used for surveillance.

Our last stop was a one-night, pre-homeward-flight stand in Moscow. Our guide said there had been a mix-up with our rooms at the National Hotel ("where Lenin stayed!"), but that she had upgraded some of us as redress for our wretched bathroom-less rooms in Samarkand. Marilyn and I were astonished to be escorted to a two-room suite, with ornate chandelier, piano plus telephone (a rarity), and the grandest view in Moscow: looking into Red Square directly at Lenin's Tomb, Kremlin walls, and the onion-shaped domes of Saint Basil's Cathedral. We immediately understood that—while all Soviet hotel rooms were surveillance rooms—this was a super surveillance room. Elbaum had arranged a farewell party for us, hosted by intellectuals who were leaders of the Jewish emigration movement (though they never would have called it a "movement"). Elbaum himself could not attend because he was scurrying about Moscow to get signatures on a petition to be presented at a forthcoming Moscow visit by the UN secretary-general. Our hosts sought our impressions of what we had learned while touring and reemphasized the importance of "making a big noise in the West."

We returned to our hotel on the Metro. At the Red Square station, we spotted Elbaum on the train. I reached into the El Al bag and gave him my last remaining Jewish star. I said goodbye dramatically with the declamation in Hebrew that Jews recite at the conclusion of the Yom Kippur fast and Passover seder: "Next year in Jerusalem!" Elbaum embraced me and exclaimed loudly, even defiantly: "Lo, b'shanah hazoht!—No, this year!" This was a memorable farewell, intensifying a 2,000-year-old declamation.

All that remained was departure from Moscow's Sheremetyevo airport. Seeking to protect Marilyn and myself from detention at the airport, I had persuaded our delegation to sit-in at the airport if any of us were detained. We were, after all, the ACLU, including two octogenarian ladies, one of them the sister of Representative Jeanette Rankin (R-MT), who served two terms in Congress and voted against US entry into both world wars. I lingered while some of our group cleared passport control. Suddenly, a uniformed officer, accompanied by five plainclothesmen asked for "Mr. and Mrs. Sprayregen." I asked the officers to identify themselves by name and rank, to which they replied "We don't speak English." They asked to examine our luggage but conducted a haphazard search. I had hidden the Leningrad and Tashkent letters in my shoe-heels. They found my notes—English words abbreviated with Hebrew letters—but could not make much of them. I have a habit of stuffing mementoes like theater tickets and train transfers into books. These attracted their attention but to no avail. Their eyes lit up when they found a photocopy (all photocopy machines in Soviet libraries were locked) in English, but it was only my directions to my firm about my pending cases. They ultimately cleared us to board.

When we had left Soviet-controlled airspace en route to Brussels, I briefed my fellow travelers on what we had been doing when we disappeared. Some were fascinated, but I sensed others felt I had abused Soviet hospitality. Only one—a Detroit lawyer—joined the work I was to do. I returned to Chicago on June 2, 1970, determined to start that "big noise in the West." On June 10, I made my first speech at my synagogue's beachfront sunrise service to celebrate Shavuot, which commemorates Moses's receiving the Law. I had told the Rabbi that I wanted to share a bottle of kosher brandy given me by Jews in Georgia and tell their story. My five-minute spiel had an electrifying effect on the worshippers. They demanded to know what could they do. I said: "Make a big noise!" This was powerful incitement to Jews who felt their parents had been afraid to speak up during the Holocaust. I subsequently gave scores of enthusiastically received speeches, lectures and media presentations; but I never reached the emotional crescendo of those five minutes.

I was debilitated with what seemed like wearying symptoms of colitis. I believed I was suffering from fatigue brought on by doing double duty as tourist and Good Samaritan, exacerbated by anxiety for my Russian friends. But a Chicago veterinarian told me I probably had ingested Leningrad water amoeba—"more potent than Montezuma's Revenge"—which the Soviets did not disclose for reasons of national pride.

On June 15, front-page headlines in the *New York Times* incited my new mission: fifteen Jews were arrested in connection with an aborted airplane hijacking. Four were found with penknives ready to board a flight from Leningrad to near the Finnish border. Korenblit and Mogilever, who were not at the airport, were among the detainees. Korenblit had told me that he opposed airplane hijacking. I later learned that the letter entrusted to me was a plea for friends in Israel to stop the hijacking. I understood that the KGB was using the arrests to intimidate Jews seeking emigration.

An opportunity now arose to make a big noise. The annual Pugwash Conference, bringing together Soviet and American scientists/academics to advance "peace," would be held on Labor Day weekend at Lake Geneva, Wisconsin—sixty miles from Chicago. Pugwash was the birthplace of Cyrus Eaton, the Nova Scotia-born industrialist and George Soros of that era, who endowed the conference. I was only a youngish lawyer, but I understood the dynamics of such conferences, partly as the result of learning from Yale Law Dean Eugene Rostow. American participants would be sincere liberals determined not to appear McCarthyite, nor to speak critically about the USSR. The Soviets would include some real scientists, but they would be directed by accompanying KGB agents experienced in orchestrating dupes.

This presented a singular opportunity to publicize the plight of Soviet Jews on a worldwide stage. Chicago friends agreed that there should be a demonstration at Lake Geneva. My original idea was outlandishly grandiose: 10,000 Americans in biblical garb would camp outside the conference for a week as "Operation Exodus," demanding "Let my people go!" In the end, all that remained of my idea was the name. I had imagined that the Jewish establishment, to which I was an outsider, was a well-oiled engine that could swiftly implement a proposal as ingenious as mine. To my consternation, Philip Klutznick—an influential leader of the

Jewish Federation—imperiously told me: "I forbid you to hold any protest meeting targeting Pugwash." Klutznick, later US secretary of commerce, was a legendary real estate mega-developer, civic leader, and philanthropist. As I came to know him, I frequently disagreed with him, due mainly to his dovishness. But I respected his brilliance and his powerful oratory.

I told Federation leaders that we would express no antagonism to visiting Soviets, indeed we would express support for the peace and détente which they advocated. But we would ask Soviet visitors to take home with them our concerns about denial of human rights to Soviet Jews. Federation leaders disagreed. Conservative in nature, many of them had been discomfited by 1960s demonstrations. They remembered that during the reign of Stalin, who had died seventeen years before, a Soviet citizen could be executed if his name was mentioned in the West. They subscribed to the notion—which I was to hear frequently—that it was inhospitable to target Soviet guests with "politics." It would take a new generation of Jewish leaders, not quite ready to step up, to actively protest. The Federation's CEO, a decent man, complained about one word that I used in a press release saying we would "confront" Soviet delegates. I was motivated to fight the Jewish establishment if necessary. We organized our own coalition to mount a protest. This proved surprisingly easy. With new and old friends, we formed a letterhead coalition without staff or budget. I spoke wherever I could, mainly synagogues and summer camps, urging listeners to turn out on Labor Day weekend to speak up for Soviet Jews. Audiences responded enthusiastically, explicitly saying they were ready to speak up, as a prior generation had failed to do during the Holocaust.

Chicago had two major newspapers—the larger *Tribune* and the smaller *Sun-Times*. A *Sun-Times* editor was married to a principal of Pugwash's influential public relations firm. The liberal *Sun-Times* editorialized "Give Pugwash a Pass," urging that peace-seeking Soviet delegates be spared political protest. I prepared a file and carried it to the editorial offices of the renownedly conservative *Tribune*. The result was a powerful editorial, proclaiming that Soviet visitors could learn no better lesson in democracy than to witness Americans protesting human rights abuses.

The Sunday set for the demonstration dawned with perfect late-summer weather. We had no idea how many people would attend. I arrived early, standing nervously in a vacant parking lot. Suddenly, chartered bus after bus pulled in from Chicago, Milwaukee, Madison, and points in between. About 4,000 chanting demonstrators arrived, many with signs showing our logo: a Jewish Star encased in chains and a lock. A client had lent me a flatbed trailer to use as our stage. The truck driver separated tractor from trailer, explaining he had been told to fear destruction in a riot. Our featured speaker was Paul Simon, crusading small-town editor who was reform lieutenant governor (and later Democratic senator) of Illinois. He eloquently demanded justice for Soviet Jews. I spoke briefly, and the crowd joined in songs. We had agreed not to picket the Abbey Hotel, site of the conference, on condition that we could send a small delegation to deliver our petition, which I had drafted. I was among those who marched to the hotel, to the military cadence of "The Song of the Jewish Partisans," with the petition. We noticed that the drapes of the hotel were closed, but we could see delegates peeking at us. The door opened and our petition was delivered.

Our demonstration attracted extensive national media coverage. It was the beginning of advocacy in the Midwest for Soviet Jewish emigration. A journalist in the hotel undertook to publish the petition under my byline in the respected *Christian Century* magazine under the provocative title "The New Serfdom." I knew the Soviets would bristle at comparison with serfs, who could not leave the lands of their masters. Soviet Jewish scientists in Riga addressed a demand for emigration to the conference. This was a good start to making a big noise, at least in the Midwest.

I allowed one detour that summer. A feisty Denver housewife named Lil Hoffman organized a rally on the steps of her state capitol to commemorate execution of twenty-four Jewish writers in Moscow on August 12, 1952. The Governor had agreed to speak. Ms. Hoffman asked the Israeli Embassy for a speaker;

the Israelis decided Chicago was proximate enough to Colorado for me to speak. I researched and wrote about the 1952 massacre, committed during Stalin's near-deathbed Jew-hating paroxysms. I gave this atrocity the name the "Night of the Murdered Poets." A whirlwind of media and political events in Denver helped me prepare for the Pugwash demo. I found that many (not all) intelligent liberals were reluctant to criticize the USSR. They feared being disparaged as McCarthyites or "cold warriors." They believed—wrongly—that the USSR was "evolving" toward respect for human rights, and that American transgressions were on a par with Russian. And some of the Jewish liberals were wary of "special pleading." I recalled Rosa Luxemburg who said: "I have no room in my heart for specific Jewish sorrows." She was hanged in Weimar Germany.

The fates of the friends I had left behind in the USSR were mixed. A few weeks after my return I received a phone call from New York. A familiar voice announced in Hebrew: "I am Mordechai, just arrived from Moscow." Just as he had predicted, his confrontational tactics left the Soviets with no choices, other than prison or kicking him out. He went to Israel, served in the army and proudly showed me excavations he had worked on near the Western Wall. Leonid Rigerman and his mother were let go after a New York city councilman took up their case. He told me that on the flight to New York, his mother—a lifelong atheist—said: "Now I believe in God!" My Georgian friends were eventually allowed to go to Israel. The Leningrad defendants did not fare as well. Dr. Korenblit was sentenced to eight years, Mogilever to four. They were both charged with not informing the authorities about the hijack plot; the KGB evidently sensed Korenblit's seething hatred for communism. I later visited both in Israel after their prison terms.

These variations revealed the KGB had no coherent plan regarding Jewish emigration. Month after month, some applicants for emigration were let go and others were arrested. All lost their jobs and educational opportunities. The Soviets may have thought such capriciousness would intimidate, but precisely the opposite occurred. Soviet Jews were saying: "How does one decide to seek emigration? Answer: he comes to one of our farewell parties." Soviet Jews now realized that many of us who had heard their pleas were making big noises in the West. When Soviet Jews whose cases we had publicized—especially "prisoners of conscience" like Natan Scharansky in 1986—were freed, we presented them on media and in public programs so that the positive results of "making a big noise" could be confirmed.

Soviet authorities, with colossal mistiming, handed down the sentences of the Leningrad group during Christmas week 1970. Two defendants—former Soviet army officers, one a pilot—were sentenced to death, although all defendants had been arrested prior to takeoff. There was worldwide revulsion over the death sentences. The Pope issued a plea for mercy. From a ski trip, I helped organize a rally at a downtown Chicago synagogue, attended by Mayor Daley the First. The publicity backlash against the Soviets was enormous. They commuted the death sentences and released a few Jewish prisoners.

In the summer of 1971, a New York scholar named Moshe Decter organized a nonofficial tribunal called "Commission of Inquiry into the Rights of Soviet Jews." This was modeled after publicized tribunals organized during the cold war by Nobel Laureate Bertrand Russell, which routinely condemned western democracies for war-mongering, and were applauded by the Soviets and some liberals. I was appointed counsel to the commission, chaired by civil rights leader Bayard Rustin. The "judges" included ex-Senator Goodell (R-NY), Nobel Laureate George Wald, Episcopal Bishop Brooke Mosley, the civil rights leader Rabbi Abraham H. Heschel, and Nuremburg prosecutor General Telford Taylor, an idol of mine whom I had befriended when he taught as visiting prof a course on FCC law at Yale Law School. I made the opening and closing arguments and presented documents and witnesses, including Leonid Rigerman. The USSR unsurprisingly declined an invitation to appear. My case flowed easily; the facts and law were on my side, and I was impassioned and prepared. The commission issued a report excoriating the Soviets for human rights violations, which was widely covered in international media.

The commission visibly irked the Soviets. An article appeared in the prestigious *Literaturnaya Gazeta*, calling the commission "a witches' Sabbath" and me "a notorious anti-Soviet provocateur." The Soviets even sent a suave KGB agent, posing as a journalist, to come to Chicago for lunch and ask me why I hated his country. I told him I bore no hatred but that several of my friends were imprisoned for seeking emigration. He said I did not know the best people in his country. We sparred verbally at the stuffy bank dining room I chose for our assignation while he ordered the most expensive Scotch and cigars and told me about his young paramour. I sometimes wonder what became of Mikhail.

I enjoyed a spectacular opportunity to make big noise—in a federal courtroom—in the summer of 1972. A synagogue youth group—including my sixteen-year-old daughter—decided to visit a Soviet-sponsored arts/crafts exhibit at Chicago's Field Museum wearing T-shirts proclaiming, over our logo: "Free Soviet Jews." By happenstance, as the teens approached the museum, Soviet officials (probably KGB) arrived. One of them placed his hand over an NBC TV camera lens aimed at the teens, which viewers saw that night. The museum denied entry to the group on the ground that "politics has no place in a museum." My instant research revealed that (1) the exhibit had been designed to show that "Under the banner of the Great October Revolution, all Soviet nationalities are free to develop their own cultures" and (2) the museum stood on county land and received large official subsidies, meaning there existed "state action" necessary for the First and Fourteenth Amendments to apply.

I filed a federal lawsuit and sought a temporary restraining order barring exclusion of the teens. If a TRO case moves quickly enough, the judge may have only the plaintiff's papers before him when the hearing begins. That is what happened. The judge was the late Hubert L. Will, who was a brilliant and a passionate civil libertarian. Peering from the bench, he asked the museum's lawyer "If ten of us judges came to your museum wearing our judicial robes to dramatize our plea for higher pay, would your museum kick us out?" The lawyer gulped and answered "Yes, Your Honor." Judge Will immediately granted the TRO, which after further hearings, ripened into an injunction. This was indeed my "dream case," linking Soviet Jews and our First Amendment. The national and local media noise reverberated, augmented by the thuggish KGB hand over the camera.

It may seem that I was participating in a series of publicity stunts to embarrass the Soviets. But a worldwide movement to free Soviet Jews was cumulatively expanding. Wherever Soviet officials or performers appeared, they were confronted by demands to "Let my people go." Some of our most effective advocates were Christian clergy. American politicians realized this was a no-risk bandwagon, and jumped aboard. The dimensions were global; e.g., in London, my new friends Lord and Lady Janner led a dignified picket line outside a performance of the Bolshoi Ballet. The size of our demonstrations expanded. When Gorbachev visited Washington in 1987, he was confronted (yes, I was still using that verb once deemed too provocative) by 250,000 demonstrators.

It was becoming clear that free emigration from the USSR was linked to great power relations with the United States. The Soviets kept turning the emigration spigot high and low depending on what they were seeking from the US. It was also becoming clearer—as my friends in the USSR had suggested—that a stagnating USSR needed trade benefits from the US under the banner of "détente." Jewish organizations were wary of explicitly linking trade benefits with emigration, fearing a harsh response from the Soviets to "blackmail." Soviet Jews and some American activists favored the linkage, but the Nixon administration, quarterbacked by State Secretary Kissinger, sought stability rather than confrontation with the Soviets and did not want their hands tied. Into this debate, there stepped the towering figure of Senator Henry Jackson (D-WA). On September 26, 1972, he gave a speech in DC to a divided conference of Jewish leaders. Because the B'nai Brith auditorium was overcrowded, I was standing on the podium, next to the senator. He came with a copy of his bill—the Jackson Amendment—explicitly linking trade benefits with Soviet concession on emigration. Jackson said: "The time has come to place our highest human values ahead of the trade dollar. I'll give you some marching orders. Get behind my amendment. And let's stand firm."

Jackson persuaded most of the Jewish leadership to stand firm behind his bill, which became Jackson-Vanik when an Ohio congressman became House sponsor. Nixon and Kissinger continued to try to undermine the amendment, but their power to do so receded as Watergate grew, On December 11, 1973, the amendment passed both houses with large majorities and became part of the trade bill. As predicted by the activists, the Soviets did not balk in anger but agreed to keep emigration at 35,000, a number that then appeared satisfactory. The Soviets released Jewish prisoners—most notably Natan Scharansky—who urged that the "big noise" continue.

During the remaining years of the USSR, the numbers of Jews allowed emigration varied, depending on what concessions Soviet leaders were seeking, e.g. 19,000 in 1988 and 71,000 the next year. Advocates for free emigration took pride that our efforts had helped open the doors. As the USSR entered its final days, the numbers swelled beyond anything we could have imagined or would have asked for—182,000 in 1990, 179,000 the next year. This was a self-accelerating phenomenon: When exit permits seemed more available, the numbers of applicants rose due to fear of arbitrary reversal. More than one million Soviet Jews settled in Israel, infinitely strengthening a small country by their mass and levels of education/skills. More than half a million settled in the US. As it became clear that anyone who wanted to leave could do so, I understood that the mission I had embarked upon in 1970 was completed.

I have made a few return visits to post-Soviet Russia, where almost everything appears to be for sale. Official anti-Semitism has been curbed, Jewish organizations operate openly, and there is freedom to travel. Wealth is displayed with brazen conspicuousness, but poverty is widespread, especially in the countryside. Massive gulags are gone, but enemies of the regime are killed with precision. On one visit, I met with former KGB officers—mostly very smart mathematicians—who owned a highly profitable firm providing information to western businesses. We discussed possible collaboration against terrorism. I traveled to Ukraine and Georgia to witness results of Russian invasions.

My priorities had changed over the years. My pro bono time became consumed by involvement in Jewish organizations, to the virtual exclusion of involvement in the ACLU. There is only so much non-billable time in a week. As the ACLU lurched leftward (as I saw it), I grew more conservative. Some would say my political thinking was maturing, others that I was lapsing into senility. But I do not agree that health care is a right guaranteed by the Constitution. I continue to defend civil liberties as a hallmark of American exceptionalism. In 1980, I crossed a Rubicon by voting for Ronald Reagan, for whom the cause of free emigration fit into his "evil empire" gnosticism (though I subsequently voted at least thrice for Democratic presidential candidates). I formed new friendships and was invited to take leadership roles in Jewish organizations. The politics of Jewish organization are as ugly as politics elsewhere, but that is another story. The fund-raising demands were expansive, but the causes were meritorious.

I was enlisted in the international work of Jewish organizations and participated in interesting and sometimes productive missions, e.g. twice as guest of the Saudi king in Riyadh, three times with Yasser Arafat (a despicable terrorist fearing assassination by his own people if he made peace), to Mubarak's palace in Cairo, to Ethiopia in the midst of a three-way civil war to help arrange emigration of indigenous Jews to Israel, to Eritrea with retired US admirals/generals seeking access to newly captured Red Sea ports, to Israel with US military delegations, as well as numerous meetings with heads of state/government in Israel, the Middle East, Europe, and Latin America, plus White House meetings. I joined in so many "missions" to Israel, always in wartimes, that I consider myself a "Jewish missionary."

My involvement in the emigration movement was, I think, in keeping with Justice Holmes's admonition that one must join in "the passion and action of his time at peril of being judged not to have lived at all." These activities allowed me to participate in work implementing values that were essential to me. One of these was to strike effectively at Soviet totalitarianism. Others were to support freedom of emigration and to strengthen Israel, which exists in a difficult neighborhood. Nor could I forget that my own family could have been trapped in the USSR had my father not emigrated in 1913. And using the American judicial system to strike blows—for freedom of speech and for Soviet Jews—was like winning a doubleheader.

My work for emigration rights and defending democracies is a way to repay our family's obligation for being allowed to find freedom/opportunity in the USA. The history of our family is stark. My great-great grandfather moved from Russia to Jerusalem in 1891. Subsequently, those who came to America mostly prospered. Those who stayed in Europe were killed, except for Cousin Volodya whom I miraculously discovered on a 2010 trip to Belarus. Twenty-seven of our cousins were murdered in one day when the Germans invaded Belarus in 1941. I can never forget or forgive that. My work in Jewish organizations links me to the eternal struggle to preserve the miraculous continuity of Jewish life.

Robert B. Stevens

East African Federation

IN MANY WAYS, WORKING ON THE GENERAL ISSUE of federation and nonfederation in East Africa was one of the most interesting times of my career.

At the time that I was recruited by the UN in the mid-1960s I was working as an assistant professor at the Yale Law School. I had first gone to Yale in 1957 as a graduate student. In those days, if you went to the US on a visitor's visa to take a job, you had to leave for a period of two years before returning permanently. During those two years I spent four months in Tanzania at the University of East Africa. This was in Dar es Salaam, where I taught at the university's new law faculty. It had just been established that year, and there were only thirteen students in the undergraduate program. Julius Nyerere had decided he wanted to train lawyers in Tanzania, rather than sending them to England or the US. There were three regular lecturers: A. B. Weston, a rather eccentric Australian, and two Englishmen: Patrick McAuslan, and William Twining, whose father had been governor of Tanganyika, as it then was. I taught introduction to law, contract law of East Africa, and legal history. I prepared by reading a few cases. It's what we lawyers do—I improvised! I found the teaching very satisfying, and I continue to do so in retrospect; the students were obviously a talented group, and several are now prominent cabinet ministers in their various countries.

Dar es Salaam at the time was a town of about one-quarter million. In the governing circles, everybody knew everybody, and Nyerere came to eat at the university. He was basically a decent, open-minded and generous man. He had been to Scotland for university and was influenced by Presbyterian principles. He was anxious that the university should not become too elitist, and indeed two to three years after I left, he sent all the undergraduates away for a year to work in the fields; he wanted them to know what it was like to work on a farm.

Tanzania was an interesting country: unlike Kenya, and to a certain extent Uganda, there had been very few settlers because it was a trust territory. This meant that legally Britain was under an obligation to lead it to independence. Kenya, on the other hand, was plagued with a long battle with the white settlers, who had powerful allies in England. The UN fairly closely supervised Tanganyika, and this was reflected in the attitudes of the government officials. Lord Twining, for instance, was a member of the Rainbow Coalition. Unlike leaders in the other parts of East Africa, he consciously invited African leaders to Government House in Dar, and looked forward to an independent Tanzania, run primarily by Africans. Nevertheless, Dar was still a colonial enclave and pretentiously British. The local club was still dragging its feet about admitting African members, so ultimately Nyerere nationalized it and turned it into the Tanzanian Youth Club. Spluttering colonials didn't appreciate that.

I arrived in 1962 with my first wife who was a historian of public health. We lived in a sublet of a house, complete with houseboy, Elias, and garden boy, Omari. Not only was this my first experience of Africa, but it was fascinating to see a country that had just become independent. At that time, before there was much tourism in East Africa, there were animals wandering everywhere: if you took the train from Nairobi to Mombasa it was quite often halted by elephants crossing the track.

After my time in Tanzania, I spent eighteen months at the London School of Economics. Then, at the end of the two years away, I returned to Yale to teach, with my permanent visa approved. At Yale I got to know Oscar Schachter, part-time professor and head of legal services at the UN. Oscar first recommended me for a job in Korea in 1961. I spent a few weeks in Seoul, working on discussions about links between North and South Korea. Of course I spoke no Korean, but somehow I managed to carry out my project to the satisfaction of the UN. Oscar then put me forward for the job of advisor to Kenya, Uganda, and Tanzania as they contemplated the issue of federation. The president of Yale, Kingman Brewster, was a bit pretentious and, delighted to have a call from the UN Secretary General, was happy to release me for regular visits to Africa over quite a long period.

There was a spirit of Pan-Africanism in the 1950s and 1960s, as African countries began to gain independence. It was a catch phrase that was big at the UN. I'm not sure of the source of the idea, but Kenyatta, Nyerere, and Obote all were interested. Everybody talked about merging bits of Africa and in one sense Kenya, Uganda, and Tanzania, since they had shared services under the British and since they all became independent within a year or two, superficially had more logic about merging than other groups in Africa. During the colonial period, they had shared trains, airlines, and banking controls. They had been meeting in Nairobi, but one of the problems was that the countries would get easily upset at procedural matters like where meetings were held.

Nyerere, Kenyatta, and Obote met in December 1961, in Mombasa. This was a holdover from the colonial period, when the leaders of the three countries had met every so often under British rule. They continued the practice to discuss matters like common foreign policy, the possibilities of working together on domestic issues and the prospects of Pan-Africanism. At a meeting in December 1961, they realized that their nations were drifting apart, and so they decided they would have one last shot at federalism and asked the UN to provide a group of advisors on the idea of federation. The International Monetary Fund sent Rattan Bhatia, an extremely good Indian economist. Rattan was their "man on Africa." The UN Development Program, through Oscar Schachter, recommended me. I accepted, and began my visits in 1966.

I went for a few weeks at the beginning of the project, then back to Yale to teach, and then I went on lots of short trips, about two weeks each. I would leave one weekend and return again two weekends later. I would fly to Nairobi from Idlewild airport—twice a week there was a direct flight to Nairobi. I stayed at the New Stanley (which was elegant and more western-ized) or the Pan Afric, which was more amateur. Rattan stayed at a fancier hotel.

The food was undistinguished, western-style food. The air-planes were TWA's 707s. I found it fascinating. I was too tired to feel lonely and the whole project was quite interesting. It was a long journey. I tried to keep a sort of diary. Not very effectively.

I also enjoyed socializing with Arthur Hazelwood, who was the negotiator for the Kenyan government, an economic adviser. He was a fellow of Pembroke College, where I later became mas-ter. Nyerere had put dramatic controls on imports, western luxu-ries largely disappeared. The only wine you could get was locally grown by Greek farmers in Dodoma. I well remember sitting with Arthur as we broached a bottle of Dodoma Red. The lights went off, as they frequently did. "It's attacking the central nervous sys-tem," said Arthur. We had a lot of fun.

Meetings alternated between Dar es Salaam, Entebbe, Nairobi, and Arusha, where the headquarters were to be. All of us grew a bit bored flying between cities, partly because East African Airways was erratic, but then when we started driving that was not without its hazards. I was with Arthur Hazelwood when we effectively crashed into an elephant. Arthur was very shortsighted and thought it was a bridge! And Ratan took a shortcut from Dar to Entebbe that ended us marooned in a rather fast-moving river, where we were rescued by some tribesmen who didn't look very impressed.

The work varied enormously. There was a ministerial com-mittee with two ministers from each of the two countries. From Tanzania, the senior minister was a man called Jamal, an Indian who was very effective and whom I liked very much. The most powerful man on the committee was the Kenyan minister of la-bor, Tom Mboya, who was very smart indeed. He'd been a trade unionist, had relatively little formal education, but was extremely effective. The Ugandan delegation was less impressive. The splits, which eventually paralyzed the country, were already appearing. These splits were between the Bantu South and the Nilotic North. In the south were a series of kingdoms. They didn't see eye to eye with each other. You never knew what their real goals were. They seemed more interested, during the early days of independence, in having a paid job, versus having a clear sense of a political goal.

I worked on both legal and structural possibilities. We had to envisage the shape of a government—what the various branches would look like, how their membership might be chosen, how transitions would be effected. We also struggled over how to coordinate legal systems, both the codes and personnel. But it became clear within a year that the whole concept was misplaced. Federation had been a wonderful theory, but in practice, after the three countries had independence and had politicians and civil servants well established in the associated positions, there was really little hope that they would give up power and influence to form a federal state. While there had been much talk of Pan-Africanism and federation, the truth was it was difficult to be serious about it; all the leaders were in favor in theory, but none wanted a merger in practice, so it all felt like a terrible hoax.

In Kenya, the Kikuyu were not interested in sharing power with the Luo, let alone with the Tanzanians, and there were similar blocks in the other countries. In Uganda, the split was between the kingdoms and the newly emerging political forces. In Tanzania, Nyerere so dominated the scene that there was little to encourage splits within the country and while Nyerere himself talked about federation, there was little enthusiasm outside the presidential palace.

It was disappointing. I got more and more frustrated and it felt like a waste of everyone's time and of the UN's money. Kenya was becoming more and more capitalist, Tanzania was becoming more socialist, and Uganda was failing as a state. After 18 months of work, when it was clear to me that we weren't going to make any real progress, I gave my notice to the UN. Uganda invited me back a couple of years later to write a report on the future of legal education in East Africa.

Although it was ultimately unsuccessful, working with these countries was a fascinating challenge. The main insight that I took away was that if you want to merge countries, merge them before they are established!

I have not been involved with East Africa in fifty years, but the dream of creating a super-state dies hard. The effort is now called the East African Community. Building on the East African Common Services Organization, the EAC was founded in 1967 to strengthen the relationships between the countries through a common market, a common customs tariff, and a set of public services. The EAC collapsed in 1977 on the heels of Kenya's demand for super status, disagreements with Uganda's Idi Amin, and the conflict between Kenyan capitalism and Tanzanian's socialism. But it was revived in 1999 as a customs union, and in 2016 the countries, now joined by Burundi and Rwanda, declared that confederation, rather than federation would be the immediate aim. South Sudan became the sixth member of the EAC in September 2016.

But the prospects for a political union still look dim.

What Lawyers Do

Biographical Sketches

JIM BOORSCH

After graduation, Jim passed the New York bar exam and started work at Winthrop, Stimson, Putnam & Roberts at 40 Wall Street, now the Trump Building. But the army caught up with him and he signed up for a six-month plus four years of weekends and summer camp stints in the New York National Guard. Returning to the firm, he spent most of his eleven years there in the litigation department, in nationwide antitrust cases, corporate opportunity, breach of contract, unfair competition, and even a replevin action seeking to seize old Buster Keaton films from MOMA. In 1970, he transferred to Mobil Oil, as a staff lawyer in its international division. As such he traveled all over the world negotiating contracts, defending and pursuing a number of arbitrations, including a tax case raising a permanent establishment charge in Australia which took him down under four times. Jim spent over three years as general counsel for Mobil Sekiyu in Tokyo, and attended many meetings of the IEA in London, Paris, Rome, and other watering holes. He took early retirement in 1990, moved up to the country in the Northwest Corner of Connecticut, but was lured back into the arena with an offer to teach at the nearby Kent School, where he spent five years teaching teenagers advanced French and constitutional law. Jim re-retired in 1997 and embarked on a vigorous program of travel that took him to over one hundred countries. He also gave three terms of seminars on the Obama Transition at a retirement community in Salisbury deep in the Connecticut woods. Jim still goes in to New York for occasional lunches and dinners, some with Yale Law School classmates, and now plans to move next year to a retirement community in Hamden, three miles from the Law School and Yale activities.

GUIDO CALABRESI

Guido was born in Milan, Italy, of a well-to-do family of Italian-Jewish heritage dating back to ancient Rome. His father's fierce anti-fascism led them to flee Italy and arrive in America as penniless refugees. Arriving in New Haven, his parents managed (not without difficulty) to become professors of cardiology and of French and Italian literature. With the benefit of scholarships (one distinctly based on affirmative action) he attended the Foote School, Hopkins Grammar School, and Yale College. After two years in Oxford as a Rhodes Scholar, Guido returned to New Haven and to the Yale Law School. He clerked for Justice Hugo Black on the US Supreme Court, and then came back again to New Haven and the Yale Law School and has been there ever since. Having been a founder (as well as a longtime critic) of "Law and Economics," he became a full professor at an "unseemly early age" and has received numerous awards and honorary degrees. Eventually, he became dean of the Yale Law School and sought to make it a place that truly exemplified decency and humanity as well as excellence. In 1994 President Clinton named Guido to the US Court of Appeals for the Second Circuit where he is now a senior judge sitting two-thirds time. He has, however, also continued to be a teacher and scholar, teaching two-thirds time at the Yale Law School and writing articles and books. His first Yale teaching was in 1955 in economics, and even after sixty-two years, a teacher is what he is at heart. In 1961 Guido married Anne Gordon Audubon Tyler, who is responsible for any number of good things that have happened in New Haven. As a cultural anthropologist, she writes about Tuscan farmers, who, in recent years, have become among the Calabresis's closest friends, together growing and pressing olives (but not in Connecticut). They have three children, and four grandchildren, whom they adore.

PETER O. CLAUSS

Peter O. Clauss was born in Knoxville, Tennessee. He graduated from the University of Chicago (a Ford Foundation early entrant after the tenth grade) in 1955, and the Yale Law School in 1958. He was a senior partner at two Philadelphia law firms: Clark, Ladner, Fortenbaugh & Young 1958–1996 and Pepper Hamilton 1996–2008. An adjunct professor at Villanova Law School for many years, he also taught law at Temple University. Peter was chair of the Sales Exchanges and Basis Committee of the ABA tax section; vice chair of the Philadelphia Bar Association and a member of the Public Service Committee of the Philadelphia Bar Association and chair of its Unpopular Causes Committee. He was also vice president of the Juristic Society. His practice, focusing on tax, securities, corporations and mergers and acquisitions, involved numerous international transactions. He wrote for several legal and business publications and lectured in continuing legal education programs. Peter was a member of the Pennsylvania National Guard from 1958–1966, as well as a member of many for-profit and nonprofit boards of directors. He is a past president of the Yale Club of Philadelphia, the William Penn Club and the First Monday Club. He was also a member or past member of the First Troop Philadelphia City Cavalry, the Philadelphia, Racquet, Merion Cricket and University Barge Clubs, and the Fripp Island, Dataw Island, and DuPont country clubs. Peter is a former regional and national officer of Phi Gamma Delta and general counsel to its international fraternity and its educational foundation. He is a former vestryman, committeeman, and lay Eucharistic minister, Christ Church (Episcopal). Peter married Elizabeth Mary Lou Percival in 1962. They have two children.

Alvin Deutsch

Following graduation, Alvin cofounded Linden & Deutsch, a boutique intellectual property firm specializing in copyrights and trademarks (primarily in the literary property, music, and theatrical fields.) His firm merged seventeen years ago with McLaughlin & Stern, where he remains an active partner. His practice took him to the USSR (1980), where he negotiated a contract giving his client, G. Schirmer, exclusive North American rights to the (then) Soviet catalog of music. The highlight of one trip was meeting Dmitri Shostakovich at a performance of *The Nose*, its previous performance having occurred in 1929 when Stalin walked out. His clients on the Broadway scene comprised the composers, lyricists, and bookwriter of *Bye Bye Birdie*, *42nd Street*, *Hello Dolly*, *Fiddler on the Roof*, and *Annie*, and the producers of *1776*, *M. Butterfly*, and Scott Joplin's only opera, *Treemonisha*. Alvin has also represented the Peter Pan copyright (in the US) and the Houston Grand Opera Company. He has represented Tom Wolfe for over forty years; Edgar Snow and the original (nonconglomerated) Maximillian Company; G. Schirmer Music; Harcourt Brace; as well as concert managers one of whose clients was Sherrill Milnes, a leading Met baritone for over twenty-five years. Alvin and his wife, Davida Tenenbaun, this year celebrated their fiftieth wedding anniversary. She is a scholar concentrating in the field of women's education in the eighteenth and nineteenth centuries, and an avid collector of rare wines and the art of Louis Legrand. Alvin has served as adjunct professor of copyright law at Cardozo School of Law; and continues to serve on the board of Goodspeed Opera House and the Johnny Mercer Foundation. He considers as his greatest honor election as parnas-presidente of the Spanish and Portuguese Synagogue in New York City (founded 1654—the oldest Jewish congregation in North America).

Stan Ebner

"Given that I had neither lawyers nor military people in my immediate family, I suppose it was inevitable that both played the leading roles for the first ten years of my professional life." Promptly drafted after law school, Stan was admitted to the Connecticut Bar and to the US Army in that order. Ten years later, facing a promotion to lieutenant colonel and a commitment he had never imagined, he resigned his commission and planned to practice law in Connecticut. That plan was interrupted, however, by a solicitation to join the Justice Department, leading to a position in the office of the deputy attorney general. The next ten years were spent at senior government levels at the Justice Department, followed by a move to Capitol Hill as counsel to the Senate Judiciary Committee and culminating with a White House appointment as general counsel to the Office of Management and Budget. Stan left that position and the government in 1976, when he joined a newly formed private consulting firm as general counsel—his first private sector job since graduating from the Yale Law School in 1958. He remained in that position for five years until he was persuaded by a corporate client to join their ranks as a senior vice president with lots of responsibilities—but none of them legal. Thus, began a career as a business executive with Northrop Grumman, where he spent over ten years until taking early retirement in 1995. Stan was reasonably content taking consulting work for around four years, but when he was offered a senior position with McDonnell Douglas Corporation it took very little time for him to accept. He remained there for around five years, but when McDonnell merged with the Boeing Company they each decided they'd had enough. Stan remains fully retired.

Bill Felstiner

Before law school Bill Felstiner went to Yale College and spent three years during the Korean War on the USS *Sturtevant* (DE-239) specializing in anti-submarine warfare. Bill Kass (YLS '60) was a shipmate. In a career characterized by one of his children as being "unable to hold a job for very long," he was successively an associate and partner with Gumbart, Corbin, Tyler & Cooper in New Haven; regional legal counsel to the USAID program in Turkey and Greece; assistant director of the USAID Mission to India; associate dean of the Yale Law School; assistant professor of law at UCLA; a research fellow at USC, the Rand Corporation, and Wolfson College, Oxford; director of the American Bar Foundation; professor in the Law & Society Program at the University of California, Santa Barbara; director of the International Institute for the Sociology of Law in Oñati, Spain; distinguished research professor of law at Cardiff University, Wales; and founder and president of the Chad Relief Foundation. He has written or edited seven books and more than seventy articles on the sociology of law. He is on the executive committee of the Santa Barbara County Legal Aid Foundation. Bill is married to the renowned polyglot Gray Felstiner. They have two sons and four grandsons. He is part owner of a boat moored in Petersburg, Alaska, and plays a lot of golf, on many occasions scoring better than his age.

Howard Fink

After graduation, Howard stayed on at Yale Law School for seven years, as a research associate, working with Professor James William Moore on *Moore's Federal Practice*. Beginning in 1959, he did six months' training with the Connecticut National Guard and later attended meetings and summer camp for five more years. During those years at Yale, he met his wife, Sondra; they married in 1963, have had two daughters, and now also have four grandchildren. Their daughter Maara teaches in the law school at the University of Toledo and their daughter Karren is a human resources manager for a major company in California. In 1965, with the recommendation of several Yale Law School faculty members, Howard secured a position as associate professor of law at The Ohio State University. He stayed there as a full professor, later a chaired professor, until his retirement in 1998. Howard has continued teaching there and at several other law schools, before and after his retirement. He created an Ohio State summer prelaw program at the University of Oxford in 1994 that continues today along with a companion summer law program for law students co-sponsored by the University of Oxford and Ohio State. He taught there many summers. Howard has written treatises and casebooks on federal practice and civil procedure and was a visiting professor at George Washington, Illinois, Wake Forest, Toledo, Emory, San Diego, and Santa Clara law schools. His articles on ante-mortem probate have resulted in several states now allowing a testator to probate his or her will before death.

Carla A. Hills

Ambassador Carla A. Hills served as United States trade representative from 1989 to 1993. As a member of President George H. W. Bush's cabinet, Carla was the president's principal advisor on international trade policy and the nation's chief trade negotiator. She negotiated and concluded the North American Free Trade Agreement, led US negotiations on the Uruguay Round of the World Trade Organization, and concluded a number of trade and investment agreements with countries around the world. Earlier, Ambassador Hills served as secretary of the Department of Housing and Urban Development (the third woman to hold a cabinet position). She also served as the assistant attorney general, Civil Division, of the US Department of Justice. Before entering government, Ambassador Hills cofounded and was partner in what is now the Munger, Tolles & Olson law firm. She also served as an adjunct professor at the University of California, Los Angeles Law School teaching antitrust law, and coauthored the *Antitrust Adviser,* which was published by McGraw-Hill. Over the years, she has served on a number of Fortune 500 companies boards of directors. She currently serves on the international advisory board of J. P. Morgan Chase. She also serves in leadership positions with not-for-profit organizations, including chair of the National Committee on US-China Relations; cochair of the Inter-American Dialogue, and of the International Advisory Board of the Center for Strategic and International Studies; honorary director of the Peterson Institute for International Economics; member of the Executive Committee of the Trilateral Commission, and cochair emeritus of the Council on Foreign Relations. Ambassador Hills graduated from Stanford University and attended Oxford University's Saint Hilda's College before going to the Yale Law School. She holds honorary degrees from a number of colleges and universities. In 2000, she was awarded the Aztec Eagle, the highest honor given by the Mexican government to a noncitizen. She is chair and CEO of Hills and Company International Consultants and resides in Washington DC.

ALAN HRUSKA

Alan Hruska, a graduate of Yale University and the Law School, was a partner at Cravath, Swaine & Moore (where he is still senior counsel), president of the Federal Bar Council and of the Institute of Judicial Administration, chairman of the Planning and Program Committee of the Second Circuit Judicial Conference, a commissioner of the New York State Executive Advisory Commission, a member of the American College of Trial Lawyers, and a director of various professional and community organizations. During the forty-four years of his practice, he handled hundreds of cases for CBS, Time Inc., Curtis Publishing, IBM, Westinghouse, Olin Mathieson, E. I. du Pont, Courtaulds, Lever Brothers, Warner Lambert, Republic Steel, Inland Steel, Studebaker, Ashland Oil, Trimble Navigation, Vassar College, Price Waterhouse, and most of the financial industry. He tried cases in state and federal courts, Tax Court, the Court of International Trade, the International Trade Commission, and the Federal Trade Commission, and argued in various federal circuit courts of appeals and the US Supreme Court. He also represented in various matters Katharine Graham, Henry Kissinger, William Paley, William Simon, Sam Walton, Arthur Watson, Thomas Watson, and other individuals. Since 2002, he has written and directed four feature films and two plays, coproduced two other films, and directed an off-Broadway production of *Waiting for Godot*. His play *The Man on Her Mind* was performed at the Charing Cross Theatre in London in 2012, his play *Laugh It Up, Stare It Down* ran at the Cherry Lane Theatre in 2015, and his most recent play, *Ring Twice for Miranda*, was produced at New York City Center in 2017. He has also written four published novels (*Borrowed Time, Wrong Man Running, Pardon the Ravens,* and *It Happened at Two in the Morning*) and is a cofounder of Soho Press, where he is chairman of the board.

Laura Kalman

Laura Kalman is Distinguished Professor of History at the University of California, Santa Barbara. She received her BA in History from Pomona, JD from UCLA, and PhD from Yale. She became dissatisfied with law school when a professor introduced her to *Marbury v. Madison* one day and *U.S. v. Nixon* the next without paying any attention to the more than 160 years that separated them. After becoming a member of the California Bar and working at a Legal Services Corporation, she decided on a career in history. When her beloved dissertation adviser, John Morton Blum, sent her to the archives to dig into the Jerome Frank Papers, Kalman realized that the legal realists at Yale had advocated alternative approaches to her legal education. A dissertation topic was born, and it became her first book, *Legal Realism at Yale, 1927-1960*. Kalman assumed that would be her last word on Yale, but she has found herself incapable of resisting the school's siren song time and again. In another book, *Yale Law School and the Sixties: Revolt and Reverberations*, she concentrated on a fraught period and its repercussions for Yale and legal education. When she is not obsessing about Yale's history, Kalman writes about the history of the legal profession and Supreme Court *(Abe Fortas: A Biography; The Long Reach of the Sixties: LBJ, Nixon, and the Making of the Contemporary Supreme Court)*; legal thought *(The Strange Career of Legal Liberalism)*; and politics *(Right Star Rising: A New Politics, 1974-1980)*. Given her great admiration and affection for Bill Felstiner, whom she met during a research fellowship year at the American Bar Foundation, the Class of '58 has a special place in her heart. Because her work has left her with an appreciation for exemplary law school deans, she is Guido's devoted fan too. She lives in Goleta and her childhood Los Angeles home with her husband, W. Randall Garr, a professor of religious studies.

Marvin L. Karp

Marvin L. Karp was born in Milo, Maine. After graduating from Yale College (1955) and the Yale Law School (1958), he was hired by a Cleveland, Ohio, law firm, Ulmer, Berne, Laronge, Glickman & Curtis, where he became a partner in 1966 and worked as a trial lawyer (serving most of that time as chair of the firm's litigation department) until his retirement on December 31, 2014. He held leadership positions in a number of professional organizations and groups, including president of the Cleveland Bar Association (1988–1989); chair of the Tort and Insurance Practice Section of the American Bar Association (1990–1991); president of the Federation of Defense and Corporate Counsel (1994–1995); chair of the American Bar Association Standing Committee on Ethics and Professional Responsibility (2001–2004); advisor to the American Bar Association Joint Commission to Evaluate Model Code of Judicial Conduct (2003–2007); chair of the American Bar Association Center for Professional Responsibility/Section Officers Conference Joint Committee on Ethics and Professionalism (2005–2009); and chair of the Ohio Supreme Court Commission on Professionalism (2012–2013). He also served on the Ohio Supreme Court Task Force on the Code of Judicial Conduct (2007–2008) and in the American Bar Association House of Delegates (1992–2010). He is a fellow of the American College of Trial Lawyers, a fellow of the International Academy of Trial Lawyers, a life member of the Judicial Conference of the US Court of Appeals for the Sixth Circuit, and a panelist of the American Arbitration Association Complex Case Panel of Arbitrators. He received the American Bar Association Andrew M. Hecker Memorial Award for Professionalism (1998), the Cleveland Bar Association William K. Thomas Award for Professionalism (2001), the Ohio State Bar Association Ohio Bar Medal for "unusually meritorious service to the legal profession and the community" (2007), and the American Bar Association Michael Franck Professional Responsibility Award (2010). He authored numerous articles and presented many lectures with respect to trial practice, business, corporate and insurance litigation, and professionalism.

Arthur J. LaFave Jr.

Jay arrived at Yale with a wife and two-year-old child directly after graduating from Williams. "I was not quite sure what to expect at Yale, but the experience was priceless, and I loved every minute of it." After leaving law school, Jay practiced for a few years with a small entrepreneurial and business-related firm in Portland, Oregon, before returning to his home in Cleveland, Ohio. There, while practicing with a traditional law firm, he met another Yale graduate, Mark McCormack (YLS '54), who had a great interest in professional golf, with friends competing on the Tour. That introduction was a career-changer. Over the next few years, Jay and Mark left that firm and started a business of providing management services, initially to golfers but later other professional athletes, models, and musicians. The business ultimately became IMG, a broadly international enterprise with a staff of several thousand, offices in some thirty countries, and an involvement in nearly all of the world's sports. They managed some events and owned others, produced their own telecasts, and distributed programs owned by others. As a cofounder (and junior partner) in this enterprise, Jay became responsible for building the business in Japan and later served as CFO and vice chairman. Mc-Cormack died in 2003. They sold most of the business to a private equity investor in 2004 and the remaining part (wealth management) to another in 2007. Jay notes: "As I write this, I continue to come to my IMG office each day where I look after the affairs of my large family and provide consulting services for an old client. My wife of sixty-five years, Carolyn, and I have six children and twelve grandchildren. My outside activities included serving as a trustee of the Cleveland Musical Arts Association (the Cleveland Orchestra) and the Cleveland Institute of Music, and as a member of the Corporate Council of the Cleveland Museum of Art. For recreation, I have a forty-foot sloop, which we have sailed extensively in the Great Lakes following a nonstop trip from Tampa to Cleveland in 1990. Recently I have added a similar-size picnic boat to my fleet."

Henry Monaghan

After graduating from law school, Henry clerked on the Fourth Circuit and then took an LLM at Harvard. At that point, he began practicing in Boston with a then small firm (but now a very large one) now known as Foley Hoag. In the early/middle '60s, he began teaching at Boston University and since then has taught at various schools. For the last three decades or so, he has been happily a member of the Columbia Law School faculty, where he is (and has been for nearly three decades) Harlan Fiske Stone Professor of Constitutional Law. In addition to teaching and writing, Henry has had a fair amount of litigation experience over the years, largely in the federal appellate courts and some in the Supreme Court.

Hugh Moulton

Hugh Moulton graduated from Wellesley High School, Amherst College, the Yale Law School, and the Harvard Business School, advance management program. He married Katie Clark, a Mount Holyoke graduate, in 1956. They have two children and four grandchildren, all of whom completed college and/or graduate school, but no known great grandchildren. Hugh was an associate and then partner at Montgomery, McCracken, Walker & Rhoads in Philadelphia 1958–1969; secretary, general counsel, executive vice president, and chief administrative officer at Alco Standard Corporation, Valley Forge, Pennsylvania 1970–1995; and executive vice president and chief administrative officer Unisource Corporation, also in Valley Forge, 1996–1999. His principal community interests have been in education and conservation. Hugh served for twenty-five years on the board of Beaver College/Arcadia University in Philadelphia, including four as board chair. He is a former president and long-term board member of Wissahickon Valley Watershed Association; former board member and board chair of the Nature Conservancy Pennsylvania Chapter; a board member and vice chair of the Montgomery County Lands Trust; founding chairman, board member, and current secretary-treasurer of the Whitemarsh Foundation; and board member and secretary of the Hill at Whitemarsh, a continuing care retirement community where Katie and he have lived since 2007. Hugh has a summer home in Chatham, Massachusetts, and a winter home in Boca Grande, Florida. He enjoys tennis, golf, travel, and American history. The Moultons have traveled extensively, the most memorable trip being a 2015 three-week trip from Greenland to Nome, Alaska, through the Northwest Passage.

GLORIA NEUWIRTH

After law school, Gloria worked on a research project sponsored jointly by Columbia University and the New York City Bar Association to determine the role of automobile accident litigation in the congested New York courts. This resulted in a book, *Who Sues in New York City*, that probably provided the impetus for "no-fault" legislation in New York. She did intermittent research in cases involving issues of pension rights of clergymen as a result of the merger of two divergent churches, as these cases wound their way up to the Supreme Court. Gloria then semiretired to raise a family of four children, keeping active with community and school matters. When her youngest turned five, she went back to school, taking courses at Columbia Law School on taxation and estate planning and administration and was able to find a part-time job (which had always been her dream). Gloria gradually became more and more involved, worked longer hours, and eventually became a partner in a small law firm. This was followed by a stint at the large firm of Kaye, Scholer in New York, after which she managed her own firm. Twenty-two years ago, she joined the firm of Davidson, Dawson & Clark where she has been happily engaged ever since. She hopes to reduce work hours at the firm by 25 percent, to make room in her schedule for tutoring in reading at a public school in East Harlem, as well as opera and other cultural activities, travel, and taking courses in various fields.

BURTON RAFFEL

Burton was born in Brooklyn on April 27, 1928, to Russian Jewish immigrants who spoke seven or eight languages. In 1948, he graduated from Brooklyn College with a degree in English and then earned an MA from Ohio State. Examining the inadequate translations of Old English poems, which did nothing to communicate their power, fueled his interest in the art of translation. He then spent two years with the Ford Foundation living and teaching in Indonesia, where he became fluent in Indonesian. After editing a casebook written by his lawyer father, he decided to study law. He enrolled in Yale in 1955 and relished his time there. But following graduation in 1958 and two years working at Milbank, Tweed, Hadley & McCloy in New York, he grew restless with law practice and left to become the founding editor of *Foundation News*, the first magazine devoted exclusively to foundations. In 1965, he returned to teaching English at the State University of New York at Stony Brook. By that point, he had already published *Poems from the Old English*, his well-known *Beowulf* translation, and *Modern Indonesian Poetry*, and was translating the complete work of Indonesian poet Chairil Anwar. His academic career took him to numerous places, including the University of Haifa, the University of Denver, and the University of Louisiana at Lafayette, where he held an endowed chair. Throughout the course of his life he published more than one hundred books, including translations from many languages, literary criticism, several books of poetry, and the novels *After Such Ignorance* and *Yankee Doric*. His interests were far-reaching, encompassing the literatures of many countries, Judaica, history, anthropology, psychology, physics, and math. After retirement, he wrote daily, read, listened to classical music, and swam. He had six children, one of whom predeceased him, six grandsons, and one granddaughter. He died on September 29, 2015. His remarkable home library can be seen at https://youtu.be/2f2l3lXNKmo.

RICHARD RAVITCH

"I am eighty-five and still not sure what I want to do when I grow up."

Dick's first job was assistant counsel to the military operations sub-committee of the House of Representatives. Next he went into the housing development business and built close to 40,000 apartments. In 1975 he assisted Governor Hugh Carey in avoiding the bank-ruptcy of the New York State Urban Development Corporation and the City of New York. Dick then sold his construction business and became the chairman of the Metropolitan Transportation Authority of New York. After four years he had to replenish the coffers and purchased the Bowery Savings Bank from the FDIC, and ran it for three years; he found the spread lending business stultifying and sold it. Since then Dick has served on boards, both civic and corporate, and several presidential commissions dealing with the subject of affordable housing. He also chaired a charter revision commission for the City of New York. In recent years he has shared offices with his good friend Paul Volcker, managed the Waterside apartments, served briefly as lieutenant governor of New York State, and taught municipal finance at the Yale Law School as well as at New York University. He is now devoted to thirteen grandchildren and to replacing Donald Trump.

David Schimmel

After Yale Law School, David was interim director of Yale Hillel, an army infantry officer in a basic combat training unit, went to rabbinical school for two years, and briefly practiced law before becoming associate Peace Corps director in Ethiopia. When he returned to the states, he served as the executive officer of the Office of Planning, Evaluation, and Research, and then was appointed director for Volunteers to America—a small reverse Peace Corps program that invited countries where we had volunteers to send their young professionals to the US—to teach, to learn, and to serve alongside American teachers and social workers. The evaluations for the program were positive for the international volunteers, their coworkers, and supervisors. The only problem was that Congress refused to fund the program after three years when White House sponsorship ended. During his final Peace Corps years, David was director of the Virgin Islands training centers where volunteers for French-speaking Africa were trained on Saint Croix and for former English colonies on Saint Thomas. Since 1968, David has been a professor at the University of Massachusetts, Amherst, where his mission has been to promote legal literacy among students, teachers, and administrators in the public schools. Toward that goal, he wrote about seventy-five articles and co-authored eight books about law and education, including *Teachers and the Law*, 9th ed. (2015), and *Principals Avoiding Lawsuits: How Teachers Can Be Partners in Practicing Preventive Law* (2017). Along the way, he was a visiting professor at Harvard's Graduate School of Education, and received the Education Press Association of America's Distinguished Achievement Award for Excellence in Educational Journalism and the Education Law Association's McGhehey (lifetime achievement) Award. David and his wife, Barbara, split their time between Amherst and Boca Raton, Florida, where they look forward to visits with their children and grandchildren.

Joel J. Sprayregen

Joel earned a BS in journalism in 1955 from Northwestern University's Medill School of Journalism. A summer working for the *New York Post* showed him that much of journalism consisted of covering what lawyers were doing. Upon graduation from the Yale Law School, he took a post that fulfilled his major aspiration to practice law as staff counsel for the Illinois Division of the American Civil Liberties Union. Joel joined Chicago's Aaron, Schimberg & Hess in 1960 as litigation associate, becoming partner in 1966 and chair of litigation in 1969 while also serving as general counsel to the ACLU. In 1970, he joined an ACLU study mission to the Soviet Union. Meeting Soviet Jews who were denied permission to emigrate, and subsequently becoming their advocate, changed the course of his life. He became a Jewish community leader focusing on international relations and holding posts including chair of the Chicago Community Relations Council and national vice-chair of both the Anti-Defamation League and the Jewish Institute for National Security Affairs. Joel served nine years as a member of the Illinois Supreme Court's Character and Fitness Committee. Among his honors is a Brandeis Award conferred by President Clinton. His litigation practice grew, specializing in complex business litigation and construction law. In 1984, Joel joined as chair of litigation Shefsky & Froelich, which subsequently merged into Taft Stettinius & Hollister, where he is presently senior counsel. He served on the boards of corporations, banks, and foundations. In his last (probably) major case, he was chair of the Administrative Creditors (i.e., post-filing debt) Committee in the largest administrative insolvency in US bankruptcy history. He pursued thirteen years of litigation, resulting in a 100 percent mediation settlement from the malefactors' D & O insurers. Joel has published extensively in legal and international affairs journals as well as periodicals. Traveling to learn and meet diverse folks continues as a major passion; he has eleven million documented miles.

Robert Stevens

Robert Stevens was born in the United Kingdom and educated at Oakham School, Keble College, Oxford, and the Yale Law School. Robert's career included both the practice of law and academic appointments in the US and UK. After 20 years as professor of law at Yale, Robert served as provost of Tulane University, president of Haverford College, and chancellor of the University of California at Santa Cruz. Robert returned to the UK in 1991, where he was of counsel to the law firm, Covington & Burling, and then became master of Pembroke College, Oxford. He is the author of numerous articles and some ten books, including studies of competition law, commercial law, social legislation, and the legal profession and judiciary in both the US and the UK. Stevens has worked as a consultant for a number of US federal government departments, and for the United Nations Development Program, in addition to serving as legal advisor to the governments of Tanzania, the Bahamas, and the East African Community. He is married to Katherine Booth Stevens, an educator and former Chair of the Oxfordshire Magistrates' Bench. They live in Oxford. Robert has three children.

Ted Vestal

After Yale, Ted wed Pat Botefuhr, a college classmate and talented painter, and moved to California during the beatnik era. He studied constitutional law and American history at Stanford and received a PhD in political science. His dissertation was published as *The Eisenhower Court and Civil Liberties* by Praeger. Following service as a lieutenant in the US Army Chemical Corps, he pursued a career in the academy and in government service. Most of his teaching was in public law, in courses on civil rights and civil liberties. The fascinating subject matter guaranteed an enrollment of talented students dedicated to succeeding in demanding courses. Many went to law school and honored Ted by staying in touch over the years. The leitmotif of his instruction and research was Yale Law School's aspirational goal of making academic work directly relevant to improving the world. Ted even ventured into higher education administration with all the comforts and pains accruing to being a dean or president. His stints in government included keeping track of the University of California budget for the California Legislature as part of a new Master Plan for Higher Education; writing a major study, "Medical Education in California"; joining the New Frontier and working in Peace Corps/ Washington for a year before moving to a two-year assignment as associate director in Ethiopia (taking with him his family, which included three very young children); serving in John Gardner's HEW, planning the implementation of the International Education Act of 1966 (see *International Education*, Praeger, 1994). His work took him to extended residencies in Addis Ababa, New Delhi, Kyoto, and Hamburg (where he had an endowed professorship). Ted was bestowed the rank, honor, and dignity of Knight Grand Cross of the Imperial Order of the Star of Honor of Ethiopia in March 2018. Ted continues to be an active Ethiopianist, writing and lecturing about that fascinating land. (See e.g. *Ethiopia: A Post-Cold War African State*, 1999; *The Lion of Judah in the New World*, 2011.)

Paul Zimmerman

The late Paul Zimmerman was a child of New York City. He grew up near the Grand Concourse and graduated from the Bronx High School of Science. A graduate of Dartmouth and the Yale Law School, Paul spent most of his professional career in public service, including stints as a Peace Corps country director in India and Iran and as an aide to Mayor John Lindsay of New York. Paul and his wife, Margot Ann Lurie, married in 1957, were insatiable travelers, navigating six continents and nearly one hundred countries. Their final journey was a return visit to Iran in October 2017, closing the circuit of six decades together. Paul died on November 20, 2017.

www.ingramcontent.com/pod-product-compliance
Lightning Source LLC
Chambersburg PA
CBHW032054050726
47590CB00001B/262